The Mystic Poetry

of

Rumi, Hafiz And Bulleh Shah

The Mystic Poetry
of
Rumi, Hafiz And Bulleh Shah

SURAIYA YASMIN

AUTHORSPRESS

Worldwide Circulation through Authorspress Global Network
First Published in 2022
by
Authorspress
Q-2A Hauz Khas Enclave, New Delhi-110 016 (India)
Phone: (0) 9818049852
E-mail: authorspressgroup@gmail.com
Website: www.authorspressbooks.com

The Mystic Poetry of Rumi, Hafiz and Bulleh Shah
ISBN 978-93-5529-101-1

Printed in India at Thomson Press (India) Limited

Preface

Sufism is a mystical movement, which emerged in Islamic history during the 8th century. It is based on the essential tenet of systematic rejection of this world as it is and the identifying of one's self through the medium of selfless love with the transcendental power called "al-matlaq" (the absolute) which could be God or a Beloved. Having rejected the mundane discourse of reason and intellect, Sufis found in poetry, especially esoteric poetry, as their natural and highly trusted medium of discourse. Since their primary object of love is God, their poetic utterances expressed itself in lyricism and ambiguity.

A lot of work has been done on Sufism by various scholars of the world such as *"Sufism-A Short Introduction"* (2000) by W.C Chittik, "*Sufism: The Heart of Islam"* by Sadia Dehlvi, "*Sufism-An Account of the Mystics of Islam*" (2001) by A.J Arberry, "*Sufism: An Introduction to the Mystical Tradition of Islam*" (1997) by Carl W Ernst. These works have contributed a lot to the Persian Sufi Poetry. Some of the notable works on Sufi Poetry includes "*The Four Gated City*" (2009) by Doris Lessings, "*Persian Sufi Poetry: An Introduction to the Mystical use of Classical Poems*" (1997) by J.T.P. De Bruijn, "*The Garden of Heaven: Poems of Hafiz*" (2003) by Daniel Ladinsky, "*The Sufi Path of Love: The Spiritual Teaching of Rumi*" by W.C Chittik, " *The Forbidden Rumi*"(2006) by Nevit O. Ergin and Will Johnson, *Bulleh Shah: A Sufi Mystic of the Punjab*" (2008) by Bob Gibbon and Sian Pritchand Jones," *Rumi Soul Furry: Rumi an d Shams on Friendship*" (2013) by Coleman Barks, "*Rumi: Works of the Great Philosopher, Poet and Mystic*" (1998) by E.H Whinfield, " *Bulleh Shah: The Love Intoxicated Iconclast*" (1986) by T.R Shangri.recent works on Sufism are *Iqbal's Approach to Sufism (2012) by* Muhammad Khaliq, *Contemporary Islamic Sufism In America: the Philosophy and Practices of the Alami Tariqa in Waterport, New York* (2011) by Julianne Hazen, *Sufi-Romantic self-Loss: The Study of the Influence of Persian Sufism on English Romantic Poetry* (2011) by Elham Nilchian, *Understanding Sufism: contextualising the content* (2014) by Benjamin G

Cook, *Early Sufi approaches to Tawba*, The Sufi journey Towards Nondual Self-Realisation (2005) by Lauren Julia Boni, *Imagining Sufism and Muslimness: The Production of Knowledge about Sufism and Its Power Against Political Islam in the United States, Canada and Pakistan* (2017) by G.M Dalphond.

Ralph Waldo Emerson, Doris Lessing, Gurdjieff, Idries Shah, Coleman Barks, R.A Nicholson have contributed a lot to the history of Sufi literature. All of them have similar ideas on religious tolerance and the importance of self-knowledge. The Sufi generally have a quest and longing for the exploration of the 'Self' in order to unfold the secrets of spirituality and divinity, while living with and accepting universal diversities, This exploration of the self is called Sufism. Emerson in his essay "*Self-Reliance*" is actually expanding on Sufi ideology when he speaks of self-knowledge and self-reliance:

> What I must do is all that concerns me, not what the people think. This rule, equally arduous in actual and in intellectual life, may serve for the whole distinction between greatness and meanness. It is harder, because you will always find those who think they know what is your duty better than you know it. It is easy in the world to live after the world's opinion; it is easy in solitude to live after our own; but the great man is he who in the midst of the crowd keeps with perfect sweetness the independence of solitude. (Emerson web)

Thus the Sufis are people who do not renounce the world rather they live in the world while secretly involved in their own mystical life of union with God. A major critic of Sufism Doris Lessing talks about the consciousness level of the human beings in her novel "*The Four Gated City*". According to Lessing human beings do not possess equal consciousness levels but they get an equal opportunity to enhance their consciousness level. So it is obvious that we all have the capacity to raise above the consciousness level that we generally possess. In another words we are unaware of our own potential. As Lessing in one of her lectures on Sufism says "Man is woefully underused and undervalued, and he doesn't know his own capacity" (Lessings, 2009). But the Sufis are the ones who realise their potential and have meditated to reach the higher consciousness level available resulting in the union with the God. Regarding the Sufi concept of evolution Lessing quotes from Idries Shah in "*The Four Gated City*":

> Sufis believe that, expressed in one way, humanity is evolving towards a certain destiny. We are all taking part in that evolution. Organs come into being as a result of a need for specific organs. The human being's organism is producing a new complex of organs in response to such a

> need. In this age of the transcending of time and space, the complex of organs is concerned with the transcending of time and space. What ordinary people regard as spoiradic and occasional burst of telepathic and prophetic power are seen by the Sufi as nothing less than the first stirring of these same organs. (492)

The Sufis are of the belief that human being are evolving but their future will depend upon the realisation of the value of their own existence. In another words human beings can only be free from the circle of the rebirth after they realise their connection with the divine.

As earlier it was mentioned earlier that the term "Sufism" or "Tassawuf" is derived from the Arabic word "Suf" which means "Wool". According to Prof. Edward G. Browne there are four theories regarding the origin of Sufism. They are: Esoteric Doctrine of the Prophet, Reaction of the Aryan Mind of the Semitic religion, Neo-platonistic influence, and Independent Origin. Scholars from the world over have described Sufism in different ways but generally most of the scholars of the world have agreed that Sufism is the inner, esoteric, and mystical dimension of the religion Islam. In the 14th edition of *Encyclopaedia Britanica* (1968), Martin Lings in his article '*Sufism*' defines it as "the name by which Islamic mysticism came to be known in the 8th century A.D. He further stated that "the influences on Sufism from outside have been enormously exaggerated. Probably the chief influence was Neoplatonism, but even this was confined mostly to terminology and to methods of doctrinal exposition".

A.J Arberry defines Sufism in his brief introduction to his book entitled *Sufism: An Account of the Mystics of Islam (1950)* in the following way, "the name given to the mysticism of Islam and "the mystical movement of an uncompromising Monotheism". Thus he is the first author to accept that though Sufism was influenced from Neoplatonic and other sources, it was derived from the Qur'an and prophetic (Muhammadan) tradition. As he said that "It is belived that the movement from within as an aspect of Islam, as though these other factors which certainly determined its growth did not exist".

Therefore it is believed that a group of disciples of Prophet Muhammad who often sat at his feet to listen to the tenets of Islam and receive Enlightenment in the faith were called the first Sufis. It is further believed that Sufism has its roots in Adam, the first man on earth as it is commonly believe by the three sects, Christian, Jews and Muslims.

> The seed of Sufism was sown in the time of Adam germed in the time of Noah budded in the time of Abraham began to develop in the time of Moses reached maturity in the time of Jesus produced pure wine in the time of Muhammad. (Graves 296)

The Sufis are called the "esoteric Christian" as they regard Jesus as a hierophant and teacher of the way. He has often been called the "greatest Sufi". In the "*Sources of Gurdjieff's Teaching*", Gurdjieff talks about the "Universal Spirituality" which is recognised by both the historical and the contemporary religious traditional teachers. As St. Augustine has asserted that the old Testament Christianity existed before the time of the historical Jesus. And Muhammad himself is said to revered Abraham, Moses, and Jesus as great teachers and prophets of the same monotheistic religion that he himself advocated. Gurdjieff while speaking of community in his book "*Meeting with Remarkable Man*", he mentions the word 'World Brotherhood' which means universal brotherhood among all human being s irrespective of their caste, creed, colour, sex, religion. As Gurdjieff wrote:

> Any man could enter irrespective of the religion to which belonged...Among the adepts of His monastery there were former Christians, Jews, Muhammadans, Buddhists, lamaists and Even one Shamanist, All were united by God and Truth. (Gurdjieff 227)

Thus Idries Shah in his book "*A Perfumed Scorpion*" calls *Sufism* as a "*flower*" or inner dimension of all religions, compatible with Islam but also existing independently of the prophetic tradition:

> Sufism has been known under many names, to all peoples, from the beginning of human times...it was transmitted by the prophet Muhammad as the inner component of all religion... it also persisted side by side with the prophetic transmission, as for instance, in the independent witness of the historical figures of Uways al-Qarni, a contemporary of the prophetic who, however, never met him. (Shah *A Perf. S.* 2-7)

R A Nicholson in his brief introduction to his book *Sufism: The Mystics of Islam* (1994) remarked: "Sufism the realities religious philosophy of Islam, is described in the oldest extant definition as the apprehension of divine realities "although referring to it as 'Islamic mystics' he still maintains the popular idea that Sufism was largely the product of diverse philosophical and spiritual influences, including Christian, Neoplatonic, and others. This definition of Sufism by Nicholson focuses on the most significant aspect of

Sufism which are diversity, universality and acceptance of all religion and creeds. Even Rudyard Kipling in his book "*Kim*", called the Sufis as the" free thinkers, simplistic or insightful"! (167)

According to the history of Sufi literature there are four Sufi orders in Sufism. They are the Naqshbandhiyya, the Quaddriyya, the Suhrawardiyya and the Chistiyya order. According to John Bennet's research, the Naqshbandi Sufis were connected with an Inner Circle of Humanity responsible for the consciousness evolutionary development of human race. Gurdjieff was a student of this school. As Ernest Scott in *"People of the Secret"* describes about Sufism and how Gurdjieff came in contact with it:

> This Sufis in Afghanistan are closely connected with these people, but no one will tell an Outsider anything more than that these monasteries exist. They say that the only outsider to have penetrated into the outer ring of monasteries was a Russian-Greek, George Gurdjieff, whose contacts enabled him to be accepted as a pupil...Said to have been trained by Bahauddin Naqshband, one of the "outer masters",Gurdjieff mastered some of the teachings and tried to teach them in the West. (168)

Gurdjieff is of the view that a comprehensive teaching of human spiritual development existed in ancient times and this teaching leads to inner freedom and liberation, which is the heart of all religious formulations and historical manifestation. But later this spiritual teaching was divided into specialisations. Thus in India it was called a 'Philosophy', in Egypt 'Theory', while in Persia 'Mesopotamia' and in Turkishtan it was refered to as a 'Practice'. In a lecture to his students at the Prieure in 1923, Gurdjieff described Sufism as a synthesis of the inner meaning of all religions.

Accordingly the inner teachings of all religions declares that the closer one comes to their own religious doctrine the more he will understand the others religion. As Gurdjieff says religion is like a radii of a circle, the close one come towards the centre, the closer they approach one another:

> The ways that lead to the cognition of unity approach it like the radii of a Circle moving Towards the centre; the closer they come to the centre; the closer they approach one another. (Ospensky 19-33)

Therefore for the Sufis the more closer they are to the religious doctrine all the religions will appear the same and they look at all the human beings as souls, which God has created in his own light.

> The essence of all religions...is the same, affirmed Mr. Gurdjieff, Fundamentally, they are all concerned with one thing-evolution. The teaching of each great master enables his pupils to follow a certain

> evolutionary path, and to arrive at a level where contact with the highest cosmic force becomes possible. At their root, all the teachings are one and the same, each having as its purpose to help us attain this possibility. (Tchekovitch 43)

Gurdjieff even goes to the extent of comparing religion with mathematics. As he says religion is nothing but elementary part of mathematics and the most exoteric that offers to the masses and which differs from religion to religion. It is due to this fact that all the messiah and the messengers were born in different time and place with different language, philosophical outlook, character, fundamental mentality, and with many other different aspects. So in order to adapt to their times they had to choose an appropriate ways to accomplish their task. As Gurdjieff quotes:

> This difference [in religions] is only apparent...and this contradiction arises from several factors. People who judge a religion in this way have not penetrated the essence of the teaching, and their judgements are bound to be superficial. Religions are actually like mathematics: it is the elementary part the most exoteric, that is offered to the masses, and this elementary part differs according to the religion. It is because of the Messiah or Messenger from above appears among people who differ in language, philosophical outlook, character, fundamental mentality, and many other temporal aspects, that he has to adapt to the times and choose an appropriate way to accomplish his task. (Tchekhovitch 45)

It is believed that Sufism developed in the 8th centuries in three major city centres of Busra, kufa and Baghdad in Iraq, as well as in the city of Bulk in Khorasan district of Persia, and in ancient Egypt. It is said that the Sufis were 'those who see this world as a hut of sorrows'. No doubt they followed the external rules of Sharia but also at the same time they developed their own mystical ideas and techniques. They even observe the discipline of little food, little talk, and little sleep, along with fasting and night long prayers for drawing themselves closer to God. The Sufis neither needed mosque for their prayer nor any form of social stability. Wherever they sat that become their prayer and resting place. They never needed to learn Arabic or any philosophy to converse with God as they used the language of their heart. They never used their power of performing magic or miracles for enhancing their reputation, indeed they regarded it as secondary to their work as they performed it merely for the benefit of the people.

Thus the Sufi path contains many stages, for example the disciples repentance, and the necessity to be the disciple of the murshid, the necessity to undergo some initial rituals following which the murshid imparts his grace, giving strict ascetic rules to follow a certain secret word for meditation. The murid or disciple had to pass through some other spiritual stations such as detachments from the world (zuhud), Patience (sabr) (Gratitude (shukur) for whatever God gives, Love (hub), Pleasure (rida) with whatever God desires to bestow, besides these they had to undergo some kind of emotional stations such as fear and hope, sadness and joy, yearning intimacy, to be granted to the pilgrim by God's grace while the final goal is to lead him on to 'Marifa' (esoteric knowledge or gnosis), 'Mahabbah' (love) and to the ultimate goal which is annihilation of personality and unity with God.

Therefore the Sufis sets out on the divine path inorder to get annihilated through his union with God. But achieving it, is not easy task for it needs a special kind of strength and stamina. As Doris Lessing says that all human beings do not possess the same consciousness level but everyone gets the same opportunity to achieve it. Which means we all have the same potential to become a Sufi but it needs greater devotion towards the divine path.

Thus the Sufis have been the true guides of mankind in all ages, who lead them to the right path of life. In today's world Sufi guides are urgently needed to lead people along the proper way. Otherwise a whole life time could be spent in dreaming about luxuries and comfortable life rather than emphasising human relations. Thus in today's world manipulation, exploitation, dishonesty, greed has taken the place of love, affection and justice, Sufism is needed as an urgent remedy of these evils of our society.

The introduction to the vast history of Sufism can be concluded with a quote from Victor Danner, who in his introduction to his translation of Ibn Ata's Allah's book "*The Book of Wisdom*" (19-22) writes: "when dealing with Sufism, it is best to leave to one side such term as '*mystic*' and '*mysticism*', it only because in the modern western world such words nowadays often leads to confusion". Victor Denner quotes Ibn Ata in his book *The Islamic Tradition: An Introduction* (2005) Where he says that 'Sufism is the spiritual path (tariqah) of Islam and has been identified with it for well over a thousand years.' It has been called 'Islamic Mysticism' by western scholars because of its resemblance to Christian and other forms of mysticism elsewhere. Unlike Christian mysticism, Sufism is a continuous historical and even institutionalised phenomenon in the

Muslim world that has millions of adherents down to the present day. Indeed if we look at the Muslim world there is hardly a region that does not have Sufi orders still functioning today. And Sufism has influenced the spiritual life of the religion to an extraordinary degree and there is no other domain of Islamic civilisation which is affected by it'.

The introductory chapter speaks of Gnostic Sufism which is rooted in the four basics i.e. Shariat, Tariqat, Haqiqat and Marufat, thus to understand Sufism we need to study the Qur'an, the Sharia (Islamic law), and above all the Prophet Muhammad to clearly understand its precepts. It also discuss Sufi origin, ways and orders followed by general introduction on poetry, influence of Persian literature on the world literature. The first chapter also discuss Sufi Poetry in detail, its characteristics and finally a brief discussion has been carried out on the elements present in the poetry of the three Sufi poet Rumi Hafiz and Bulleh Shah. The main portion of the book explore the Sufi Poetry of Rumi, Hafiz and Bulleh Shah.

Suraiya Yasmin

Acknowledgements

First of all I Acknowledge, the grace of Almighty Allah, Without whose love, care and guidance I would not have accomplished my research work. I thank my divine for guiding me silently by proving good health with spiritual, emotional and psychological strength in completing my work.

I would like to express my heart-felt gratitude and appreciation to my Superwoman Prof. Sujata Gurudev, Head, Deptt. of English, NEHU Tura Campus, Tura. Had she not been there with me all the time this work would have not been accomplished. I sincerely thank all the person behind my work to make it a successful one.

I am grateful to my family and friends especially my father Abdus Sobur Akond. There is a saying that 'behind every successful women there is one man' and that Man is my Father, whose constant encouragement, motivation and support has given me enough strength to carry out my research work. Lovingly, I thank my mother Aleya Begum for her emotional and moral support for which I could devote my time to complete my thesis. Last but not the least I thank my only brother Arif Akond for his constant support, encouragement, love and liberal attitude, without which it would have not been possible to complete my writting. Therefore I humbly thank my family members and friends for their love, faith and believing in me, in everything that I took up in this entire journey.

Suraiya Yasmin

Contents

CHAPTER 1

Introduction

Sufism dates back to antiquity, before the emergence of the prophets like Abraham, Jesus or Muhammad. As its central precept is mysticism of creation, originating with God's creation of the universe and human race along with Adam. Sufism came to light at the time of Prophet Muhammad. As it is believed that his followers were the first mystics or the Sufis or the followers of gnosis (mystical knowledge). Some people call themselves Sufi while Sufism is a broad category where some adherents do not follow Islam and the religious laws. Other believe that to become a Sufi one needs to follow the outer laws, morals and ethics of Islamic religion. To become a Sufi one needs to follow the outer laws, morals and ethics of Islamic religion. Sufi master Muzaffar Ozak comments:

> Sufism without Islam is like a candle burning in the open without a lantern. There are winds which may blow which may blow that candle out. But if have A lantern with glass protecting the flame, the candle will continue to burn safely. (Fadiman 4)

Therefore, Sufism without Islam is like Hinduism without Vedanta. Without following the religious morals and ethics one cannot be called a Sufi. Sufism without Islam is like a building without having no proper base and which can be demolished by an earthquake. Before starting and adopting the path of Sufism one needs to follow the Sharia or Islamic religious law which includes honesty, charity and kindness towards the poor, love and service to humanity as epitomised by Prophet Muhammad. The Sufis look towards Prophet Muhammad as their role model as he showed humanity to balance worldly and spiritual life. This is evident in the fact that prophet Muhammad had married, raised children, settled political issues, led armies and also preaching and instructing his followers about Islam. Islam means "Submission to God's will". Qur'an describes Islam as a monotheistic tradition which has its root from Abraham, Moses and Jesus. As prophet Muhammad had himself was belived to have said, "I have not brought you a new religion. I have brought you the religion, in an unchanged, untampered with way". (Fardiman 4) To serve humanity implies having to bear all humiliations in order to save them from ignorance. Historically at that time the Arab world was fully plunged in heinous crime like murder, rape and genocide etc. Moreover, to be a Sufi the disciple needed to follow a spiritual discipline as a hard shell capable of holding its mystical experience. The Sufis believe that religion is the tree and its roots are the religious practices. The branches are the mystical experience while the fruits include the truth or God. So without the roots i.e. the discipline one cannot grow and reach the fruit. Therefore, it is the moral and ethical values of Islam which provides the perfect climate for the Sufis to attain spiritual fruition. The primary goal of the Sufis are progress on the path of self-realisation, devotion, love of God and humanity.

Sufism is so abstract that it cannot be grasped in words nor in sentences, it can only be understood by going through its stories, poetry, art, rituals, calligraphy, exercises, readings, dance movements, prayers and also by studying its preparatory stages. Sufism is above all a universal expression of love, love for mankind and God. Love not only expressed towards God but also his creation as they wish to exemplify the fact that loving creation is to love the creator. To be a Sufis is to be a lover of truth. Another definition for Sufism is to follow the path of truth. Which leads one towards the union with the divine. Sufism implies a systematic rejection of the material world and (involved) deeper and deeper into spiritual world. Therefore following the Sufi path means to follow the path of truth. And it's a spiritual path which leads one towards the union with the divine. Indeed it a systematic rejection of the material world and in the spiritual world. Self-control, diverting oneself of all ego is the ultimate goal of the Sufis leading to divine union. While divine union is the prime goal for the every follower of Islam. For the Sufis its important to know in conceptual terms the meaning of that divine unity and that is why they proceed for the Gnostic view point i.e. knowledge of the unseen. Divine union is the prime goal for the ordinary follower of Islam but for the Sufis it is important to know the reality or meaning of that divine unity and that is why they proceed for the Gnostic knowledge (knowledge of the unseen).This research project has been selected not only from the Academic point of view but to establish beyond all doubt that Sufism is perhaps one of the Greatest expression of love and peace the world has witnessed.

Terminologically the term "Sufism" or "Tassawuf" is derived from the Arabic word "Suf" which means "wool". However it has several other associations like "wuf" (pure), "aff" row (one who stood in the first row with the prophets), "uffah" or verandha (porch i.e. those who studied and worshiped with the prophet the holy Quran away from the worldly affairs. Another important connotation of the Sufis is that roamed from door to door bagging for alms and that is why they were also called the Dervish which means door. Sufi "faqir" which means begger i.e. having their sole frocus not in the worldy things but upon their belief that they were nothing and totally empty without their God. Further the Sufis believe that God send his messengers to this earth. According to Quran there are 1,24,000 messengers who have been sent to earth by God and further the Sufis believe that at all times there is a messenger of God present upon this earth. In Chapter 10, Sura Yunus it is clear that in every nation and community there had always been a messenger:

> And for every ummah (a community or a nation), there is a messenger, when their messenger comes, the matter will be judged between them with justice, and they will not be wronged. (Qur'an 10:47)

This has given Sufism very liberal in its outlook as the Sufis had opted for different ways, languages and traditions in order to fit in to the tradition and cultural environment of people. The liberality of the Sufi Islam from the fact that all the messengers of God are like the rivers which originated and flowing into the same source, the ocean.

Since there has been awakened souls in all the times so it is not possible to restrict the wisdom and illuminated souls to any one historical period or Sect. Sufi is a very broad category which is inclusive of all who responded to the Divine Messengers of all ages like Abraham, Moses, Jesus, Zarathustra, Buddha, and Muhammad. We can say that the Sufis are the one who has not hesitated in their responding to these messengers of all ages. Thus a true Sufi is not only a follower but has an innate divine wisdom which in Sufism is called "Ihsan" a stage of mind where one can experience the divine presence in everything and everywhere. Thus before the advent of Prophet Muhammad they were called Ekuanul Safa (Brothers of purity) and after his lifetime those who follow his Shariat (Islamic law) were designated as Sahabi Safa (Knights of Purity). However the prophets or messenger can be categorised as Sufis if they possess the mystical divine knowledge of heart called "Ihsan" which established a divine communion with God. Thus the Sufis world view admits of no differentiation all of mankind is ultimately One. The boundaries and separation self-erected since we are ultimately waters from the same rivers flowing into the ocean. Thus Sufism removes all the barriers of religion, rules and regulations in order to unite with the divine. Inayat khan the great Sufi mystic was once asked by his teacher in 1907 to establish a Sufi institution in the west, His reply underlined the fact that the corpus of Sufism could not be limited to a particular time and place.

> Every age of the world has seen awakened souls, and as it is impossible to limit wisdom to any one period or place, so it is impossible to date the origin of Sufism. (Minhas:5)

Thus while many Sufi scholar believe that Sufism is not possible without its Islamic roots, there are some including Inayat Khan who believes that Sufism has Multi-religious roots having its existence from the very beginning of human creation when God created Adam, the first man by breathing in his human frame. According to Inayat Khan the Sufis are men of wisdom whose mysticism is beyond the understanding of common people. The Sufis kept themselves apart from humdrum existence, imparting their mystical knowledge and wisdom to the selected few who are eager to know and ready to take on the ardours of discipleship. Robert Graves in his Introduction to Idries Shah's "The Sufis", says that the Sufis were ancient freemasons whose origins could not be traced or dated. Another reason nor do they for their mysterious origins is that they abjured all identity except union with the divine. They concentrated and focused solely upon their spiritual development. Unlike many the Sufis do dogmatic sects do not focus upon any particular place of worship or sacred city nor any religious dogma for they firmly believe that God dwells everywhere and in everything take any interest in the research for their identity for they want only one identity that is to unite with the divine. Instead they concentrate in their spiritual development. The Sufis do not bother for any worshiping place or sacred city nor any religious dogma for they believe God dwells everywhere and in everything that He has created.

> Thus Sufism is universal with an omniscient; omnipresent; omnipatient, attitude towards the creator while outwardly seeing the Sufi seems to love from a heightened consciousness level to obey all the outward religious law but inwardly they are beyond all these rules and regulations of the

> physical world. They do not even like to be called as Sufis but they accept it good-humouredly for their followers. An interestingly anecdote about Rumi's master-cum friend Sham-e Tabriz is that he once forbid Rumi from reading the old religious book of his father Baha-uddin – Baktiyyar. This was because Shams wanted him to grow without the strange hold of Laws. Even to this day while the Sufi schools are generally established in the name of the Sufi masters there is no graduation degrees in these schools. scholars are made to stay connected with their masters and fellow beings to impart in order, share and develop the knowledge and wisdom of Sufism.

Thus it may be said that while Sufism existed from time immemorial it has come to light after Prophet Muhammad. Likewise the Sufis believed were two dimensions to the revelation of the Quran to Prophet Muhammad by the Archangel Gabriel. One is the Word of Quran and another is the divinely inspired knowledge which had been put in the heart of Prophet Muhammad who could not read or write. To the Sufi it is indeed that wisdom the heart is supreme. This (brings) us to another meaning of Sufism which qualifies the fact that purity, alone who are pure at heart. The Quran that God has made our soul with all the knowledge of right, wrong, good and bad at the time of our creation. But it is that pristine purity is lost during our sojourn on this earth resulting in the contamination of the soul. But this when we try to get back to that pristine state God purified state can restored through a path of enlightment. As it is mentioned in Sura Ash-Shams (The Sun) in the *Qur'an*:

> He indeed shall be successful who purifies himself and he will indeed be successful who purifies his soul, and he will indeed fail who corrupt his soul. (The Quran 91:9-10)

Therefore in order to get divine approval one needs to go through the rites of purification. Thus the Sufis follow certain steps in order to purify themselves from all the evils that beset man; greed, jealousy, hatred, grudges, selfishness, sinfulness, desire etc. In Sura Al Baqarah (The Cow) it is mentioned clearly that God is compassionate and merciful to those who repent for their sin and purify themselves. When Adam asked for his forgiveness He not only forgiven but further that he and his descendants would be guided and he would receive the Divine Grace.

> Get down from this place(the Paradise), then whenever there comes to you Guidance from Me, and whoever follows My Guidance, there shall be no fear on them, nor shall they grieve. (The Qur'an 2:38)

Thus the Sufis strongly belief in repentance. Therefore we can say that all the enlightened beings or whoever has acquired that special knowledge of heart which takes one nearer to the divine are the Sufis. But it is clear from the various evidence that Sufism was a name given to the companions of Prophet Muhammad, the Prophet of Islam (surrender to God's will) and hence to those who follow the path which he followed i.e. Shariat, which implies follows, Tariqat, Haqiqat and Marufat.

Sufis are the follower of both the Qur'ran and the teachings of the Prophet Mohammed, but they believed that the way to salvation could not be possible only by the mere declaration of the clergymen, whose teachings are restricted within the religious jurisprudence. The Sufis declare that Islamic Law (Shari'a) should be followed by Islamic Way (Tariq'a) inorder to assist the Seeker (Salik) in his search for Truth (Haqiq'a) Which he cannot reach without being in the state of Mysticism (Maruf'a). William Chittick's comments on Sufi ways:

> Sufis understand 'Law' or Shari'ah in its widest sense, as embracing 'knowledge' and all the theoretical teachings of Islam. The 'Way' or Tariqah is then the method of putting the Law into practice. And the Reality or Haqiqah is the inward states and stations attained by the traveler in his journey to God and in God". (Chittick *Sufism* 22-34)

According to the Sufi tradition a Seeker (Salik) has several stages or stations to come across and to achieve perfection of self. A station can be attained by observing and exercising certain discipline and practice, but a state is nothing but a submissive state of mind, which is controlled by sensations and not of conscious choice. The Sufis believe that anybody can attain divine knowledge but if someone desired to go through Sufi ways one must follow the Sufi path for which requires a guidance from a Sufi Sheikh or Murshid. The disciple who travels that path will be called as "Salik" or traveller and road itself is called as "Suluk". The disciple acquired all the knowledge from his murshid which he indeed received from his Sheikh and in this way the process continues. The process is called silsilas. It is said that this silsilas in Sufism has started from Prophet Muhammad who as a Sheikh to Ali and Abu Bakr had transmitted the mystic tradition which they imparted to their follower.

In this way the Sufi way or Silsilas has been transmitted from the master to the disciples. In the beginning the disciple is a seeker or 'talib' then a 'salik' and then a Gnostic or 'arif' (possessor of mystical knowledge). In one occasion Prophet Muhammad happened to say"

When someone has no sheik Satan becomes his Sheik". Initially there is a ceremony called Ba'ya or the murid where the murid holds his Nurshids hand and takes an oath of allegiance with some repetition of prayers and shijra (spiritual lineage of the order). After the ritual the Murshid takes the Murid as his spiritual son and observes his every action whether good or bad, suggest him trains him to meditate in order to help him in his spiritual development. The murshid teaches the murid to surrender himself to his murshid so that he will learn to surrender himself to the divine. Once Shams-e-Tabriz had tested Rumi's Submissiveness for his master. He asked for a woman for him Rumi offered his wife Shams declared her his sister. Shams asked for a young boy Rumi offered his son and Shams accepted him as his son. Then ordered Rumi to get some wine though it is forbidden in Islamic law, he fetched a glass of wine but Shams threw it away and said that he was testing him. Rumi was a man of law but when he met Shams he realised his limitations and embraced him. Rumi believes that no matter what we are if our companion is a holy person we become one. Rumi quotes in his Mathnawi on the teacher – disciple relationship:

> Whoever travels without a guide
> Needs two hundred days for a two day's journey. (Schimmel *Mystical* 19)

In Hadith Qudsi, Prophet Muhammad affirms God's word as it is mentioned that God himself has said that when the believer wins his heart he became the ear of his believer hear, the eye by which he sees, the hand by which he grasp and the foot by which he walks.

> My slave seeketh unremittingly to draw night unto Me with devotions of his free will (nawafil) until I love him; and when I love him, I am the Hearing wherewith he Heareth, And the Sight wherewith he seeth, and the hand wherewith he Smiteth, and the foot whereon he Walketh. (Bhukhari 37)

Therefore, to be called as Sufis or to get favour of God the Sufis needs to go through certain ways namely the Shariat (Laws), Tariqat (Ways), Haqiqat (Truth) and Marufat (Mysticism). Again the Shariat consist of certain laws which have the basic five pillars to have faith in the assertion that there is no god but God and Muhammad is his messenger (La Illaha illal lahu Muhammadur Rasul Allah), offering of five times prayer, fasting during the month of Ramadan, Zakat (Charity) and Pilgrimage to Mecca.

The Sufi Tariqah (Tariqat) includes Tawbah (repentance), Faqr (Poverty), Zuhud (piety), and Dhikr (remembrance of God) Faith in

God (Tawakkul), Patience (sabr), gratitude (Shukr), Contentment (rida) and love (mohabba). As Sharia is to clean up the outer life but Tariqah is designed to clean up the inner self. Tawbah or repentance makes us pure. The Sufis believe that God likes the repentant and forgives their sin.

Therefore, the first and foremost criteria to become a Sufi, is to go through Tawbah (repentance). God is the most merciful and compassionate and surely he forgives those who repent for their sin. In Qur'an Sura At-Tawbah (The Repentance), it is mentioned that the believer must destroy the non-believer, which does not mean one to be killed physically but by preaching and teaching about God to kill their inner evils. But many scholar has misinterpreted and mistranslated the Qur'an for which many criticise the holy Qur'an. This is the most controversial verses of Qur'an. So, to understand this particular verses one must consider the age and situation of the time when this Sura (Verses) has revealed to the Prophet. As at that time the believer of Prophet Muhammad and his religion is very few and so the majority of the non-believer inflicted terrible torment on Muhammad and his followers (including women and children) so whoever believed him and on his religion and came to the rescue, thus the notion that war with the non-believers is loved by God:

> But the messenger and those who believed him
> Strove hard and fought with their wealth and their lives
> Such are they for whom are the good things, and it is they
> Who will be successful.
> Some Arabs of the desert came with ready excuses,
> Asking for leave to stay behind. But those who had
> Lied to God and his Prophet stayed at home doing nothing
> So punishment for those who disbelieve among them will be painful.
>
> (*The Qur'an* 9: 88-90)

Secondly, in order to understand this verse one must understand that God is the most merciful and kind to his creatures for he is the one who created us. So just like our parents who punish us for our misdeeds but can't kill us or direct to someone to kill them, God cannot order his one child to kill the other. So we can say that fight against them is self defence and for the safety of their woman and children from the hand of the Zalimun (wrong doers). Once in the battle of holy fight against the tormenter of Muhammad and his followers the enemy soldier had spat on Ali's face the son in law of Prophet Muhammad when he was about to stab him, Ali left enemy free later when questioned why he left that enemy he said that he was fighting for the holy cause of protecting his people from the hand of the tormentor, but if he would have killed him it would be a reflection of his personal anger and surely God is with them who are pious and innocent and not with the Zalimun (wrong doers). So if that was the ideology of Islam then how can the so called Jihadis be considered as the follower of Islam. The word Islam itself means peace. Therefore Islam does not permit violence. Instead it directs us towards inner Jihad (fight with all the inner instincts or, nafs i.e. ego, hatred, jealousy, greed, desire etc).

> When the sacred months comes and have passed, kill the Mushrikin (inner evil)
> Wherever you find them, (in whatever situation it come out).
> And capture them and besiege them, and prepare for them each and every ambush.
> But if the repent (inner self) and pray to Allah (God) and give alms (Zakat).
> Then leave their way free. For sure, God is Oft-Forgiving, Most Merciful. (9:5)

Therefore, only one who is not mature ethically, morally and spiritually will mis-interpret this verses of Qur'an as the rebellious and violent one. But we must understand that God cannot suggest any harmful deeds for his creatures for He loves all creatures undoubtedly. So God through this verses tells us that if one can kill all their Nafs (i.e. ego, hatred, jealousy, greed, desire etc.) during the holy months (Ramadan) they can also do so in the other month of the year. And if one repents for his sin God will surely forgive him. So the Sufis repent for their sin before they start for their further journey towards the Sufi path.

Poverty is another important observance for the Sufis. They believe that Poverty brings one nearer to God. Prophet Muhammad himself had a life of extreme poverty. Prophet Muhammad himself proclaimed: 'Poverty is my Pride', he even prayed to the lord in this way: O God make me live lowly and die lowly and rise among the lowly. He further said that on the resurrection day god will say "Bring ye My loved ones nigh unto Me"; When the angels will say that who are Thy loved ones, god will answer "The poor and the destitute". (Dehelvi, 128:2010) The author of the Sufi manual *Kashf al Mahjub* Uthman Hujwiri commented on Poverty in this way: Know that poverty has a high rank in the way of the truth and the poor are held in greet esteem by God. The Sufis believe in long fasting for they believe it makes them humble in their behaviour.

Zuhd or piety is another station of mind that the Sufis need to attain. Zuhd means complete devotion toward God by keeping oneself away from all the temptations and attachment of this world. For this one must fight with all the temptations which exist inside us called Zahid. Prophet Muhammad gave the name of this inward fight of ours as Jihad e Akbar (the higher struggle). Which means fight with our inner nafs (instinct) not with the outer world. In Qur'an Sura Yusuf (Joseph) when the woman tried to seduce Yusuf and put the blame on him. Yusuf is ready to be tried by his master and Zulaikha's husband. As he said: And I free not myself (from the blame). Verily, the human (self) is inclined to evil, except when my Lord bestows his mercy (Upon whom he wills). Verily, my Lord is Oft-forgiving, most Merciful. (12:53) which means we humans are not free from sins but we can be rescued from it if we ask his guidance in every sphere of our life. Therefore it is clear from the above verse that God saves us from all the sin if we ask him to keep us away of all the sins. So the Sufis firmly devoted themselves to God for their guidance. Long night prayers and fasting is another way to have control on one's instinct.

Dhikr (Zikr), is the way of the Sufis to get connected with the divine. The Sufis believe that the souls had a very intimate connection with the divine more than we can even imagine. Before the birth of humans we all were existed in the souls world where we had been connected with the divine but after we are born we have forgotten our origin. So the Dhikr helps us to connect with our previous state of mind where we can somehow remember our previous life in the soul world. It is also important to remove the veil of self-ego which acts as the main veil between God and its creation. Therefore in order to remove such veil the Sufis practice the remembrance of God by reciting its 99 beautiful names. Nevertheless, a defense of rituals such as *dhikr* was put forward by no less than the brothers Ahmad and Muhammad Ghazâlî in the early twelfth century. The defense depended upon maintaining the strict distinction between the spiritual and the profane, or, as J.T.P. De Bruijn writes, the defense was "not without certain restrictions which were to prevent such expressions of mystical ecstasy from becoming entangled with the sinfulpromptings of the lower soul."16 The ecstasies of *dhikr* are thus affirmed as defensible spiritual practice, but would seem to bring with them the risks of their contamination by a profane ecstasy and a profane love that is a necessary consequence of the traditional association of music.

Dhikr is of three types one is Group Dhkr (halqa), Silent Dhkr (dhkr e khafi) another vocalised rhythmic chant (Dhkr e jahri). Dhkr consist of Repetition of the 99 attributes of Allah (God).Before starting Dhikr one must clean oneself by Wudu (wuju), sit in a clean place surrounded by good perfume of rose water, wear proper cloth which will be strictly in adherence with the Islamic dietary laws. In Qur'an Sura *Al-Muzzammil (The Enshrouded One)* it is mentioned clearly that God asked his servant to recite his name: And remember the name of your Lord and devote yourself to Him with a complete Devotion. (73:8) Then again in Sura *Al-Baqarah (The Cow)* He says: Remember me, I will remember you, and be grateful to Me and never be ungrateful to Me. (2:152) Therefore it is clear that God wants us to remember him. Prophet Muhammad too gave emphasise on the remembrance or recitation of divine name in this way:

> It is pronouncing Thy Name
> That I must die and live. (*Bhukhari* iv 187-188)

Therefore in this process of remembrance the Sufis get awareness about their nothingness and gradually detached themselves from all the egos, greed, anger etc. which are the actual veils between divine and them. Sabr or patience is another attributes of Allah among his Ninety-nine (99) attributes. God loves them who possess this qualities and God had tested particularly His Prophets. It is said that Victory will be there for them who had patience in all the sphere of life. Rumi writes in this regard:

> Patience O Father, is an iron shield
> On which God has written 'victory has come' (Schimmel Mystical 30)

Patience had been a priority with God to test his messengers. Whethere it be prophet Yunus, Yusuf (Jeseph), Musa (Moses), Abraham, Isa (Jesus) or Muhammad.

Tawakkul or faith in the divine God is the main tool for the Sufi path. Which again revolve around in the first pillar of Islam i.e. to have faith in the line La-illa-ha illallahu-Muhammadur Rasul Allah (there is no god but God and Muhammad is the messenger of God). The Sufi disciple are trained to believe that one should not rely on anybody and on anything except the Almighty and the sheiks are only the path finders. In the *Qur'an* Sura Abasa (He frowned) God says:

> "Then let man look at his food(How we provide it), for what we pour forth water in abundance, And we split the earth in fragments, And produce therein corn, And Grapes and nutritious plants, And Olives and Dates, And enclosed Gardens, dense with lofty trees, And fruits and fodder, For use and convenience to you and your cattle. Then when the day of resurrection will come, man will flee from brother, mother and father, wife and children, for that everyman will only think about themselves, the believers face will be bright for the news of getting paradise and the disbelievers face will be dust-stained. (80:24-40)

So that day no one but Allah (God) can help the humans from the horrifying hell (Dujak), where man and women will be punished and burned several times for their sins and disbelief in God.

Shukr (gratitude) and contentment is another great station that the Sufi disciple must attain to reach Marufat. The law of universe says that the more we will be thankful the more we are going to receive. The Sufis always remain grateful to Allah no matter what they are going through. Rida or contentment is similar to Shukr, So the Sufis remain contended and give their gratitude towards God for they believe that everything and everyone good or bad comes from the divine as a guide to teach us lesson of life for our good.

> Gratitude is the wine for the soul. Go on. Get drunk.
> Wear gratitude like a cloak and it will feed every corner of your life.
> Be grateful for whoever comes, because each has been sent as a guide from beyond. (*Quote by Rumi* web)

Mohabba or love is another station that the Sufi should reach. Which is possible only when the Sufi free themselves from all desires except the love of God. In this stage nothing can trouble them except the union with God. Rabia-al basri is another great example of selfless love of God. As she said:

> Thy love is now my desire and my bliss
> And has been revealed to the eye of my heart that was athirst
> I have none besides thee, Who dost make the desert blossom
> Thou art my joy, firmly established within me,
> If thou art satisfied with me, then
> O desire of my heart, my happiness has appeared.
> (Nicholson *Studies in I. M.* 32)

Therefore, the Sufis experience certain stages in the form of stations (*maqaamaat)* and states (*ahvaal)* while on the journey for complete absorption in God and in the path of love. It is in these stages that he realise love (muhabba) and is equipped with certain qualities of mind which helps to reach higher stages of consciousness.

It is believed that God himself has created us because of love. So the Sufis disciple is to love God without expecting any reward from him except the union with Him. F. Holdone Devis describe Sufism as a religion of love with a creed and dogma. Prof. K.D Bhargawa says Muslim mystics may be regarded as the lovers of supreme beauty but also there is a convergence of an East and west term thought in the fundamentals of love and admiration for supreme beauty, 'There are minor differences in their ways but they tend to move in same direction and sing the same prayer for the union with the beloved.' (Tarachand 50)

Having passed through all the stages of Tariqat the Sufi attains the State of Marufat or (Mysticism) which is followed by their realisation of the Haqiqat (Truth)The ultimate goal of the Sufi life is to be united with the ultimate Reality, viz. God, a union which is referred to as 'the divine Onenes'. According to the Sufi concept of God and its creation which they termed as 'Wahdat-al- wujud' (Unity of Being) which mean from one being all other being got their existence. The Sufis concept of 'union' with God takes places after the Sufi Salik pass through the stage of fanna and baqaa where a fanna is a state of self-loss or self-denial or death of the self (annihilation) and baqaa is a permanence in the real Other (eternal existence). After the cessation of the self and the union with the truth the Sufi does not die physically but becomes aware of the outer world again but he is not the same person any more.

Böhme's notion of cessation of self in order to attain divine union without leaving the way of the world and God resembles the Sufi state of *fanaa* and *baqaa*. As Böhme has said:

> The only true way by which God may be perceived in His [...] essence, [...] is that man arrives at the state of unity with himself, and that, [...] in his *will* – he should leave [...] self'. (Hartmann 54)

If we only leave our selfish nature, then the divine will dwell in us and ignite our soul with its flame of light and love:

> The human selfhood will then follow in the joy of humility, and become able to see what is contained in time and in eternity. [...] The soul is then no longer her own property, [...]. In such a state of calmness [...] should the soul then remain, like a fountain remains at its own origin, and she should without ceasing draw and drink from that well, and nevermore desire to leave the way of God. (Ibid 56)

In this regard P. B. Shelley exclaimed: Man's soul is but a part of 'one harmonious Soul', a 'Soul of the Universe', a river flowing 'to the sea'. (Shelley, 1820), Wordsworth said God is a 'one mighty whole' which contains within itself all beings a pantheistic oneness of the beings with God 'when he says:' All beings live with God, themselves | Are God, existing in the mighty whole (Selincourt and Gill xxxiii)

Wordsworth again argues in *'Lines Composed a Few Miles above Tintern Abbey' (1798),* 'a spirit, that impels All thinking things, [...] | And rolls through all things' (101-03), (Wordsworth, 2000). Coleridge too is of the view that it is 'God | Diffused through all, that doth make one whole' and human beings are 'Parts and proportions of [that] one wondrous whole!' (Coleridge 128)

Seyyed Hossein Nasr renders a broad ontological reason for the logic behind the reality of Sufism in its relation with our being. 'Sufism', he remarks, exists to enable us to become what we should really be, [...] to become ourselves', that is, 'to become that archetype or essence which is our [...] inner reality'. (Nasr 3), This state is only achievable through the subject's excessive love for the ideal Other, with whom the subject yearns to assimilate himself, and through his loss of self into the Other. In other words, the subject attains the 'inner reality' of his own self only when his essence dissolves into the 'sublime Essence' of the beloved and thereby becomes one with her/him (Fackenheim 214). Therefore in the process of 'fanna' and 'baqaa' the Sufi attains a stage where there is no veil which separates them from the divine.

Therefore we can conclude the main motive behind the Sufis attaining of the state of Haqiqat in Djavad Nurbakhsh words on Sufism 'a way towards the absolutely Real'. (Nurbakhsh, 1978: 204). Thus a Sufi starts off on his journey for the absolute Real, (*Haqiqat*) with the aim to discover divine love.

Therefore, the Sufi literature speaks about a number of stages in the Sufi quest for perfection. It also emphasise on the loss of self through love for the Other, which is called in Sufi language as '*fanad*' or annihilation of the self in the ultimate Being and the mystic's reaching of the station is his personal endeavour and progress towards the divine, but the state is a spiritual state of mind. Al-Qushairi, remaks on states as; gifts to the Sufis for their hard core devotion; the stations are earnings. (Arberry, 75) The station include, renunciation, silence, fear and hope, sorrow, endurance, trust, and satisfaction and the final stage of the station end with the announcement of the Sufis servanthood for the divine.

There are nuemerous Sufi orders in the world in this thesis the intention is not to describe about the different orders of the Sufism but the Sufi poetry. Therefore, a brief discussion has been made on these Orders. The most important and major orders which are mostly followed in the South Asia are: The Quadriyya order, The Chistiyya order, The Naksbandiyya order and Suhrawardiyya Order.

The Quadri order was stablished in Baghdad by Shayk Abdul Quadir Jilani (1077-1166 AD). He was known as the master of masters or Pir e Dastir and was also awarded the titles of Muhiyuddin (reviver of the faith), Qutub Rabbani (the spiritual asis established by the lord), and Ghawt al-A'zam (The greatest helper, the greatest saint).The People of Sind affectionately called him the "Putar mithe mahbub jo" (the blessed son of the sweet Beloved Prophet). The Quadri order focus upon the following: first to follow all the obligatory religious prayer of Islam, second is the voluntary prayers, Third is the Dhikr, remembrance of God (chanting 99 name of Allah), Fourth is to observe the five pillars of Islam, and fifth is the Tariqah (the spiritual way to reach God).

The word 'Naqshbandiyya' consist of two words 'Naqsh' which means engraving or engraving the name of the almighty in the heart of the worshiper and 'band' which means bonding, bonding between the individual and the divine. Therefore the Naqshbadiyya order's main moto is to tie the bond with the divine. The Naqshbandiyya order is named after Hadrat Baha-uddin Naqshband (1359 AD). Shaykh Ahmad al Faruqi al Shindis described the Naqshbandi order as the "Mother of all Tariqah. The Naqshbandi order were given different name in different time period. It was called 'Sadiqiyya' from the time of Hadrat Abu Bakr as – Siddiq to Hadrat Bayazid al-Bistami and the name 'Al-Tayfuriyya' was given to this order from the time of Bayazid to Sayyedina Abdul Khaliq al Ghujdawan and from the time of Abdul kaliq al Ghujdawan to the time of Hadrat shah Naqshband it was called as 'Khwajaganiyya'.

The Naqshbadiyya Order consist of prayer in every action with devotion and sincerity and clarity by following the Sunnah of Prophet Muhammad. It believes in maintaining the highst level of deeds and gives personal freedom to all interpretation. This order emphasise on complete self-purification by following all the Sufi tariqas which is very essential to feel and realise the divine presence. It ends up loving the divine and getting back love from the divine.

Therefore the Naqshbadiyya order is the easiest, cleanest, simplest and wisest way to reach God.

According to Khawaja Moinuddin Chisti the highest form of worship is 'to redress the misery of those in distress, to fulfil the needs of the helpless and to feed the hungry' (The Hindu, 12 October 2007) popularly known as Khawaja Ghareeb Nawaaz which means the caretaker, Supporter of the poor. He is the one who brought the silsila of Sufi tradition in India in around 11th century. The Chistiya order has been founded by Khawaja Abu Ishaq of Syria who settled in the village Chist, near Heerat in Afghanistan. Khawaja Muinuddin Chisti was born in 1141 A.D at Sanjar, in Sijistan present Iran. He is the descendant of Prophet Muhammad's grandson Imam Hassan and Imam Hussain. He got the title of 'Garib Nawaz' (Emperor of the Poor) from the beloved Prophet Muhammad. As when he Went to visit his graveyard and convey salam (greetings) to prophet Muhammad a reply came,' Va alaikum as salaam ya Garib Nawaz' and it was there where he received spiritual inspiration to settle in Ajmir of India and hence he got the title of Garib Nawaz and settled in Ajmir.

When Moinuddin and his spiritual Uttman went to Kaaba the Shaykh prayed for Moinuddin then a heavenly voice came, 'O Moinuddin, I am pleased with you and have accepted you. Ask for whatever you desire and I shall give it to you. Moinuddin replied, 'O Allah, accept those murids (disciple) who will follow me and those who descend from me' Another reply came, 'O Moinuddin, you, all your murids (disciple) and the murids (disciple) who will be descended from you until the day of judgement, I accept them all'. Then Muinuddin had himself promised to his people in this manner:' Whoever is my murid, and whoever is the murid of my murids and whoever is the descended from me until the Day of Judgment, Moinuddin will not step into paradise if he would be given without his followers'. (Curie 22)

The Chisti order follows the seven principles, notably the financial dependence on alms and farming, renunciation of material things, sharing of wealth to the needy, respect all the religion, independence for financial help from the political patronage. He strongly believed in love and tolerance among the people of all religion and that is why he had attracted several people who embraced his religion. He even opted for their way of dance, music and culture in order to make them understand him and his way to

God. He said that the pilgrims walked round the kabba (worship house at Makkah) but the divine knowledge possessor knows that God dwells in the heart of the believer so they circle their heart. He even cured several people from deadly sickness. Love to all the humanity and hate to nobody is the main moto of Chisti order.

The Suhrawardi Order was founded by Shaykh-al-Shayyuk Shihab-al-Din Abu Hafs Umer Bin Muhammad al Bhukhari al Suhrawardi Baghdadi. He was born in a town of Suhraward near Zanjan in Iran, he was a great philosopher and was imprisoned by Shalahuddin and was given death sentence at the very young age of around 36-38yrs as he was accused of heresy. The Suhrawardi order was later developed by his nephew Umar as-Suhrawardi and it has been brought in the sub-continent by Shaykh Jalauddin Tabrizi, disciple of Hafs Umar Suhrawardi. Bahauddin Zakaria was the one who established this order in India.

The Suhrawardi Order has been well accepted in Uchch, Gujarat, Punjab and Delhi. Later it became popular in the Bengal province, The Delhi Sultan's such as Alauddin Khilji and Muhammad Tuhlaq paid great tribute to this particular order.

In the ninth century, Arabic was used as a vehicle for mystical expression in verse, followed closely by Persian beginning in the eleventh century. Later the Sufis composed verse in other mother tongues such as Turkish and early Hindustani in the thirteenth century.

In this part a brief discussion has been made on the impact of Persian literature to the rest of the world which is followed by the discussion of Sufi Poetry specially the Sufi Poetry of the three major Sufi poet Rumi, Hafiz and Bulleh Shah. Raymond Schwab argues that the influence of oriental literature on the Europian has its beginning with the translation of Anquetil du Perron's *Upanishads* and the *Avesta* in 1771 and 1786:

> It was from Persia, through Anquetil, that everything began to open up: with Persia as the base, everyone from scholars and politicians to polemicists built up the East-West parallel, and the number of discoveries multiplied, as did liaisons between scholarship and creativity. (Schwab 6)

Warren Hastings (1732-1818), the first Governor-General of Bengal, in around 1764 in his discussion of Persian literature and its influence on English literature and its people says 'the cultivation of Persian literature might with advantage be made a part of the liberal education of an English gentleman' (Macaulay 545).

Hossein Nasr asserts that it was first in the late eighteenth and early nineteenth century that the West had shown its interest on the Orients and is because of the Sufi literature and Sufi Poetry. Nasr adds to his argument by emphasising on the fact that it was through the universal spiritual appeal of the Persian Sufi literature which is dominated by the spirituality, philosophy and doctrines of Prophet Muhammad and other Sufis had attracted the attention of the west. He remarks that the influence of Sufism in Europe is because of the writings of Persian Sufi poets and philosophers such as, Jalal-ud-din Rumi, Attar, Sana'i Sa'di, Shamsuddin Muhammad Hafez, Mahmud Shabestari, Shah Ne'matollah Wali, and Jami. (Nasr 3*)* They are famous for their spreading of Sufism in both Persia and other Islamic countries. It seems that the reason behind the scholars of the west to take interest and translate the Persian literature is mostly of the Persian's own admiration in the work of their Sufi Poets.

William Jones, Orientalist, Jurist and Welsh philologist had his great contribution in translating Persian literature in English. In his essay *On the Mystical Poetry of the Persians and Hindus,* published in the third volume of Asiatick Researches (1793*),* talks about the similarities that exist among the Persian Sufi literature, the seventeenth-century European theology, and the Indian Vedantis. He also suggests that all these three ideology has same belief on mens' soul being a part of divine soul and will go back to it 'absorbed in the divine spirit, that the love of God, who is the perfect truth and beauty, is real love, and that the beauties of nature are resemblances of the divine charms' (Jones 457).To prove his point on the omnipresent nature of God Jones illustrates examples from Hafiz works on his Divan, Rumi's Mashnavi and Nezami's Leili and Majnum. To Nezami's *Leili and Majnun* he called a *'vowedly allegorical and mysterious',* According to him the Sufis are full of desire for the divine love but without the presence of carnal affection, spread the love among people without any greed of material or physical possessions. (Jones 458)

William Ouseley was another Orientist who translated a large number of Persian poems, anecdotes, and memoirs into English. In his *Persian Miscellanies: An Essay to Facilitate the Reading of Persian Manuscripts* (Ouseley, 1795) and *The Oriental Collections Consisting of Original Essays and Dissertations, Translations and Miscellaneous Papers* (1797), Ouseley brought several translations from Persian poets such as Ferdausi, Attar, Hafez, Sa'di, Maulavi, Nezami, Jami, Saeb, Khosro,

Anvari, Orfi, and Khaqani. Ouseley also translate the famaous legend on *The Loves of Khosru and Shireen.*

Among other British Oriental scholars of the age is Francis Gladwin and John Nott. Gladwin has translated many Persian Sufi Poetry of Poets like Hafiz, Sa'di, Farroki, Nezami, amir Khosro, Anvari etc. in his book *The Persian Moonshee* (1800). He also in his dessertation *on The Rhetoric, Prosody and Rhyme, of the Persians* (1813) given an explanation on the poetic measurement and style in Persian poetry. John Nott too had translated in English seventeen ghazals from the *Divan* of Hafez with a brief and comprehensive introduction on some accounts of Hafez's work.

Poetry is the source of entertainment. Infact, it is a mixture of our thoughts, emotions and imaginations. It is neither the complete absence of reality but with little colour of imagination, rhythm and tune which adds charm to it. Different person has given different definitions of poetry. Dryden says poetry gives instructions and side by side delights us. Other poet like Johnson, Coleridge and Wordsworth says Poetry is a mixture of pleasure and truth. P B Shelley says that poetry is the record of the best and the happiest moment of the happiest and best mind. Therefore we can say that the Sufi poetries are also the records of the Sufis happiest moment of union with the divine. The oldest Sufi writings could be found first in eleventh century were in New Persians.

Sufi Poetry is generally dominated by mystical themes and any kind of mystical themes can be called as non-rational and poetry is non-rational. It is frustrating for those who try to understand and analyses poetry in logical, rational and utilitarian ground. Because poetry is something which can be felt and experienced rather than thought about. Before the beginning of modern age, poetry was usually read and sung and was orally transmitted to others. Therefore people did not think and understand instead they visualise, felt its meaning by its metaphors, imagery, symbols etc. Sufi poets give importance to metaphor as it helps convey message that is hidden and is beyond the reach and understanding level for the general people of this world. Metaphors are very important poetic elements which helps evoking sensibilities to the readers or listeners. Sufi poetry uses certain metaphors which would help understand it better. Sufi Poetry is being written to enlighten the inner self, to be aware of the reality, the connection with the divine. Intoxication is an important metaphor generally uses in Sufi poetry to define a spiritual state of mind where one is completely get drunk in divine love. Transformation took place and enters into the reality where no one but the divine exist. Intoxication is not only a metaphor used in poetry but it is also a state of mind.

Sufi poetry affects not only the exterior but also the interior of the human mind, which completely transforms a human. Another element of Sufi Poetry is the utilisation of imagery which is being used to arouse feelings of beauty, peace, grief, tension, humour etc. Which creates a world which gives a complete experience of the entire life in a moment of time. Therefore metaphor and imagery helps than to think it. With emotional responses poetry also arouse the spiritual and moral responses by listening or reading to the poetry consisted of the prophets Hadith or sayings or different stories related to different prophets from different religion or faith. And this feelings arouse in us the feelings of faith, emotions, of joy and sorrows. And if we are little aware of ourself (self-awareness) then the spiritual awakening may take place after listening to such poetry.

The important characteristic of Sufi Poetry is to depict the relationship between the creator and the creation. In Sufi poetry the feminine word is being used to describe the feelings of emotions and love between the creator and its creation. The Sufi poet who used the feminine language in their poetry are Sayed Muhammad Hafiz, Bulleh Shah, Sultan Bahu, Khawaja Ghulam Farid and Mian Muhhamad Bakhsh. Another is the love theme in Sufi poetry. The love poem generally has two characters involved one is the lover another is the beloved. In general love poem, the love occurs between two humans but in Sufi love poem love occurs between human and divine. Sometimes to make us understand the real love for divine the Sufis represent the human physical love in their poetries. No matter if they portrays the physical human love affair in their poetries but in reality they represent the spiritual in the disguise of physical love. In Sufi love poem the lover is in love with the beloved in such a way which brings its destruction. In Sufi term which is called as 'Fanna'.

Another important characteristic of Sufi love poem is the excruciating pain of the lover. In this type of poem the lovers has to suffer the pain of separation before they could get a glimpse of the beloved. History has been the witness of such separation between beloved and lovers. As Majnum has to bear the pain of separation for Laila, Zulaikha for Joseph (Yusuf), Mahmoud for the ailing Ayaz (because homosexuality is forbidden in Islam), Forhad for Shree. And these separation is not only for the passionate lovers but for any form of love. Such as father-son love, sister-sister love, human-animal love bond, Human-God love. In every love relationship there exist a separation if the emotion is extreme. As there is a popular saying that too much of anything is harmful so is love feelings. Best example for father-son relationship is the relationship between Prophet Jacob (Yaqub) and his son Prophet Joseph (Yusuf). Whose separation was destined by God as it might be important for His plan to execute. As Joseph was required for the Missories to bring them in the right path as they were the idol worshippers. And moreover anything which goes to its extreme whether proud, love feelings, or anything then suffering is a must. So was the case with Joseph and his father as Jacob loved Joseph more than any other of his son and hence was destined to suffer the pangs of separation. Pain is another great important element in Sufi love poem as it is because of pain and suffering one realises the depth of truthful love and also the happiness of union.

The third feature of Sufi love poem is the unconventional love. The most unconventional love is the love of Rumi and Shams, Mahmoud and Ayaz, Bulleh Shah and Innayat Khan as these are unacceptable love in the society as homosexuality is forbidden in any kind of society. This happens because of the lack of consciousness level among people. As it was not easy for normal human being to understand their love for each other. Therefore it is not possible for a normal human to comprehend the way of the Sufis whose consciousness level is beyond the reach of anyone.

Another major elements of Sufi poetry is the use of symbolism. Symbolism is a very important features of Sufi poem. As through the help of it one can understand the mystical poetry of the Sufis. The word 'Nightingale' has two meaning it is used for divine music, and for pilgrim who travels. Night stands for the material world which is gloomy for the free soul to move to the world of brightness. In other word the Sufis want to move from the dark gloomy world where there is only day which is an illusion and night which is gloomy to the world of divine presence. The word tree symbolises something which lure us to keep away from the divine. As Wordsworth says in his poem *Prelude* that when we are born there exist nothing but the divine that is why every human being is born in a state of complete innocence but gradually this mother earth lures making us forget our reality (Wordsworth). The Veil is the symbol of hindrance which comes between the divine and its creation. The mole represents the attractiveness of the divine, lamb symbolise the state of being innocence, white dove symbolise peace, eye brow symbolise the arched entrance of a mosque. The owl symbolises as satan, pelica symbolise Christ sacrifice on the cross, Swallow symbolise the incarnation of Christ, stork symbolise chastity, lion symbolise fire, mirror symbolise marry, sepent symbose for earth, cedar symbolise Christ, clover symbolises trinity, raven symbolise air. When Hafiz and Rumi refers beloved they means God.

The Sufi love poem has some common features. To appreciate Sufi poetry, it is important to acknowledge the role of pre-Islamic Arabic poetry in the formation of Islamic culture. The pre-Islamic poetry were mostly dealt with semi-magical, semi-prophetic manifestation of idolatry, self-ego, worldly life and human war against God. And therefore the follower of Islamic Monotheism considered those poetry as the poem of the 'jahiliyah' (ignorant or disbliever). Prophet Muhammad was too against such pre-Islamic poetry as he thinks those poetry is not worthy in building up a better society but he appreciates the Sufi poetry of Hassan Ibn Thabit. Later a sense of awareness spread in their poetic expression where only truth and nothing must reveal. In Qur'an Surah "Ash-Shuara" (The Poets) seems to disfavour the poets but it was only for those who denies the message revealed through Prophet Muhammad and lies through their poetry:

> Except those who believe (in the oneness of Allah) and do righteous deeds, and remember Allah much, and reply back(in poetry) to the unjust poetry. And those who do wrong will come to know by what overturning they will be overturned. (*The Qur'an* 26:227)

Therefore we can say that the Sufis were the strict follower of Shariat and hence they reveal only the truth and nothing else in their poetry. Annemarie Schimmel in his book "*As Though a Veil; Mystical Poetry in Islam*" outlines about the three types of Sufi Poetry in these way:

> We may discern here descriptive poems, in which the Sufis tried to tell of their experiences in the mystical states (ahwal); technical poems with often complicated word plays, poems, and allusions; and popular poems which as will become clear, often prefigure the mystical poetry in the non-Arabic areas. (18)

Arabic and Persian Sufi poetry cannot be separated from the tradition of court poetry. The ode (qasida) and the lyric (ghazal) were cultivated at the courts of the former chalipha governors in eastern Iran. However it was the quatrain (ruba'i) that was preferred for the expression of brief mystical insights. But the language that they used were direct simple and paradoxical.

Sufi poetry as was popularly misunderstood was not all about wine drinking, but it often used the shocking technique of reference to wine and to idolatry, to convey an ultimate goal for which respectablity and righteousness were to be sacrificed. Wine of course which was required for the court ritual of Persian kings, symbolises the intoxication of mystical love. The primordial covenant of the Qur'an, which fixed the relationship between God and humanity, is often re-called by a single word from the Qur'anic text; since humanity affirmatively answered God's question, "Am I not your lord?" (alastu- be-rabbikum in Persian).

However the Arabic and Persian Sufi poetry is inseparable from the tradition of poetry produced in the court. In terms of their social environments it might seem that the poetry recited in Sufi lodges, which celebrated the divine love and the intense master-discipline relationship, had little in common with the formal odes that professional poets composed to honour and praise their noble patrons. But if one take a closer look it would reveal that much of the poetry produced in court was saturated with the same imagery used in Sufi circles. Sometimes the same verse can be read in different situations differently for examples the praise of ordinary wine means simply the earthly passion. While in another context it could be interpreted mystical intoxication and divine love. Even the verse which are recited in Sufi lodges were first composed in a courtly settings. It is equally possible to read these poems as addressed to a royal patron, to a Sufi master, to God, or to a beautiful young boy who pours wine in a tavern.

Sufi poetry strictly follows the forms of rhyme and meter. There are four main poetic forms in sufi poetry they are: the ode (qasida), the lyric (ghazal), the quatrain (ruba'i), and the epic (masnavi). Sufi verse followed a strict system of quantitative meter, based on long and short syllables. The many possible meters, which from two to four syllables in a foot, were also the theoretical basis for Persian, Turkish, and Urdu poetry in Arabic script, although earlier poetic traditions in those languages may have been non-quantitative; this situation resembles the use of Greek quantitative meters (iambic pentameter, and so forth) to describe the stressed verses of English and other Europian languages. And the basic unit in all these case is the single verse, which is always divided in two; poetry is generally written with two halves in parallel columns. So in the ode, the ghazal and in the quatrain, the two halves of the first line rhyme, and in following verses only the second half of the line preserves the rhyme. The structure is therefore:

a a
b a
etc.

From this formal point of view the only difference between these forms is their length. The quatrain consist of only two complete lines or four half-verses. The lyric is customarily from six to twenty lines, and the ode may be from twenty five to several hundred lines in length. Both Arabic and Persian are far richer in rhymes than English, so that is why the composition of a long ode with a single rhyme is not so difficult a feat as it might appear. The epic form which originated in Persian bardic tradition, resembles the couplet (masnavi is the Persian pronunciation of the mathnawi, an Arabic term meaning doubled). Here the two halves of each verse, rhyme, but each succeeding verse takes a different rhyme, as follows:

a a
b b
c c
etc.

The epic form can be extended to truely enormous lengths, since it is not limited to the resources of a single rhyme.

Sometimes the readers assume that the Sufi poems are to be understood mainly as autobiography as a personal and individual document of inner experience.But generally the literary critic like R.A.Nicolson and Coleman Barks suggest that one should avoid this biographical fallacy. The height of Sufi poetry can be explored in the writing of Rumi, Hafiz and Bulleh Shah. As Daniel Ladinsky describe Rumi in his poem "The purity of Desire-100 Poems of Rumi" in this manner:

> Good poetry, like music or sweet touch, can doctor us up, be an antidote for an hour or longer, help us to get dressed for another day – combat the blues enough to mount the horse again; and may be even aid one in lying down the insidious weight of some old grudge or deep-rooted anxiety. Herein enters Rumi.... draws us near to his – and our own-inner light...From head to toe this guy is blazing. He is like a cyclone one wants to be drawn into... (Ladinsky 1)

It is said that discussion of Persian mystical poetry would be incomplete without a mention of Jalal-ud-din Rumi (1207-1273). He was born in the city of Balk in Afghanistan. The meaning of his first name (Jalal-ud-din) is Majesty of Religion. He was known as Mawlana in Iran and other Islamic countries and as Rumi in the west.The celebrated Persian poet Jalal al-Dln Muhammad Ibn Baha Muhammad (1212-1273) – known as Rumi in the West and Mawlana 2 Iran, in the Persian and other Islamic countries. Qolam-Hussein utters that the critics who admired Rumi as the most influential poet of the world are Hegel, R.A. Nicholson and A.J. Arberry (210). Several contributions has been made on the scholar study of Rumi's mystical work. Many song writers specially American singer-songwriter Madonna, has used Rumi's poetry for their songs and musical performances.

Rumi's poetry gives an impression of colourful and lively world where everyone can relate themselves to his poetry irrespective of caste, creed, faith etc. (Mannani 143). In order to make spiritual points in his poem Rumi had used many immoral stories as mentioned in the interview of Leonard Lewisohn with Shusha Guppy. His humorous lyrical narratives and stories serves the same spiritual function as the profane images. But they also act as the agent to cancel the blindly accepted ethical points and religious rituals and rules. Despite his grave philosophical ideology Rumi's poetry is mostly less rigid and more colourful and lively. His creativity and resourcefulness in using of metaphors and other figures of speech, refined and elegant diction, peaceful tone, clear and vivid continuous simple, humble and plain language, with beautiful and joyous rhythm adds to his Fascinating spiritual poetry. Critics, Philosopher and scholar including Yusufi are of the view that, 'no other poet in the canon of Persian poetry has been able to introduce as many varied rhythms as Rumi has' (211-214).

Rumi's poetry aims not only to instruct but also to entertain his reader. The Non-Persian too acknowledge the enthralling and captivating quality of Rumi's poetry. Shams-i Tabriz is his spiritual master and guide who introduced him the mystical path of love and freed him from the religious boundaries and jurisprudence. Rumi declared about himself through his ghazal: "My hand always used to hold a Koran, but now it holds Love's flagon. My mouth was filled with glorification, but now it recites only poetry and songs" (Divan-i Shamsi Tabriz 24875-76). Shams, wandering dervish, from the city of

Tabriz was unknown to Konya. One day Rumi accidentally met him in Konya When Rumi was returning after his sermon in the mosque. The detailed of Rumi-Shams meeting have been discussed in the second chapter of the book. It is this time when Shams queried Rumi about whom he considered more capable of having a greater palce with God the Prophet Muhammad or Bayazid Bistami (Mystic) that the Shari'a and Tariq'a came face to face. And this very question shook him and put in a new realm of life. (Mannani 22)

And it is said that before this encounter, Rumi was very serious in his profession as a clergyman and a rigid follower of Islamic Jurisprudence. According to William Chittick, Shams "transformed him from a sober jurisprudent to an intoxicated celebrant of the mysteries of Divine Love poetry" (Chittik *The Sufi Path* 3). Rumi and Shams love grew in time because of their constant companionship which was further increased with the deep pain of his separation with him when mysteriously Shams had disappeared from Konya. In the memory of Shams he even wrote his collection of sonnets in his name as Divan-i Shamsi Tabriz. Rumi was the founder of the sama' or whirling dance of the Sufis which help them get detached from the material world which is comprised of the movement of body parts in certain rhythm. Rumi's poetry has the quality of being called as Sufi Poetry.

Rumi became the founder of the Tassawuf-i ashiqanah (mysticism of love) from a Tasawuf-i zahidanah (pious mysticism). Abdul-Karim Soroush, states that Rumi and Ahmad Ghazzali, are the two mystics who balanced beautifully the love and Sufism in their Poetry (34). Generally the Sufis are scared of the God but Rumi sees God as an epitome of love and generosity. The poetry of Rumi gives us the universal message of brotherhood. Through his poetry he suggest the reader not to go with only the outer level meaning (Zahir) of the world and its phenomena rather he suggest to go beyond and search for deeper meaning (Batin) which is hidden.The important metaphors that Rumi uses in his poetry are the pair of coexisting objects like foam and ocean, picture and painter, and dust and wind (Chittick 21). Multiplicity of all existence is but the characteristics of one being which had split once to unite again. And in order to understand Rumi's poetry one must understand the multiplicity and separateness of our existence. Masnavi strarts with the poem with the concept of separateness. As in "*The Song of Reed*" in which the reed celebrates pain in separation of its reed-bed. (*MasnaviI* 9-10).

Rumi in his poem mainly talks on the everyday experiences of our depression, sadness, anger or the feeling of being. According to him they are guests in human mind, and we must welcome them as our teacher.

It is believed that Rumi was of royal descent as his mother belonged to a princely house whose roots could be traced to the immediate family of the prophet Muhammad and his father Baha-ud din Velad was the descendent of the caliph Abu Bakh. He has written almost 65,000 verses which consist of intoxicated Sufi poetry of love, separation and the joy of union with the divine. One of the reasons behind his popularity and universal appeal in both the Islamic world and in the western world is the lyrical beauty of his outpourings of love for the divine. As Jawid Mojaddedi, a scholar of early and medieval Sufism at Rutgers University and an award winning Rumi translator quotes of Rumi:

> Rumi was an experimental innovator among the Persian poets and he was a Sufi master. And the combination of mystical richness and bold adaptations of poetic forms is the key to Rumi's popularity... (Ciabattari)

Rumi's major works are Diwan-e shams-e Tabriz (named in honour of his great friend shams of Tabriz, consisting of 40,000 verses), and the Masnavi (called the Persian Qur'an, a six volume poem). His poetry can be further divided into various categories: the quatrains, and odes (ghazals) of the divan, the discourses, the letters, and the six sermons, *Fihi Ma Fihi* is consist of his speeches recorded either by his son sultan Velad or some other disciple. *Majalis-i-sab'a* is another work containing seven sermons. It is said that his *Masnavi* is considered as the most influential text in the Islamic world after Quran. And the original text in Persian was so appealing that in some institutions during the Ottoman empire were devoted to its study.

Rumi's poetry often expresses the dialect of love, separation, union, hope, fear, pain, and joy. Often considered the ultimate poet of love. Lee Briccetti, executive director of Poet House, co-sponsor of national library series in the US that features Rumi says:

> Across time, place and culture, Rumi's poems articulate what it feels like to be alive. And they help us understand our own search for love and the ecstatic in the coil of daily life. (Ibid)

According to Rumi love is the only reason that made the creator to create this beautiful universe. And there is no separate religion and nation for the lover accept the beloved because for the lover nothing exist accept the beloved. While speaking about Rumi in one of his interview Coleman Barks says:

> I feel there is a strong global movement, an impulse that wants to dissolve the boundaries that Religions have put up and end the sectarian violence. It is said that people of all religions came to Rumi's funeral in 1273. Because they said he deepens our faith wherever we are. This is a powerful element in his appeal now. (Ibid)

Therefore in today's world of terrorism and religious violence, it is very important to have the liberal view about religion which Rumi possessed and showed through his poetry several hundred years ago. As Rumi quotes:

> It is love that makes God to create this cosmos.
> Love's nationality is separate from all other religions,
> The lovers religion and nationality is the Beloved (God)
> The lover's cause is separate from all other causes
> Love is astorable of God's mysteries. (Naini 12)

Rumi further felt that if we do not love anyone we will never know the pangs of separation. Therefore it is important to be in love in order to realize the pain of separation. He also asserts that language is not enough to explain the joy of union with the divine and it is love that makes the lover weaker and the beloved stronger day by day. So the lovers can only feel the height of love but cannot express it in words. In his Masnavi Rumi tries to explain it:

> If you should speak and try a hundred ways to express it,
> 'Tis useless; the mystery becomes no clear
> A horse of wood is useless on dry land,
> It is the special conveyance of voyagers by sea,
> Silence is this horse of wood,
> Silence is the guide and support of men at sea.
> This silence which cause you annoyance.
> Is uttering cries of love audible to the spiritual. (Whinfield 326)

Therefore one should not trust in their tongue to express love for the beloved as there are so many other ways to express love beyond words. In his teaching Rumi says:

> However much we describe and explain love,
> When we fall in love we are ashamed of our words.
> Explanation by the tongue makes most things clear,
> But love unexplained is clear....
> Naught but love itself can explain love and lovers!
> None but the sun can display the sun. (Ibid 5)

Through his poem from Diwan, Rumi says that silence can make our heart speak better and it is the inner bond that draws one person to another, not the words. As there is a universal rule that whatever feelings a person possess against another person then the other one will also starts thinking the same for him. So we should always possess a feeling of love for each other because it is love that turns even the bitter into sweet, copper into gold, drugs into wine and pain into medicine.

> Be silent, that without this tongue the heart may speak,
> When I hear the speech of the heart, I feel ashamed of
> this speech. (*Arberry Mystical Poems of R. 9)*

According to Rumi a heart can express its love for the beloved a hundred times better than a mere word of our mouth. When a man once asked Rumi, 'Why is it you talk so much about silence?' He answered: 'The radiant one inside me has never said a word.' *(*Barks Rumi Soul Furry 196*)*

The translated poetry of Rumi by Coleman Barks published by Harper Collins publisher in New York 2001, has made the thirteen century poet of the Seljuk empire one of the most widely read poets across the world. As Hutson Smith writes about Rumi in the book of Coleman Barks *"Rumi Soul Fury: Rumi and Shams Tabriz on friendship"* in this manner:

> If Rumi is the most read poet in America today, Coleman Barks is in good part responsible. He ear for the truly divine madness in Rumi's poetry is really remarkable. (1)

The next Sufi poet that would be discussed here is Khwaja Shams ud-din Muhammad Hafiz (1320-1389) of Shiraz. In the Islamic tradition the name Hafiz is a honorary title given to a person who has memorised the entire holy Qur'an. His poetry deals mostly the intoxicating love of God. He often uses the wine as the symbol of love and has the power of intoxication. Scholars are at a loss wheather to consider Hafiz as a mystic or a libertine a good Muslim or a skeptic or the combination of all these. But as a poet he was dearly beloved and has often been referred to as the "Tongue of the Invisible". Ralph Waldo Emerson in his book "*Essay on Persian poetry*" published in 1858 called him as 'a poet for poets'. Parvin Loloi Pursglove in her thesis (1983) has written on the various translations of Hafez and their influence on English literary work. In the article, *Byron in Persian Costume*' (1988) She talks on Byron's interest in Persian literature and reading. And it is none but Hafiz, who mainly had his influence obout Byron's work through the agency of William Jones. Hafiz in his poetry expresses his experience of the mystical love for his beloved God. He was initiated into the Sufi school of Attar at the age of twenty one and there after skills in poetry converted from being a poor baker to a court poet. However his controversial writings and teaching led him to flee from Shiraz to Isfahan for his life. Eventually, however on public demand the Shah pardoned him and allowed him to return to the city. Hafiz's poems were divided into two-line couplets, and all of these couplets were put together in a bunch known as ghazel.

> "Neither Hafiz's body nor his life can deny for all his mischief only heaven awaits him". (Nisarg 3)

For Hafiz, he is not only a Sufi poet but also a great outspoken person of his time who could not tolerate the hypocrisy in the society. So he remained misunderstood by the court authority and also by the people. Thus he remained a controversial figure, saint or libertine.

Till date it is not easy to comprehend and understand the multi-faceted poetry of Hafiz. The important thing of Sufi poetry is the recognition and identification of self, God and the union between them, and so the Sufi Poets uses various beautiful images to explain these unity. The Sufis sets their journey in the search of the Self and of its unity with the Other to avoid alienation. According to the traditions of Neoplatonism and Sufism this inner urge for the unity aroze in us from the original separation from the Divine. Neoplatonist belief in the doctrines that, 'all entities originate in and emanate out of an undifferentiated unity'. 66 Sufism, too believe that all creation 'was of an undifferentiated unity interrupted by material creation which resulted in the separation of humanity (as lover) from God (as Beloved)'. Such separation of man from God creates an inner desire to return to the origin. This rupture is not only between the lover and the beloved but also with one's own inner Self. Therefore it is because of this estrangement the soul longs to return to its original state.

Hafiz is among the Sufis who asserts that the souls intoxication of God is similar with the body's intoxication with wine. Coleman Barks says about Ladinsky's translation of Hafiz's poems in the book '*The Subject Tonight Is Love: 60 wild and sweet poems of Hafiz*"

> There are universes inside Hafiz, a lineage of masters. Daniel Ladinsky follows the Playfulness; the rascal moves well. (1)

Hafiz urges us to view this world though his eyes to realise the presence of God in everything in this world. Therefore according to the Persians Hafiz's poems were not classical literature from a remote past rather it is cherished love, wisdom and humour from a intimated friend.

Bullah Shah Qadri Shatari was the greatest sufi mystic poet of punjab. His pure life and high spiritual attainments has made him famous among all nations. It is not known exactly when and how long he lived, but most scholar agree that it was during the period from 1680-1758. His family is believed to be related to the generations of prophet Muhammad. His family was from Uch Gilaniyan, i.e. modern day bhawalpur. Later his family moved to Malakwal near Multan. He completed his studies from Qasur under the sufi master Inayat shah. Scholars from the world such as Ralphwaldo Emerson and Innayat khan called him "The Sheik of Both the world", "The man of God", "The knower of spiritual Grace".

> Because of his pure life and high spiritual attainments, he is equally popular among all communities. Scholars and dervishes have called him 'the shiek of both the worlds,' 'The man of God', The knower of spiritual Grace' and by other equally edifying titles. (Puri, and Shangari web)

Inspite of his saintly qualities Bulleh Shah was not allowed a buried in the community graveyard for his unorthodox and radical attitudes towards religion. No doubt Bulleh shah was the follower of Shariat but later in life he became a radical because of the harsh policies of the Mughal emperors towards the non-muslims. To become a good muslim one had to follow the five pillars of Islam: bearing witness (believing the kalema; la-illaha-il lal la-hu muhammadur rasullulla), offering five times prayer in a day, fasting during the month of Ramadan, charity (paying of zakat) and pilgrimage to Mecca. Initially Bulleh Shah was the orthodox follower of Islam but gradually when he understood the mystery of all the religion he realised that all these external religious laws were of no use if our heart is not pure from all the hatered. As in his poem Bulleh Shah affirms:

> I gave up the mosque, I gave up the temple, No skipping meals nor Ramadan fast. I forgot ablutions and prescribed prayers. I'm sacrifice unto Him as long as I last. (Duggal 155)

Sufism in many ways a heretical and dissident spiritual movement which was suppressed by mainstream religion. Bulleh Shah was also one of those who had to suffer for his unorthodox religious view.

Even his family members were not spared. His sister had to pay for his liberal view by being forced to remain a spinster all her life.

> "Goodbyes are only for those who love with their eyes. Because for those who love with heart and soul there is no such thing separation." Rumi.

CHAPTER 2

Love and Separation in the Poetry of Jalal-ud-din Rumi

> Divine wisdom decreed us lovers of each other;
> all the particles in the world
> are fated to be in love with their mates,
> just as amber attracts straw. heaven says to earth; Welcome,
> we are magnetised to each other." *(Helminski 4391)*

No doubt the popularity of Sufi poetry is because of its translation in western languages and perhaps for its secular appeal. The Sufi poet who has written expensively on the theme of love were Rumi, Hafiz, Omar Khayyam and Farid-ud-din Attar. Sufi literature was decorated by Rumi with his mystical imagination and intuitive insights into spiritual reality expressed beautifully with subtle style that the way Persian language should be. When Rumi met the great Persian mystic Attar in Iran, Attar predicts "This boy will open a gate in the heart of love and throw a flame into the heart of all mystic lover." (Clarke). Attar showed the way to Jalaladdin Rumi, the greatest poet in the Islamic world, whose Mathnavi has been called by the fifteenth-century mystic, Jami, "The Qur'an in Persian tongue".

For the Sufis love is the most important term which is being used to show their intimate affection for their beloved, master, divine and prophet Muhammad. For the Sufis it is a matter of pride to be called as a lover. They are also called as lover or Ashique (Muhibb) and friend (dust, yar in Persian) of God. The Sufis has the great power of affection for their beloved that is why they were given a title of 'master of the heart' (Persian Sahibdi or ahl-i-dil).

A mad desire for something is another form of love. Wherein one forgets oneself and remembers the other. The thinking, liking of the others becomes the thinking, liking for the others. Thus the Sufis forget themselves and remember only the Divine. Divine love is something where one merge his sense of self with the divine energies and ultimately all self-identity annihilated. In divine love one has to surrender the self which is like a drop of salt in a vast sea of divine energy. Therefore the self has very little or no existence if one merge in the sea of divine energy. Human being often mistook the mortal love as the real love which is just the image which leads us to the real love. Spenser is of the view that earthly love is temporary and the divine love is permanent. In his poem *'Four Hymns' he says:*

> But only that is permanent and free
> From frayle corruption that,
> doth flesh ensew.
> That is true beauty: that
> doth argue you.
> To be divine and borne of
> heavenly seed. (Spenser web)

Even though John Donne had written mostly on sensual romantic love. His *Holy sonnets* showed his passionate and argumentative love for God. As he says:

> Yet dearly, "I love you", and would be loved fame
> But am betroth'd unto your enemies:
> Divorce me, "untie, or break that knot again:
> Take me to you, imprison me, for I
> Except you, enthral me, never shall be free,
> Nor ever chaste, except you ravish me. (Donne web)

So even Donne did not escaped of the feelings of the divine love which he has portrayed through his poem. Poet like Herbert and Vaugan was not behind in showing their divine love for God in their poems. Aurobindo Ghosh in his famous poem *Savitri,* the mythological story of Savitri and Satyavan celebrates the theme of earthly love through the beautiful lines of his poem:

> Love must not cease to live upon the earth;
> For love is the bright ink twist earth and Heaven,
> Love is the far transcendent's angle here;
> Love is man's lien on the Absolute. (Ghosh 633)

Dante, Plato, St. Augustine and Neo-Platonist believes that sensual love is degraded form of spiritual love. But Fraud felt spiritual love is the result of a suppressed profane love.

> Libido is an expression taken from the theory of emotions. We call by that name the energy regarded as a quantitative magnitude...of these instincts which have to do with all that may be comprised under the word 'love'. The nucleus of what we mean by love naturally consists (and this is what is commonly called love, and what the poets sing of) in sexual love with sexual union as its aim. (Strachey 20-30)

But Freudian concept of love is not applicable in case of Sufi love for their divine. As all the Sufi saints lead happily wedded lives along with their divine love.

The lovers sees the beloved in everything and even in themselves. As Majnum starts loving the gazelles in desert as its eyes resembles Leili's. And he even kissed the dog from Leili's palace thinking that it belongs to Leili. But later when Leili herself comes he tells her to go back "as I found the real beloved". Similar was the case with Zulaikha and Prophet Yusuf (Joseph), the son of prophet Yaqub (Jacob) whose descendants were called as 'Bani Ishrael'. Here in this story, which is mentioned in the holy Quran one can see the dynamic phase of love and separation between father and a son and a lover-beloved. Through this story God perhaps tries to show to humanity that separation is a must in order to realise the sweetness of union as from his childhood Yusup (Joseph) was the most lovable child of his father which made his other siblings envy him and hence planned to kill him. So in order to fulfill their wishes to separate Joseph from his father they (ten brothers of Joseph from other mothers) conspire and takes him far land and beat him severely and threw him into a well, where the water is not consumable. Then may be by God's wish he was rescued by a saudagar (businessman) who happened to pass by and is sold him in Missore (Egypt) to Kutifar, the Aziz-e-Missore (a Minister of Missore). It is said that the separation between Joseph and his father was destined by God in order to bring out the real qualities of Prophethood for both Joseph and his father Yaqub (Jaqob). Therefore Rumi's separation from Shams was also destined for his maturation. As Shams said that it was necessary and needful for Rumi to get 'cooked' and so he had to leave for Aleppo for good. So that after the return of Shams Rumi could avail the benefit of being with Shams. Rumi himself summarised the result and benefit of his separation in this words:

> The fruit of my life is no more than three words-
> I was raw, I was cooked, I was burned. (Chittick *The Sufi P. of L.* xiv)

And in case of Yaqub (Jacob) to understand the sacrifice of Ibrahim (Abhraham) for his son Ismail. And also to understand that God is above all and everything on earth and heaven. In between his forty years of separation with his son, Yousuf (Joseph) Yaqub (jacob) left all his necessary work and made a separate house from his home and stayed in solitude, perhaps which was not tolerable for God so in order to make him understand his real reason for his life that it was not for him to love only his one son and forget the real (truth) God. As God Did not want him to forget his real motive to lead the Bani Israel (descendants of prophet Ibrahim) or humanity in the broader sense.

Love acts as a transformative force for every human being which change us completely. For Rumi too love acts as a transformative force which transform him and changed him from a religious professor to a famous Persian mystic poet. It is love which switch us to the law of universal unity which even makes us realise that we all are connected with each other. While searching for Shams, Rumi could find his true self. There is another story which resembles the separation of Rumi and Shams. It was of Zulaikha, the wife of kutifar and Joseph. Zulaikha was the wife of that particular Aziz-e Missore (Prime minister), Kutifar who bought Joseph as their bound servant. Zulaikha eventually fall in love with Joseph for his physical and mental beauty. But at the beginning her love was mere a lust but after being rejected by Joseph her love went through different stages as it grew more and more which even made her insane. She even called her Joseph by different names just like the Sufis called their God by different names. Which even makes general people misunderstood them. Rumi too uses different names to call his friend Shams and God. Rumi spoke about how Zulaikha called her beloved Joseph by different names.

According to Rumi love is an eternal realisation. Love has got an important space in Sufi tradition as well as in Islam. Scholars have the view that Rumi's poetry conspires to engage the lover in their love for their beloved and the prime goal is annihilation. In fact, Rumi tried to plunged us in a state of mind where nothing but the truth exist. Rumi was completely true to himself and was deep in his Self-realisation making him an enlightened lover. He is the one who brought awareness on the notion of love among the poets and Sufis. Rumi was also given the title 'Qutb' or 'the pole of love'. Rumi, could see himself plunged in the ocean of divine love and bounty and he was so much under the spell of love that he could not see anything but graciousness and abundances of love in God. He has a strong faith and belief in the greatness of love and so never compares it with anything. According to him, love has a great influence in our life and it has its power to shape and direct everything. Jone, quotes eighteenth-century Jacques Necker's account of love in the following manner:

The brightest ornament of our nature, love, enchanting and sublime, is a mysterious pledge for the assurance of those hopes; since love, by disengaging us from ourselves, by transporting us beyond the limits of our own being, is the first step in our progress to a joyful immortality; and, by affording both the notion and example of a cherished object distinct from our own souls, may be considered as an interpreter to our hearts of something, which our intellects cannot conceive. (Jones 459-60)

Seventeenth-century English theologian Isaac Barrow describes love as:

> an affection or inclination of the soul toward an object, proceeding from an apprehension […] of some excellence […] in it, as its beauty, worth, or utility, and producing, if it be absent, a proportionable desire, and consequently an endeavour, to obtain such a property in it, such possession of it, such an approximation to it, or union with it […]; with a regret and displeasure in failing to obtain it, or in the want and loss of it; begetting likewise a complacence, satisfaction, and delight in its presence, possession, or enjoyment, which is moreover attended with a good will toward it, suitable to its nature; that is, with a desire, that it should arrive at, or continue in, its best state; with a delight to perceive it thrive and flourish; with a displeasure to see it suffer or decay: with a consequent endeavour to advance it in all good and preserve it from all evil. (Jones 446)

The lover's great compassion and urge for the beloved is perhaps because of the attraction that created by the beauty and excellence of the beloved. But the characteristics of the beloved being as perfect that Burk underlines is not universally as the Beloved is prone to suffering and pain for the lover too.

The perfection of the beloved is described vividly by Edmund Burke in his work *A Philosophical Enquiry into the Origin of Our Ideas of the Sublime and Beautiful (1757)* where he affirms that perfectness does not come from beauty and beauty is merely the quality of flesh and body can be perceived through our senses. According to Burke beauty is a characteristic associated with the female sex which also symbolises weakness and submission. Therefore Burke's concludes that we are in love with something which really submits to us. And we love someone who loves us more and from whom we can get a sense of relief and security and happiness.

Burke's view on loving someone inferior or who is submissive to us can be challenged on the basic of the two points: the first one is the unattainability of the object of love second is the shifting of power from the subject to the object of love. Beauty plays a significant role in celebrating the superiority of the beloved and the influence of the beloved remained on the lover due to the separation which brings about a melancholic urge for union with the beloved. Jones argues obout Burke's notion of beauty as weak and inferior in his *Poeseos Asiaticae Commentariorum Libri Sex (1774),* where he says that the beauty of the beloved has such power to ' rob his soul of rest'. Therefore Jones's notion of the beloved as a source of powerful contradicts with Burke's idea of loving the beloved for her submissive nature. It also contradicts Barrow's notion of the subject's desire for union with the beloved as an act of possession. Jones further claimed that it is the lover and not the beloved who submits to the other. Here Jones in his song depicts how the subject desires for the beloved for her beauty which gives immense delight and joy and hence it a tremendous power and influence on the subject. Therefore one can deny Burke's notion of beauty as weak and inferior but rather the super quality to attract the subject towards the beloved. Jones's stanza goes in the following manner:

> O! when these fair, perfidious maids,
> Whose eyes our secret haunts infest,
> Their dear destructive charms display,
> Each glance my tender breast invades,
> And robs my wounded soul of rest,
> As Tartars seize their destin'd prey. (Jones 61)

Therefore it the love for the absolute beauty which has all its power for the love and attention of the lover including Rumi and all the divine lover who decreed for the love of their beloved. Rumi highlights his notion of love in his *Mashnavi VI*:

> "Love has a thousand (not 500) feathers, and each one soars over the Throne beyond the Pleiades""(182)

Burke's notion of beloved as submissive is applicable here in the relationship of Rumi and Shams as both of them were submissive to each other. As in one occasion it could be seen that both Rumi and Shams bow down to each other in such a way that nobody could understand who is the master and who is the disciple.

> What can I do when
> Love appears
> And put its claws
> Around amy neck? (*Quotes by Rumi* web)

But it is not applicable in the divine love as it is not for the divine's submission the lovers goes insane and crazy in the love of the divine. Infact in divine love Jones notion of the power of the beauty of the beloved is applicable. Therefore one can conclude that Burke's idea of the beloved as weak and submissive is applicable in the mundane love but not in the divine love.

Rumi declares that we should love with our heart and not with the mind. So that love would make us free from all our egos, hatred and jealousy which is the barrier between us and divine. According to Rumi when we are able to remove our ego from our soul we can look clearly and can see the real inside us. Our soul is like a mirror if there would be dust we could not see our image in it. Similarly if we cannot remove our ego, hatred, jealousy, greed from our soul, it is not possible for us view our real self.

All your unfulfilled desires
Are from your greed
For gain of fulfilments
Let go of them all
And they will be
Sent as gifts. (Ibid)

Franklin Lewis asserts, in connection with Rumi, it is when burnished of all its rust that 'the mirror of the soul perfectly reflects the attributes of God'. (Lewis 417). The Sufi's heart thus becomes 'an unstained mirror' that reflects 'the Divine light and reveal it to others'. (Schimmel 13) As shams quotes:

"This is the work of heart, not the work
Of mind
The mind constricts, love unbinds
The mind says, Don't let go overflow.
Love says, Be free without formality." (Shams Qoute web)

Rumi transforms when he met Shams. Shams says to Rumi that he would never realize the depth of his love and suffering which he was going through before meeting Rumi until he himself steps in it. Therefore if we do not step forward towards divine love, we cannot receive the love of divine for us.

Be thirsty heart, seek forever without a rest. Let this soundless longing hidden
Deep inside you be the source of every word you say. (Rumi Quote web)

Rumi's poetry expresses the intoxicated love, the pain of being separated from the beloved and the joy of union with him. Rumi's poem have appeared in various format and in different languages of the world. Rumi expressed in his poem the deep yearning for ecstatic love that he felt in the presence of Allah:

> Love has taken away my practices
> And filled me with poetry. (Barks The soul of Rumi 104)

Though the concept of love is very common it seems very difficult to explain or describe in words. William C. Chittick comments on love in his book '*The Sufi Path of Love*':

> Love cannot truly be expressed in words. It is fundamentally an experience
> Situated beyond the narrow confines of articulated thought but an experience
> More real than the universe and all it contains. (194)

Love can be regarded as one of the most important themes of poetry. Poets of all ages have used this theme in their poetry enormously that without it poetry becomes dull and gloomy. The main reason for the popularity of love theme is because of the fact that every human being has experienced love. But it is notable that not all love stories are similar. Every story has its uniqueness and hence it is the most interesting topic among the poet of all ages and places. Research on love poetry reveals that there are varieties in love themes as there are different beings on earth. The important love themes in poetry are love for the country, love for mankind, love for the nature, love for God or spiritual love and sensual love. John Stallworthy in his book *Love Poems* comments on love theme in this way: 'There are as many definitions of love as there are poets' (John, 1981:2). C.S Lewis in his book *The Four Loves,* talked about the four types of love in human life. One is affectionate love, another is friendship, the third one is eros (Ishq) or passionate love and the last one but not the least is the charity love or love for God and its creations. So love may come into our life in all these four forms. Here in this thesis the eros love or the love for the worldly beloved leads one to the spiritual love for the divine beloved. Poet like Emily Dickenson, Kamala das, Christina Rossetti and Sarojini Naidu have the perception that divine love both compliments and substitutes human love.

Rumi's quest for the ultimate Other makes him follow certain steps like passionate love (Eros); desire (eshtiyaaq) for the beloved, solitary journey (enzevaa) to get the love object; which is followed by the idealisation of earthly beloved as the divine and exchange thoughts and feelings which is called Raabita; then realisation happens of one's origin, the ultimate truth (Shawq); separation from the self to be one with the Whole; then fanaa or loss of the self; and to die mentally before the physical death is to unite with the beloved.

Romantic philosophers, J. C. Friedrich Von Schiller (1759-1805), speaks about the popular theme of love and separation that our journey is like a circular one which starts with the fall of the Adam and will end with the return to our divine Home. Therefore the history of mankind itself is a proof that we have been separated from heaven or our divine to learn goodness, virtues, humility to be capable for our stay in heaven or divine. (Abrams 206-207). Hence according to Schiller, the fall of Adam's fall is a historical fall and from it we can conclude that human bestowed with several pain and difficulties learn to be good soul with their good deeds (Ibid). Therefore based on the above discussion on Schiller it can be summarised that Men are separated from his true Home and in their brief journey of life they are bestowed with difficulties, hardships, pain, sorrows, joys, annoyance, to put them in the path of perfection. This in nothing but a process of attaining of original innocence.

Henry Bayman in his *The Black Pearl: Spiritual Illumination in Sufism and East Asian Philosophies* (98-100) elaborates on the themes of separation and union. Here he describes on the philosophy of the creation and creators. He affirms that behind every creation there is a reason and so the reason behind the creating the huge universe was the human and behind creating man is the preparation of man to stay in His divine realm. In order to give an example he illustrates a very good example by saying that parents send their beloved children to school, colleges university to learn their assignments, and come back with knowledge, manners etc. to benefit society similarly God send his children on this world to learn to be humane and to know about God (*marifat Allah*), and then return to Him. Therefore the main goal of God's creation is reunion with him:

> Were it not for the ocean of pure love
> What reason would I have to forge the
> Heavens? (*MasnaviV* 2739)

As it is the incompleteness which makes us to look for the things which can complete us and hence continues our growth. And if we feel that we have received what we were longing for it may hinder our growth in the spiritual realm. In Islamic theology it is believed too that humans are born with the innate knowledge of God as the child utters some words which they might have learnt during their stay in heaven and gradually they tend to forget the permanent for the transience. Shams of Tabriz says in this regard:

> When I was a child I saw God
> I saw angels;
> I saw the mystery of the higher and the lower worlds.
> I thought all men saw the same. At last I realized
> That they did not see.... (Shafak 1)

As Christopher John Murray, the Romantic Neoplatonic philosopher follow the same principle that 'all creation originally existed in a harmonious unity (the One), then fragmented (the Many), and now longs to return to a state of unity'. (Ouseley 52) Since we are separated from our origin we have the quality of the Real in our subconscious zone and hence could feel the cosmos within ourselves.

Like the Sufis the romantics were too experienced the divine by idealising through the earthly beloved. Poet like Shelley, Wordsworth, and Coleridge have expressed in their literary works the theme of longing of the self for union or oneness with the supreme God. According to Shelley, man's soul is but a part of one harmonious Soul, a Soul of the Universe, a river flowing to the sea (Reiman 400). Wordsworth, in *Lines Composed a Few Miles above Tintern Abbey (1798),* views God as one mighty whole which contains all other being in Him and all beings contain Him that means a sense of pantheistic oneness of the beings with God when he says: All beings live with God, themselves | Are God, existing in the mighty whole (Gill xxxiii). Coleridge too had the same view on God that it is God | Diffused through all, that doth make one whole' and human beings are Parts and proportions of [that] one wondrous whole! (Jackson 128) at all events it struggles to idealise and to unify. It is essentially vital, even as all objects [...] are essentially fixed and dead. (Ibid 313)

Therefore Rumi believes that love is the only reason behind this creation of the universe:

> Its waves of love that makes the heavens
> turn
> Without that love the universe would
> Freeze:
> No mineral absorbed by vegetable
> No growing thing consumed by animal
> No sacrifice for anima for Him
> Who inspired Marry with His pregnant
> Breath
> Like ice, all of them unmoved, frozen
> Stiff. (Masnavi V 3854-9)

In *The Qur'an* Surah *Al-Maidah* it is said that God will send a people whom he will love and they will love him. (5:54) Perhaps the messengers, the Sufi saints or the enlightened lover of God whom God has accepted as his lover are included here.

Rumi shows his gratitude for the unconditional love that comes from God in our life to set it in the right direction. And in order to do that He break us and then mould us just like the iron smith and gold smith does with the iron and gold to give a perfect shape he wants to give. Rumi says the same through his poem "*Your Blessings Is Unconditional*":

> Grab hold of our skirt
> And pull us nicely over to yourself
> You never lead the heart in the wrong direction.
> You always keep your word, never giving up,
> Pulling everyone merrily along to your place.
>
> (Ergin, *The Forb.* R. 12-15)

Therefore, love is not only a word to explain but to understand it one needs to experience it. Since time immemorial love and separation have been the inevitable part of human existence. It has not only started right after our birth but from the time we were just a soul and was ready to depart not only from heaven and all its comfort just to unite again with the divine. Naji Oueijan speaks on the separation from our real self in his 1999 article *Sufism, Christian Mysticism, and Romanticism* in the following manner:

> Separation from the self involves a detachment from the material self and other, and an attachment to or a fusion of the spiritual self with the spiritual other; the former involves pain and suffering, the latter redemption and reconciliation.

Right after we are born we experience the continuous process of love and separation, right from leaving our parents for school then our friend in school, college and university. And not only this we continue to meet, depart, love and then separate from each other. In our youth too we happen to fall in love and separate from them. In our old and middle age we separate from our children when they go for their higher studies and job. We separate from our parents when they leave for their heavenly abode. And a time comes when we separate from everyone and everything on earth for our own heavenly journey. Therefore, love and separation is a continuous and non-ending happening in our life. And this separation is a never ending process as one ending leads to another beginning which leads us to the main divine ocean.

The meaning of love is not only confined among the lovebirds or between a male and a female partner. Indeed it has a different states and stages. It is a kind of feeling and emotion which one possess for different person or thing in their life. In fact it's an emotion which arouse out of strong attachment for something or someone. And emotion could be for our food, for mates, for parents, for children etc. And it has its different stages too. Sometimes it starts with attraction and mere lust for someone if it continues it may come across several stages. It can be sum-up in Andrew Marvels words that love grows with time. As he talks about the different stages of love in his poem *"To His Coy Mistress"*:

> My vegetable love should grow,
> Vaster than empires, and more slow;
> An hundred years should go to praise
> Thine eyes, and on thy forehead gaze; (Marvell ebook)

Though the lover here is a beginner whose love can be called as a mere lust for his beloved. Who tried to convince his beloved for the physical love making but he also says that one day it will grow to the extent that he will only bother about her heart and not the physical anymore. Therefore, we can say that love grows with time and so was the case with Rumi and Shams whose love for each other grew in the course of time. Love can also be instance or medium. When we don't get the thing or person we desired for we realised the intense of our love for that thing or person. Love can also be defined as unconditional love which is selfless concern for one another. Everything has got its two side love has it too. In one phase love is beautiful and in another it is cruel too. It is said that where there is love there is pain or separation. Without separation one cannot understand the depth or intensity of love. Therefore, love is a beautiful and crafty element that God has been using as an instrument to run the universe. He also uses the element called separation to break, polish and clear the human heart which has been polluted by desire, greed, proud etc. Rumi says if you have the guts to break than only you proceed or dare to love for love never comes alone. As it may make us or it may destroy us. C. S Lewis says on love in the book *The Four Loves* in the following manner:

> To love at all is to be vulnerable. Love anything, and your heart will be wrung and possibly broken. If you want to make sure of keeping it intact you must give it to no one. (Lewis web)

Not only human God too gets pain because of the sin of his creatures. According to Christianity God send his only son on earth and has to make him die for the sins of his creatures. A mother is ready to bear all the pangs and pain of bearing her baby nine months in her womb along with the unbearable labour pain of child birth just to see the little face of her child. Similarly despite all our sins God loves us and waits for the day when we will glorify Him.

Rumi's yearning of ecstatic love is not only for God but also for his beloved friend and master Shams of Tabriz, who indeed introduced him in the mystical path. Here we can be sure that Shams was his earthly beloved through whom he could realise his love for the real. Keats views friendship as divine attribute which brings happiness and says love acts as an agent of transcending this feeling as it leads us to the divine path. Rumi was totally lost in this new found love that his master revealed, and all his great attainments were blossoming through that love. In fact, after he met Shams everyday was a miracle and a new birth for Rumi's soul. As Rumi himself describe his condition through his poem "I Died as Mineral":

> "The outcome of my life is not more than these three lines; I was a raw material, I was cooked and became mature; I was burned in love." (*Rumi Quotes* web)

However for Rumi it is Shams who recognised the hidden qualities in him and the friendship between them became one of the mysteries. As Henry Thorau quotes about friendship in his book "*Walden; or life in the Woods*":

> True friendship can afford true knowledge.
> It does not depend on the darkness and ignorance.

Keats in his *Endymion* (1818), asserts that our happiness lies in 'that which becks Our ready minds to fellowship is divine' (Book I, ll. 777-78). According to Keats friendship is 'the crown of all [enthralments]', there still is another 'orbed drop of light' whose influence 'genders a noble sense' and that is 'love' (Cook 798).

Annemarie Schimmel (1978) in *Triumphal Sun: A Study of the Works of Jalal-uddin-Rumi* writes on Rumi's life and his various thoughts and ideas with reference to his poetry. He presents Rumi as a well-grounded in Islamic Jurisprudence and also as a spiritual master. She also acclaimed that through Shams the divine sun showed its fascinating beauty. Indeed, he viewed the whole world from a new perspective. Schimmel asserts:

> The true dervish has to cut the neck of egotism, of selfishness, of I-ness so that he may experience one day the mystery of God's action through him similar to the prophet, who was addressed in the battle of Badr "Thou didst not cast when thou cast' (Sura 8/17). So long as the self is still conscious, it is comparable to a cloud which covers the moon, but selflessness is cloudlessness.Wonderful is Rumi's simple line which I am so submerged in not-being (*nisti*), that my beloved keeps saying: 'Come, sit a moment with me!' Even that I cannot do. (309-10)

The mystical disappearance of Shams is believed to be his sacrifice of his head for his mystical friendship. The word mystical or mysticism can be defined in the words of Swaty Samantaray (2013), in her article "*Demystifying Mysticism: A Comparative Study of the Poetry of William Blake and Rabindranath Tagore*" where the author comments that Mysticism is nothing but a spiritual journey to unveil the truth, which would be followed by the union with the divine. But each would experience different Mystical experiences. However, researcher have found that many of the mystics had experience notable similar mystical experiences irrespective of their race, religion, social orders, or cult.

It is Shams himself who had desired to get a friend or companion like Rumi for which he was ready to sacrifice his own head. Shams said "I prayed for someone who could endure my company: a voice came: what you give in return? My head! The one you seek is Jalal-ud-din of Konya". After Shams met Rumi, Shams disappeared and this mystical disappearance of Shams is a symbol of sacrifice that Shams wanted to give for getting a friend like Rumi. And after Rumi met Shams he became a changed personality as "I prayed for someone who could endure my company: a voice came; what will u give in return? "my head"! The one you seek is Jalal-ud-din-After Shams he became a changed personality Annemarie Schimmel quotes "Rumi turned into a poet, began to listen to music, and sang, whirling around hour after hour". Perhaps this is exemplified by the whirling dervishes. Therefore in this regard Golpinarali in his book *Introduction to Aflaki qualifies (648):*

> Rumi was like a pure clean lamp, where the oil was poured in the holder and a wick placed therein, ready to be lit; and Shams was the spark to set it afire.

Rumi says there is a soul inside our soul hidden under a stream of water and to reach that soul we have to look for it. Through his poem *Childhood friends* Rumi asserts that no matter how clean our soul water looks but at the deep down there are some dirt or unstirred hidden matter on the bottom. We always need a channel or hole to drain those waste from our soul. And it is said that sorrows, sufferings, pains, imperfections makes those holes in us. Our spiritual guides and mentors are the one who acts as a doctor to operate those holes with a bandage and though those bandage the divine light enters to make the water more clear to see the hidden divine soul.

Your stream water may look clean,
But there's unstirred matter on the bottom.
Your sheikh can dig a side channel
That will drain that waste off. (Barks, *The Essential* R.142)

And for Rumi, Shams was the one who dug the hole in Rumi and make the light to pass on it. Suffering is needed for the stubborn and ignorant to be knowledgeable in the path of truth and that is why God gives us a shake to put us on the right track. Earth is like a mother's womb where each one of us stay to complete our shape. Rumi says there is a secret window through which every night we travel to the unseen world but a thread is fasten to it and so we come back again to learn and mature to be free forever.

In the poem *'The moment you are With yourself'* Rumi says if we will think about ourselves we will suffer disappointment but if we will start thinking and doing thinks selflessly we will be happy forever. As Rumi was thinking to get his friend Shams and was in search him, therefore suffering was must as it was his selfish desire to reach his friend. As he states in his poem *The Moment You Are With Yourself*:

The moment that you are with yourself,
You are under the clouds of sorrow;
And the moment that you are selfless,
The moon will come to your side. (Helminski, *Love's Rip*.11)

And all of our try to be restfulness makes us restless. We must be so hardworking that rest will search us. If we start searching for things we will never get it. Therefore it is better to stay empty and selfless because then only all the things of our desired will come to us a gift.

All of our displeasure is due
To your seeking pleasure
Abandon pleasures, and austerity
World become a pleasure to you.
All of your frustrations are due
To you seeking your wishes
If you didn't, all wishes would
Come to you like offerings. (Ibid 12)

So when we learn to deal with our desire we can control them. If we would no longer desire anything we would attain all those desired automatically. Hence our suffering will end and we would be in a state of complete joy.

After every separation or pain there lies happiness. Just like the night there is a dawn followed by bright shine morning. Rumi too exchanged the same notion of the happy days after the days of pain. As he says through his poem *Life is coming to the Rose Garden:*

The roses have bloomed
To heal the pain of the thorns.
Water carriers souls.
Life is coming back to the rose garden.
Leaves bring you news
Of the fruits.
Don't scratch your head.
Come soon to the garden. (Ergin *The Forbidden* 138)

Rumi through the poem *The Rose's Plea*, where rose symbolises human being, pleads to God not to give it any pain or thorn, then in reply God says that without crushing the fruit how can you expect the juice.

The Rose turned to God and begged for mercy,
"Don't make this cold winter
Your commandment to us."
God answered,
How do you get the juice
Without crushing? (Ibid140)

The one who runs away from the suffering which is God's plan to make us mature is a thief and is walking towards the hell. In the poem *One Who Runs Away,* Rumi says:

A Lover swallows the bleeding heart like a lion.
Without great suffering, can one ever be lionhearted?

(Helminski, *Love's Rip* 99)

We cannot reach God until unless we go through pains and suffering then a new self will rise and shall walk on the right path. He further says that our troubles will stay with us until unless we will surrender ourselves to the almighty.

Your troubles will stay with you
Until you become God's drunkard
You can't capture Joseph of Canan
Unless you u dress up like a wolf. (Ergin, *The Forb.* R 154)

Rumi's friendship with Shams has become an extraordinary history. As both of them has sacrificed a lot for each other. Rumi met Shams in around 1244. Shams was a fierce man and was in need a companion who could be his voice to the world. So he wandered every corner of the East in search of his soul friend Rumi. Shams was called by the people of his time as 'parinda' (flier)'. He got the title because of his wandering nature from one place to another opting different occupation in different place. Sometimes as a coblar and sometimes as a teacher to teach Quar'an. Rumi was a teacher of theology and a learned man and he sacrificed his status, and other relations for his new found love of friendship. So love means to sacrifice not to get. Even in the relationship of Radha and Krishna there is sacrifice. It is believed that both Krishna and Radha had chosen the path of separation in order to experience the pangs of separation and also to measure the depth of the love for each other. One can summarise Rumi's condition after he met Shams in the following manner:

> I am in love with you.
> What's the use of giving me advice?
> I have already drunk the poison.
> What's the use of candy?
> They say bind his feet in the chains,
> But they can't bind up my crazy heart. (Helminsky *The Pocket Rumi* 9)

Shams was in search of love i.e. Rumi who could receive all the message that he wanted to convey to the world. And Shams was a person who called a spade a spade and hence lacked a good communicative skill. In the novel cum manuscript of Rumi *The Fourty Rules of Love* it is mentioned that Shams was praying to almighty for somebody who could be his voice. As Shams was not an ordinary person, he had some special qualities as he had some special means to communicate with the divine. When he asked for his soul friend an inner voice asked him, "what will you give in return?" My head, said Shams. Then the answer came "The one you seek is jalaluddin of Konya, son of Bahauddin of Balk. "The reason that we can't call Shams vision as dream because once he asked God not to give him any dream so that he would not get confused it with his vision. Shams was directed through his vision about his meeting with his soul mate Jalal-ud-din Rumi. Whom he can meet in Antolia. But Shams had been convinced to sacrifice himself i.e. his life for his new found friendship.

After Shams arrived in a darvish institute where he was given a direction to meet Rumi by a Sufi master. When he reached Konya he stayed in a sugar merchant shop in a disguise of a businessman. One day he happened to meet Rumi when he was riding on a donkey, Shams asked him about the greaterness of Muhammad and Bistami. Shams words "money changer of the current coins of esoteric significance, knower of the names of the lord, tell me who is greater, Muhammad or Bistami?" Rumi answered "Muhammad is incomparable among the saints and prophets." Shams said "then how is it he said, we have not known you as you should be known,' while Bestami cried out, How great is my glory!?"

Here the analysis comes that while searching for the truth or divine inside one must be outside the door to be inside. For Muhammd he could see himself inside while he was outside the door and also saw himself when he was inside but for Bistami and Mansur they were already inside the door so it was a bit difficult for them to recognise the truth. In the night of Miraj (mystical night journey of prophet Muhammad) when Muhammad was initiating into the unseen or all the mysteries related to the other world. Gabriel (angel) was accompanying Muhammad in his journey and at a point he said that he was not allowed to cross the door and if he would do he will be burnt into ashes. From the above evidences we can summarised that God has privileged us with different positions and status not only to human to human but also to angels.

However Rumi realised the depth of Shams questions and so felt down to the ground. When he got his consciousness, Shams answered in this way. "For Muhammd, the mystery was always unfolding, while Bestami takes one gulp and is satisfied." Then the two went for a mystical conversation for weeks and months which is called "sohbet".Rumi spend almost three and half years with Shams in Konya. In between the period Shams left Rumi for he thought was required for the maturity or spiritual growth of Rumi. Which can be possible only through the pangs of separation. Shams was found and then again went missing for the second time and was not known where. Perhaps it was because of his promise to sacrifice his own head as a forfeit for his mystical friendship with Rumi. Franklin Lewis believes that perhaps Shams left Rumi to give a final punch for his spiritual growth. One day in his search for Shams, Rumi reached the road of Damascus then he realised that he was looking for none but himself. Then he came back in konya and started writing down all he learned from Shams. In fact all the poetry of Rumi has sprung from the mystical friendship of the two. In the poem sublime Generosity Rumi described how transformation took place in him through his love and friendship for Shams. Here in this poem Rumi explained how he went to Shams and was denied for getting the certificate for the Sufi path:

> I was dead, then alive.
> Weeping, then laughing.
> The power of love came into me.
> And I became fierce like a lion.
> Then tender like the evening star. (Barks *The Essential* 134)

Here Shams told Rumi that he was not ready for his spiritual journey as he has got his wings for it. But Rumi desired for Shams wings to fly on for his spiritual journey and finally Shams gave him his wings to Rumi.

> The soul at down is like darkened water
> That slowly begins to say Thank you, Thank you. (Ibid135)

Therefore it is Shams friendship that list up Rumi's soul steering it towards the path of divine love. One could see the intense love and respect that these two possess for each other in the following lines:

> When I am with you, we stay up all night.
> When you are not here, I can't go to sleep. (Ibid 106)

He says nobody would under love if he himself were not in love. As Rumi's love for Shams made him realise his love for God, he uttered that God too love us and hence we love him. In his Mathnawi Rumi qoutes that when he was asked about love by someone he answered in this way:

> Someone asked, "What is love?" I answered, "Thou wilt know when thou becomes I lost in) Me." Love is uncalculated affection. For that reason it has been said to be in reality the attribute of God and unreal in relation to (man who is) his slave. He (God) loveth them (yuhibbuhum) is the entire sum. Which (of them) is really the subject of the word yuhibbuhum, they love him? (Nicholson, *MathnawiI* 221)

Therefore we can say that we all possess the knowledge of the divine prior to our birth but when we are born very few of us can remember about our real origin and may be Shams of Tabriz was one of them who had the mystical power to remember the pre-existence. And as we are separated from our divine we have the inherent tendency to return to our origin, therefore we feel the emptiness and unfulfilled in everything we get. In *Mathnawi-I* Rumi speaks about the inner pull or desire to our divine origin in the following manner:

> Anyone who has
> remained far from his
> roots,
> Seeks a return (to the)
> Time of his union. (Nicholson *Mathnavi*I 4)

For Rumi the earthly love for his friend Shams could make him realise for his real love of divine. Rumi neither neglects the earthly love or beloved because he says that all our earthly love for our earthly beloved is even a stepping stone towards the divine love. Because, in that process we will realise the depth of the original love that God and his creation possess for each other.

Therefore whether it is a love for the divine or love for the human both can burn tremendously to help us in the path of divine love. Rumi through his poetry suggest us to drink the wine of divine energy till it completely make us drunk. Which will help us view the heaven on earth. People desired to get the heaven after their death but the Sufis are the impatient one to see the heaven after death and hence desired to see both God and heaven on earth itself.

> In your light I learn how to love.
> In your beauty, how to make poems.
> You dance inside my chest where no one
> Sees you, but sometimes I do,
> And that sight becomes this art. (*Quote by Rumi* web)

Another example we can site here is of Zuleikha, who was madly in love with Joseph (yusuf) for more than thirty years. She even became blind in the wait for her beloved Joseph and stars thinking like him. But after her long wait of thirty years of separation she became one with Joseph being unaware that her love for Joseph was the mirror image of the real love for her divine.

> Love is a mirror.
> In it you see nothing
> Except your reflection.
> You see nothing
> Except your real face. (Ibid)

In the love story of Joseph and Zulaikha, which has extracted from Quran one can see the different phase and stages of love where the love begins with the mere desire of the physical pleasure and finally reach to a stage of being happy only at the far distance smell of the beloved. And most astonishing phase of her love can be seen when she met Joseph after her thirty years of wait she no longer desired him but the divine. As when she get to marry her beloved, Joseph, she denied in the beginning and went for prayer for her new found divine. We can say that she found out her real love which she was searching in Joseph all the year. That is why she no longer desired Joseph's love and presence instead she sits in prayer for forty days in search of her divine love for God. Rumi too found himself or his love for his divine when he was in search of his friend Shams for the second time.

In this heart's journey one is a stranger to oneself, the more one will try to know oneself the more stranger he will become to himself. Once Bayazid kept himself away from the crowd and sit for meditation in a mountain cave, his mother came and enquired about him then he replied in a strange manner from inside that he himself is looking for him for several years and didn't find yet. Rumi uttered the same in his poem *A Stranger to Myself*:

Enough stop beating the drum
And crafting words for others.
I've become a stranger to myself.
Please don't ask anything more of a stranger. (Ergin, *The Forb* R 159)

Therefore we can say that mortal love leads us to the real love for our divine. Rumi like Bayazid and Mansur experienced that there exist nothing but God in them. He calls people crazy who does not feel that kind of tugging in their heart. He even says that when he was in that state of mind, he felt like he is neither from sky nor from earth and neither made of fire nor water but become one with the divine. In this state he feels himself in everything and everything in him. The Sufis believe that all the creatures of God are same soul put in different frame of body and that is why we can feel the pain of other creatures. But knowingly or unknowing we try to fool ourselves in order to fulfill some of our selfish needs. But the Sufis are so drunk in the love of God that they do not feel any difference between God and them.

I became Jesus to that moon.
I rose up and passed through the skies.
I am the drunk Moses.
God himself lives inside this patched cloak. (Ibid 160)

In the "*Conference of Bird*", too Farid-ud-din Attar talked about his journey in search of God where he described that he found himself when he was in search of God.

Rumi describes through his poem *"Where You are"* that before love touched him he was plunged in rules and regulations of the outer world but after it touched him in the form of Sham's friendship he became alive. He even compared himself with a lifeless piece of reed which is silent with the lips of Shams. Rumi says:

I am like a lifeless piece of reed,
Ever silent when your lips are not around.
But if u play me like a ney,
Your breath turns me into divine melodies. (Nasr *MathnawiI* 113-16)

Rumi through his *Rubaias* asserts that lovers do not finally meet instead they are in each other. And we should not search our divine outside but inside of us. Rumi even suggest the Sufis who deserts everything and roam around the world in-search of the divine, not to search for their divine outside somewhere but inside of them. And when they will find that jwell soul inside them they will be called as enlighten being. And if we are in love with God, He too be in love with u

There's a jewel in the mountain of your flesh
Go and find the mine of that jewel
O wandering Sufi, search if you can
But not somewhere outside
Look for it inside yourself
God is in your being from your head to your toe nail
Once who doesn't know who you are
What are you looking for beside yourself. (Ergin, *The Rubais* 54)

Therefore in order to know God one must know himself first. In the poem "A Helper of Heart" Rumi explains that our heart is responsible for its reaction for different situations and circumstances because it is the broken heart where God's treasures are buried in. And for God it is more precious to make a broken heart than to go for pilgrimage. And if we serve the heart like slave the road towards the divine will be more clear for us. He also says that it is the process of helping the hearts which lead to the greater wisdom. As he quotes:

Don't look down on the heart,
Even if it is not behaving well.
Even in that shape, the heart
Is more precious than the teachings
Of the exalted saints.
The broken heart is where God looks
How lucky is the soul that mends the heart!. (Ergin, *The Forb* R 116)

Rumi says in his poem *Hidden from the Eyes* that our heart is a water bag and God is the carrier of that bag and so we cannot see the carrier but he asked us to watch the action of the bag bearer. Which means whatever happens in our life controls by the carrier of our heart but we cannot see him just like the smell of the aloe wood is itself for its burning. According to Rumi the journey of love to separation then to union is a step by step process as he states in his *Masnav III*:

> "(That) from the stations of asceticism to the passing away (from self-existence), step by step up to union with God" (*Masnavi* III: 4235)

Most of the Persian Mystical poets have exchanged the similar view on the theme of love, separation and union. Sheikh Mahmood Shabistari (1288-1340) has his contribution with several beautiful poems on the theme of love, separation and union between divine and human:

> The traveller on the path,
> 'Tis he who knows from whence he cometh;
> Then doth he journey hastily,
> Becoming as pure from self as fire from smoke.
>
> (Lederer 40).

However, many researcher believed that Rumi's *Masnavi* serves best the topic of love, separation and union. Moreover the main theme of Rumi's *Masnavi* has been summarised in the prologue which speaks on the separation of the reed flute from its reed which symbolise our separation from our origin and it goes like this:\

> "Listen to the reed how it tells a tale,
> complaining of separations" (*Masnavi*I 1).

However before the separation happens there must be some love or attachments and Rumi's *Masnavi* explains it candidly:

> A man in love, no matter what he says
> The smell of love wafts love-ward from
> His mouth
> He speaks jurisprudence, what
> Emerges?
> From mystic poverty a sweet effulgence
> He blasphemes, the scent of faith arises
> He offers doubts, no doubt we grow more
> Sure. (Ibid 2880-82)

According to Rumi love is the astrolable of God's mysteries and the animating force of creation (Ibid 110). Rumi proclaimed that no matter whatever way a lover choose be it through law or blasphemy or scepticism to reach the truth are all adds to the meaning of love of divine. Like other Sufis Rumi too uses the language or symbol of earthly beloved to represent the divine beloved in the poetry. Rumi view love as both eros (Ishq) and agape (Mahabbat) which he talked in his *Masnavi 5*: Agape then describes what's real, Eros, too. (2168) Which means the feeling for earthly beloved leads us to the divine beloved (Ibid 111).

Rumi in his series of *Masnavi* describes the love between God and human in the following manner:

> Love grows in the garden of human perfection. (*Masnavi*-V: 2742-44)
> Exalts the earthly body above the seven heaven. (*Masnavi*-I: 25)
> In the realm of free will and pre-destination,
> divine wisdom made human beings
> Lovers of one another. (*Masnavi*-3;4400-4403)
> Everything is the beloved and lover is just the foil. (*Masnavi*-I:30)
> Hence illusionary separation of subject and object. (*Masnavi*-I:22-24)

For Rumi love is his religion. He believes that the blade of love cuts the outer covers of the soul and keeps the lover separated from the sins. Rumi says through his poem *Someone digging the Ground* that this body of ours is a guest house and whatever comes to us whether sorrows, sufferings, pain, joy, depression, meanness, dark thoughts, shame, the malice should be welcomed with honour and laughing at the door as these are sent as a guide from the divine realm to sweep our house and empty it to be fill it with some new and great delight.

> Welcome and entertain them all!
> Even if they're a crowd of sorrows,
> Who violently sweep your house
> Empty of its furniture,
> Still, treat each guest honourably.
> He may be clearing you out
> For some new delight. (Barks *The Essnt* R. 109)

Therefore each one of us must be courageous enough to deal with all the darkness in our life. Because these are the weapons of God to clean up and make us ourselves. When we annihilate or surrender ourselves to our beloved God there lies a shining moon of our spirit. Rumi says he was beating the drum of love for his beloved for so long with the song, "*My life depends upon my dying*," (Rezwan 128) which keeps his body alive and lively.

Hence love matures and grows through separation and separation from the worldly beloved is the image of real separation from our truth(divine). In order to get the union one should not just call the divine into their heart but should also feel his sensation through their sense organ in the form of some relationship. Hence in case of both

Shams and Rumi they were tied up and feel the divine in the relationship of friendship.

Therefore in loving the creature we love the creator. For Shams it is the earthly love of desiring the company of a friend (Rumi) leads to the realisation of real love which frees one from everything of this material world. However similar was the case with Rumi after his separation with Shams realised his true search for the divine. In the poem *"Don't talk of Love to the Body"* Rumi says that we should not love these physical world as it is illusionary and not permanent and God is the ruler or owner of this game of life. So we should surrender ourselves to this omniscient power if we won't do that we will suffer a lot.

O Love! Don't discuss Love with the body.
That charming hypocrite is not of this flock.
He would welcome you with open arms
But laugh behind your back!
Go to the graveyards and hear for yourself
The laments of the carnal self. (Helminsky, *Love's Rip.* 20)
Rumi summarised his initial stage of love for Shams in this manner:
I said:
O friend, are you truely my beloved?
I Gaze at you and see that you are my soul. (Ergin *The Rubais* 62)

He also says that why to love the creation if the creator exist. In other words why to love the things which is perishable or destroyable indeed one should love the eternal or the divine which is the supreme truth of our existence. So despite loving the shadows one should recognise and love the original which is not subjected to change in any way.

Why continue admiring the water color?
O heart, behold the painter!
Behold the Moon and the Sun!
Why be stumbling among moon shadows?
But say you're following the scent of flowers,
But there's garlic up your nose! (Helminsky *Love's Rip.*17-18)

To Rumi suffering of this world is a blessing for the next and he welcomes suffering hole-heartedly because it is where God's treasure is hidden. As he says:

If you are a friend of God, fire is your water.
You should wish to have a hundred thousand sets of mothwings,
So you could burn them away, one set a night.
The moth sees light light and goes into fire. You should see fire
And go toward light. Fire is what of God is world-consuming.
(Barks *The Essent.* 97)

He further says:

Outside the freezing desert night
This other night inside grows warm, kindling
Let the landscape be covered with thorny crust.
We have a soft garden in here. (Ibid 98)

Rumi further says that to understand love one must go through separation and love is neither aware of its beginning and ending instead it does not has its starts and end because it is eternal and in the resurrection day everyone will be out of temple accept the lovers. Here the lover means the divine lover. In this regard Rumi has expressed through his collection of poem *The Rubias*:

So many people search for love
On the day of resurrection
But everyone except the lovers
Will be dragged out from the temple. (Ergin 128)
My love is purer than clean, clear water
I'll play any love game you want
Ordinary love is so fickle
It changes from moment to moment
But the love for my beloved
Goes on forever. (Ibid 178)

The love for the material world is just a fickle and does not last long. Rumi says if we love someone who is subjected to change or demolish will bring suffering but if we love the eternal we will not suffer. So, we should surrender ourselves to the divine or supreme soul who can transform all the evils into good and who is the ruler of both the world.

I Was a slave and a donkey driver; I became sovereign and a lord. (Helminsky *Love's Rip.*68-69)

Rumi was heartbroken and shattered in the separation of his earthly beloved Shams but he never went back to his former position of prestige and honour and remained to the path which Shams had shown. However before transformation had occurred Rumi and his friend Shams had undergone close communion of admiration and affinities in their process of Raabita which is an exchange of thinking and feeling by visualising interiorly the object of love which is further becomes a way to remember the divine presence in order to experience the ecstatic love. During this separation Rumi gradually proceed to the mystical stations. In Shams' separation, Rumi was confussed about his condition and hence utters these words for Shams:

In my hand there was always the Koran
Now I seized the lute out of love!
In my mouth there were always words of laud
Now it is poetry and quatrains, and songs.... (*Divan* 2351)

It was Shams personality which has its effect in the transformation of Rumi and not mere his ideas and doctrine.In the earliest year of his life Rumi was influenced by this learned father and his Sufi disciple Sayyad Burhan-ud-Din Tirmizi. No doubt these two great personalities in his life has inspired him tremendously but Shams had come as a light in human form who transform him totally. However it was for Shams image and grief of separation which haunted Rumi throughout his life which resulted in form of his literary work of *Divan-i Shams-i Tabrizi* which is comprised of lyrical and passionate image of Shams in ecstacy and in grief and *Masnavi* which is again of separation and union. Rumi's Divan is consist of 40,000 lines in lyrical verse and no doubt its spoken by Rumi but sounds to be the voice of Shams:

Sun of truth and faith, pride of Tabriz!
Speak!
But it is your voice that mouths all my
Words. (*Divan* 2056)

The imagination of the beloved in Sufism is the mental faculty which comprised of image', form, or idea and is termed as '*khiaal*'. *Khiaal* is then contains with images and ideas in the mind of the Sufis. According to William Chittick the imagination in Sufism receives the images and ideas not only from the mind and the memory, (Hanif, 2002:230) but rather 'from a separate World of Imagination' (Nasr 33).

Human being are tend to act or behave like the person they meet or spend time with. And at a point we realise that they starts behaving like the person they meet or is with. We catch up the behaviour and action of them easily with whom we spend most of our time like best friend, siblings, spouse, mother and father. Sometimes we bring out those qualities and behaviour and sometimes not. Similarly in case of child when they mix up with another child they immediately copy the behaviour of the other. So when Rumi was with Shams he became shams and hence if we will seek God's company and spend time in Dikr or prayer we will start thinking like Him. In *Mathnawi* Rumi says:

Since the true believer is a mirror for the true believer, his face is safe from defilement. The friend is a mirror for the soul in sorrow; breathe not on the face of the mirror, O my Soul! Last it cover its face on account of thy breath, though must swallow (suppress) thy breath at every moment. (Nicholson 30)

Sir Phillip Sidney in his the *The Countesse of Arcadia* expresses the behaviour of the lover and the beloved in this way:

My true love hath my heart, and I have his,
By just exchange, one for the other given;
I hold his deer, and mine he cannot miss,
There never was a better bargain driver.
His heart in me keeps me and him in one.
My heart in him, his thoughts and senses guide;
He loves my heart, for once it was his own;
I cherish his because in me it bides. (Hadfield 44)

In the last four lines Sidney exchange somehow similar notion about love, lover, beloved, heart, oneness with the Sufis. Where the lover gradually starts thinking like the beloved. In fact, the lover completely surrenders to its beloved and hence annihilated. As many Sufis including Bistami and Al-Hallaj calls themselves as the ultimate reality. which is completely forbidden in Islam. But by those words they meant that there exist nothing but the divine as they have completely surrendered themselves to the divine and hence nothing remains except the divine inside the veil of skin. Many religious clerics claimed that the claiming of Bayazid and al-Hallaj is similar who claimed himself as God. But that was not the fact with these Sufis as they were the strict follower of Shariat by after being gone through all the Sufi path they reached the final spiritual stage where nothing exist but God or truth called "Annihilation'. Rumi like other Sufis believes that there exist nothing accept the reflection of the divine on this earth. Which literally means I, we, He, She is equal to divine because all are made of divine light. In Rubais Rumi says when we are completely clean we can see our beloved's face instead of our own. And probably because of that Mansur and Bayazid could see the divine image in them and uttered those forbidden word.

When your heart is cleansed of everything you
Think you are
You'll see yourself as an old beloved soul
It's not possible to see your face without a mirror
So gaze at the beloved
Let his face become your mirror. (Ergin, *The Rubais* 88)

Therefore the World of Imagination is at a higher level than the 'rational mind' and the 'individual human faculty of imagination determines the form in which images present themselves to the consciousness'. The Sufis could access to this higher world 'through the visions he may receive on the spiritual path'. (Hanif 231-233)

The image which the mind possess is the mundane and mechanical one but the imagination which Coleridge talked about is the spiritual one. The imagination, as Coleridge asserts, is that 'living power of all human perception' that 'diffuses' to 're-create' and 'struggles to idealise and to unify'. (Nilchian 33-67)

Like the Sufis, the Sufi-Romantics too are being obsessed in love with the Other transform themselves into the Other.The subject and object fuses in such a way that the subject dissolves into the object and becomes the Other. Rumi says if we can let go things we wanted for long we may receive them in an unexpected way. He further says that if we attain absence from our self there is a hidden energy of God which pulls us towards union. Rumi describes the love of God in such a beautiful manner in his *Rubais*:

> The secrets of the minds attainments
> Can only be found in madness
> Whoever has become insane with love
> Becomes the wisest one of us all
> Whoever gets familiar with the mysteries of
> The heart
> Becomes a complete stranger to himself. (Ergin 38)

Moreover Rumi in his poem "*I Died as a mineral*" says that if he will not deny his existence he will never be able to unite with the divine and so he would have to die and take birth several times. But if he will realise his own self and reach a higher spiritual level he may not go through the same pain of life and death. As Doris Lessing says that all man do not possess the same consciousness level but all get the equal opportunity to gain it. Thus Rumi wanted to reach that consciousness level where he could unite with God. As Rumi writes in his poem "*I died as mineral and become a plant*':

> I died as mineral and become a plant,
> I died as plant and rose to animal,
> I died as animal and I was man.
> Why should I fear? When was I less by dying? (*Quote by Rumi* web)

Which means from just a mineral we became vegetable, from vegetable we became animal, and from animal we became human being. And about this journey we are completely ignorant, do not even know that we have to go through a hundred different worlds to reach our destiny if we will not surrender ourselves to our God just like Mansur, Rumi and other Sufi saints. Rumi further talks about the concept of existence and absence in a very detailed manner in his Rubais:

> Hear this if you can:
> If you want to reach him
> You have to go beyond yourself
> And when you finally arrive at the land of absence
> Be silent
> Don't say a thing
> ecstasy, not words, is the language spoken there. (Ergin *The Rubais* 22)

However, it is the earthly Aashiq-Ma'ashooq (lover-beloved) relationship, its separation and longing for each other leads to the path of divine presence through the process of Raabita. For the Sufis love means to give preference to the other before himself. And therefore Rumi's Divan-i-Shams-i Tabriz is the example of giving preference to Shams rather than to himself. The essence that the Sufis discovers as their divine is from experiencing the earthly relationship. Such example of removing of duality can be seen in Rumi's Diwan:

> I have put duality away, I have seen that the two worlds are one.

In the mystical divine love or the earthly love there should not exist a veil between a lover and beloved or a duality among them but should exist a sense of oneness (Tawhid). The sense of having or distinct identity is itself a barrier to the relationship of divine love.

> Remove the veils and tell the nacked
> Truth
> Who sleeps in carnal embrace with their
> Cloths/! (*MasnaviI* 138)

Rumi further says that the beloved exist everywhere and in everything it is just the lovers illusion which brought us the separation of the subject and the object (*MasnaviI* 30) The possibilities of the feeling of oneness can be possible only after the renunciation of the material life. "Go, renounce that person in order to contemplate the being of Him" (Nicholson).

Majnoun, too like Rumi were in search of the supreme whole by idealising the earthly beloved which is followed by dissolving in the idealised One or divine. Shelly in her poem *Epipsychidion* (1821), says Nigel Leask, speaks on the psychological quest for the idealised

Other in the form of a ideal woman for the search of the soul within a soul (Roe, 145):

> For in the fields of immortality
> My spirit should at first have worshipped thine,
> A divine presence in a place divine; (*Epipsychidion*, ll. 133-35)

However Shelley too seems to borrow the idea of idealisation of the earthly beloved for the divine and finally dissolve into the Other from the Oriental or Sufi sources which he portrayed through his *Alastor*. Where through an idealised visionary maid becomes the epitome of ideal beauty and the source of divine light.

In this poem Shelley celebrates the bliss of union through introducing the idealisation of the beloved and the urge to return to the blissful state of our origin which has its likeness to the Sufi idea of longing for a return to its original state of unity. Shelley's *Alastor* tries to take us in such a state of mind which makes us to feel our inner urge to return to the origin.

After he met Shams week and month they shut themselves in the closed room for retreat. But it was not being liked by Rumi's followers. Rumi's relationship with Shams was a resemblance of Rumi's relationship with God. As the earthly loves are the mirror of the original love for the divine, Rumi's love for Shams was too the same. For Rumi Shams was the stairs to reach God. Rumi and Shams were on the path of direct contact but the orthodox religious mind would not accept that idea instead they believe that only Gods messenger can have a divine contact with the divine. Therefore Rumi and Shams' ideologies and friendship could have not been possible to accept for the general follower of Islam and hence they had to part away from each other.

As love has to pay so does Rumi and Shams. As Shams his head and for Rumi his peace of mind and eventually had to become a changed personality including forgetting all his old self which was comprised of all rules and regulation implanted in him by his father Baha-ud-din Balkh. With love there will always be a pain (separation) as with the rose there is a thorn. Rumi described this forfeited nature of love through his poem "*The Pull of Love*":

> I pulled a thorn from the fence of His
> Garden,
> And it has not stopped working its way into
> My heart.
> One morning a little of His wine
> Turned my heart into a lion hunter. (Helminsky 37)

The Sufis believe that we are the part of the divine soul that is why we always feel inside a separation, a gap or emptiness in us. And that is why no matter how much we earn or get we are never satisfied with our achievements. But the Sufis are the impatient one to wait to fill that emptiness in them and desire for that divine whole in their life time. Being unaware of it, human being feel that attachment and therefore get involved in love with the worldly things. People in the hope of getting that fulfillness in them. And hence meet disappointment in life like mirage in the desert for the travellers. They also search for their whole in the form of relationship like in beloved, mother, father, siblings etc. But this affection or longing is only the image of the real love which we possess for our whole or divine. And in order to understand that divine love or union one must surrender oneself to the divine will so that the currents or divine force would sweep us away towards the path of union with the divine. The Sufis believe that if we surrender ourselves to the divine will, we will be able to listen to our inner voices very eloquently which would lead us to union. The union is a state of mind where we return to our original whole (divine).

Once we are aware of the original reason of our very existence and realise our true self this union beckons us back to our original state. The very nature of our impulse of union with the divine is quite similar with the impulse to get our mate, partner or beloved in the world. It is mentioned in Quran that whatever is there in heaven including river, mountain, stream, emotions, love though in smaller amount, God has put everything of it in us while sending us for our earth's journey. Self-realisation or enlightment happens only when we unveil ourselves. Which means unveil into nothingness. In the process of unveiling we will realise that we are nothing and we know nothing and the word "I" removed from "Me" and then we can see the ultimate truth in the mirror of our heart. Rumi explains that if we could get rid of ourselves we could view the truth as clearly as water in the river. He says:

> If you could get rid
> Of yourself just once,
> The secret of secrets
> Would open to you. (Nilchian 33-130)

Hence we can say that everything we have on this earth is a symbol or image of the original including our love for our beloved, friend and parents. In fact, these love of ours is mere an image of the real love that we possess for our real love for our divine. Rumi through his poetry urges us to walk the path of union because that is the only station where we can overcome our sorrows and suffering of separaton.

Rumi and Shams kept themselves locked up in room away from one and everyone and in solitary engaged themselves with prayer, fasting with forty days of Chillah Kashi (austerities) (Shibli pp. 13-14). It was the pick time of Rumi's life when he met Shams-e-Tabriz. It is his presence which helps him to transported to divine energy. After this belief stay with each other Rumi became Shams's disciple, a wandering dervish who had abandoned the material world for the mysteries journey to the Eternal. Coleman Barks summarised their friendship in the following manner:

> Their friendship is one of the mysteries. They spent months together without any human needs, transported into a region of pure conversation. (Tsolak web)

Rumi being influenced by this wonderful dervish had a great attachment with this Sufi mentor and hence written all his and Shams experience of love, separation, anguish, spiritual vision and ecstatic union with God in his collection *Diwan-i-Shams-i-Tabriz. Since* Shams was a man of few words and silence he chosed Rumi to speak for him. And if someone has the urge to know Shams one must read *Arasteh* (conversation between Rumi, Shams and God) which is derived from Rumi's *Maqalaat.* The main theme of this work is the idea and concept of self and the cosmic self and their separation at the time of birth and through Shams Rumi could see his universal Self which was separated from its cosmic self.

After Shams was taken away from him, Rumi became a lover in pain and in anguish of separation desired for his love object Shams. And set out for his journey to get his beloved friend Shams. To Rumi Shams became 'the light of his body', his inner being, which was unfolding to him, a free universal God like man or truth and also became his every source of happiness. Shams, an illumined spirit, acted as a mentor to unfold Rumi's inner self to him and torn all the veils that comes between him and his divine self:

> When he (Shams) stimulated my thought from the depth of my psychic sea, the phantom of light arose. Shams was the light. Shams was the light of the eyes, the clarity of reason, the brightness of the soul and the enlightenment of the heart. (*Arasteh*)

However, the absence of the earthly beloved creates restlessness, despondency and a desire to possess the object of love which further makes the lover realise the nostalgic separation and a wish to return to its lost origin.

Among us who are too busy loving the worldly beloved and forgets the real beloved, God, in order to make them realise of their true self God takes that things or objects of happiness from that person so that they will realise the true self. Therefore in this regard Rumi explains artistically in his Rubais in this way:

> Whoever sees you with the eyes of heart
> Goes ecstatic
> But the blind person stays lost in thought
> Hundreds of branches from the secret worlds are
> Dropping roses at your feet
> Why do you cut down the tree of contentment? (Ergin *The Rubais* 26)

Perhaps though the above mentioned line from his poem Rumi was asking lord about his reason to separate the lovers when they are happy and contended and even worships the lord in their happiness. Therefore Rumi's poetry mirror back to us this ocean of woven speech too in-intricate and dynamic for any grammarian to untangle.

> If you want to know God, enjoy the company of lovers.
> If you want to be thought a great person,
> Learn some subtle point and say it with many variations
> As the answer to every questions If you want to live your soul, find a friend like Shams and stay near. (Mascetti 4)

Rumi believes that all the love we possess for each other is in reality the love that we possess for our God. Though people love one another and the different beautiful objects of the world, Rumi says these are merely the reflections of the divine beloved. These worldly love is just a distraction from the truth. And when we will realise the truth we will seek to re-unite with our beloved God to whom we really belong to.

> First you empty the lovers at the hand of separation,
> Then you fill them with gold to the tops of their heads.
> (Chittick *Sufism* 22)

Rumi says, at that moment our joy will be exactly that of a lover who re-unite with his beloved after being felt the torturous pangs of separation from his beloved. As in every human being there is an inner urge to meet their divine and heart is the only station where one can have that meeting. And people are always in search of that meeting in the form of relationship. That is why even though people are get cheated, happen to fall in love again and again. It is the heart and not by the intellectual means that one can attain that meeting with our divine. As Ouspensky has rightly comments on it in a letter that heart is the only way and hope to reach our divine and not the intellect of ours. Human heart is a place where God has a secret meeting with its creation. God has set different phase of love in human heart. As it comes in our life in a form of different relationship. Rumi through his poem *'Folks'* suggest us to be in love in such a way which will free us from all and everything in our life. He says the lover must keep on pursuing their love. Through a disciplined regular practices as it will act like a calling bell at the divine door who atlast opens it to see the person outside on the door.

> Submit to a daily practice
> Your loyalty to that
> Is a ring on the door. (Barks *The Essential* 101)

Rumi's poetry connects us to the emotional centre with the divine. Human reality is the incompleteness, emptiness, non-existence and non-being so we are always in a state of mind to break free from all this desire and dream of this material world.

> In the existence of your love,
> I have become non-existent.
> This non-existence, linked to you,
> Is better than all existence. Rumi (*Quotes by Rumi* web)

The Sufis believes that the human heart is only the comprehensive reality of humans and the way of love is the only way to annihilation. And because of this non-existence we are not aware of our true self and hence ignorant of our reality. Rumi says in his poem *Bouyancy* that the journey of love is like sailing to the ocean without knowing where and when to reach. Which means complete surrender is the only way to stay away from pain. It is said that when don't think about ourselves God thinks about us. We are weak and may stay in unconsciousness but it is never too late to be awake again. Therefore instead of lamenting on our guilt we must assured ourselves that God is caring and tender like our mother who forgives us no matter what we do once we surrender and repentant:

> So the sea – journey goes on, and who knows where!
> Just to be held by the ocean is the best luck
> We could have. It's a total waking up! (Barks *The Esst.*105)

Plato's Symposium, Aristophanes elaborates about the idea of our return to the original source by citing the example of the myth of Zeus who cut beings, into two separate parts longs to unite to each other. Rumi's poem *Ney-Naame from his Masnavi which* was first translated by William Jones as 'The Song of the Reed' consist of 51 *beyt* (couplet) in this poem the lover reed (*ney*), is separated from its native land, the reed-bed (*neyestaan*), where it had belonged. Therefore the poem *Ney-naame* is the story of the reed's melancholic complaint of its return to the origin which is again represents man's yearning to return to its truth, its long lost origin. The reed-flute (*ney*) is symbolically a soul's yearning to return its origin (Jones, 446). Reynold Nicholson comments on Rumi's story on the reeds as the voice of the personified reed could be perceived as the soul of the poet himself who is filled with divine inspiration, singing the songs of the 'deified' perfect man who is one with the divine. (Nicolson 20-21)

This very word resembles the saying of Sri Krishna to Arjuna in *Gita* where he describes about the existence of supreme soul in the soul of human being. And that is why our soul has the urge for the union with the supreme as we are the part of the whole. Therefore as the flute is made of the wood and so it cries for its separation in pain and agony in a hope of union with the wood it belongs to. So does the human soul which is never satisfied no matter what does it acquire or gain in their life there always exist an emptiness or desire in human and that is the urge for the union with the truth.

In fact this love and pangs of separation and his search for earthly beloved friend Shams makes him realise his talents in his poetry and also his true self. But the fact is that language is not enough to express the mystical longings and union for the beloved.

Similarly it is the pangs of separaton of Leili-Majnum and Majnum's failure to fulfill his love for Leili, Majnoum while wandering for her reached Leili's native mountain where he being intoxicated in the love of Leili composed several of his Ghazel and poem on his lady love Leili:

From the pain of grief and fire of love
He did not rest unless on that mount
He clapped the hands while roaming up there
Tumbling and uprising like the sots
He warbled on and ran here
And there in rapture. (Sattari 282-285)

The theme of love, separation and longing is the most dominating theme in Rumi's poetry. But these separation is not only with his divine God but also with his master Shams. In fact in whose separation he could understand his real Self or the presence of divine in him. As after Shams departure Rumi uttered:

> Why should I seek? I am the same as he.
> His essence speaks through me
> I have been looking through myself! (Nihat web)

Despite all hindrance Rumi din't give up his search for his friend, and travelled to Syria. Interesting thing is that he finally found his beloved nowhere but"in his own heart, radiant as the moon." Then he had started writing his poetry under Shams' name:

> The primordial Moon is his face, verse and ghazal are his scent –
> Scent is the portion of him who is not intimate with the view.
> Maulana complied, and it is said diately improvised the first eighteen couplets of the
> "The Spiritual Couplets." It is the so-called "Song of the reed": Mathnavi
> Harken to the reed how it complains and how it tells the pangs of separation. (*Mathnavi I.*I)

Not only the Sufi mystic who brought this notion of union with the divine but also some Christian mystic including Jacob Böhme. Böhme's notion of sacrifice of self-will to be united with the divine without leaving the way of God resembles the Sufi states of *fanaa* and *baqaa*. According to Böhme, the best and true way to perceive God, may be to perceived in His [...] essence, [...] is that man arrives at the state of unity with himself, and that, [...] in his *will* he should leave [...] self'(Hartmann,1919:54). It is only in that state that man enters into divine union with Christ, so that he sees God 'Himself'(Ibid 55). He is all, and whatever you wish to know in the All is in Him. Once we step out of all our selfish will (desiring), then will the Holy Spirit of God take a living form within ourself and ignite the soul with its flame of divine love:

> The human selfhood will then follow in the joy of humility, and become able to see what is contained in time and in eternity. [...] The soul is then no longer her own property, [...]. In such a state of calmness [...] should the soul then remain, like a fountain remains at its own origin, and she should without ceasing draw and drink from that well, and nevermore desire to leave the way of God. (Hartmann 56)

According to the mystic tradition the self-desires to dissolve into the other in beauty or truth which is lacking in the phenomenal self. It is a process of uniting of the self to the cosmic self and get annihilated. Hence it is Jones idea of the power of divine beauty which makes the subject die into the other and not the Burkean's idea of Beauty of the other whose weakness and submissive nature makes fall for the other.

The difference between the two mystic tradition i.e. the Christian and Islamic Mysticism is that in Islamic mysticism the mystic achieves the state of *fanaa* and *baqaa* through idealisation of the earthly beloved in place of divine. The Romantics too had exchanged the similar notion of idealisation of the earthly beloved as the divine.

However it was very clear that while searching for Shams, Rumi could realize that he and Shams are the same and hence the divine in them are also same. So Rumi decided to seek the union with the beloved at the cost of his own cessation which is also called in Sufi language as *fanna* or annihilation. Enlightment is something where we are not just a mirror element of this vast universe of God but a very special creatures of God. Rumi's poem reads:

If you're nimble on God's path
You'll rise up to the sky
Your real place is on that throne
Are't you ashamed of just being a shadow
Dragging along on the ground? (Ergin, *The Rubais* 45)

According to Rumi enlightment is a state of mind where there is nothing called good or bad deeds and to reach there one has to sacrifice his self into the Other. And that state of mind is called enlighten mind:

There is a place beyond good and bad deeds both
But this is not the place for every young and
Pretty novice
The price for the one who wants to get there
Is to give his life.
And sacrifice his heart. (Ergin *The Rubais* 46)

Rumi described the secret behind our birth, death and annihilation through his poem *You Can't Get away.* Here he declared that we come, go and pass this world in confusion and it will continue until unless we realise the value of annihilation. For annihilation to take place in us we must go through the separation and pain. Adam and Eve who were too not ready to live in the spiritual realm of God and so were send here on this earth to learn through sorrows and sufferings.. Here he told us about the importance of knowing our lord.

He doesn't open his door
Until you become dust at his doorstep.
You can't pick up a rose
Until the thorn has pricked you. (Ibid 154)

Rumi asserts that once we start this journey to God there is no right and left but the straight path which leads to the beloved. And to get the divine, one must surrender and sacrifice the self into nothingness and then realise the ultimate truth.

Rumi used the 'sama' as a meditation to connect himself with the divine. The term '*sama'* in Arabic means 'listening' the Sufis practice this Sama in order to experience a state of ecstasy and spirituality., D'Israeli called Maulaviyeh dervishes as 'Mevleheh dervise', who are involved in the ritual of whirling dance which is again resemblances with *fanaa*, and in both the Sufi loses consciousness (self). But the difference between them is that sama is just a ritual and *fanaa* is a higher state of love. D'Israeli's depiction of such Sufi states as *fanaa* and *samaa'* throughout his romance shows his soft corner for Sufism.

The self is always in a urge to return to its origin by dissolving in the supreme One in essence. In the process of *fanna* the self is annihilated and becomes one with the other or dies in the other. In Persian Sufism, the lover achieves the state of *fanna* by idealising an earthly beloved in place of the divine.

"I am naught, God is all; there is no being but God". (Chande 79)

During *fanaa* the Sufi loses his self and assumes to be the Real and becomes the Real. In this particular state of mind the beloved like blood flows in each and every veins of the lover and emptied the lover and fills every inch of the lover's body and soul and nothing is left and left him in a state of nothingness.

Love entered me
And become blood in my veins
Emptied me of myself
And filled me with the beloved
Every single particle of my body
Is soaked in the beloved
My name is all that's left of me
He became the rest. (Ergin, *The Rubais* 45)

The idea of becoming the 'Other' by idealising the other can be found in the tenth century Persian Sufi Mansur Hallaj's whose heretical utterance '*ana 'l-Haqq*' (I am the Truth), which led to his execution. A century prior to that, the Persian Sufi Bayazid Bastami had exchanged the same state of *fanaa* and uttered the same by proclaiming ' I am God' or 'I am Thou' or 'I am He whom I love and He whom I love is I' is nothing but his ecstatic state of mind or a self-annihilation in the divine. Therefore *fanaa* or loss of self in

Sufism, is an ecstatic state of mind where self is annihilated due to excessive love for the beloved.

Bastami uttered long before Hallaj made on the notion of unity as 'the ultimate identification of the worshiper and the worshiped, or the lover and the beloved '(Fatemi 162)'. Which Hallaj made much more later with the declaration of *'ana 'l-Haqq'*, Four centuries later Rumi declares the same:

O my Soul I searched from end to end:
I saw in thee naught save the Beloved;
Call me not infidel, O my soul, if I say
that thou thyself art He. (Fatemi 165)

He invites the people of all religion and faith in the journey of self-realisation and union with the divine. And that is why he was loved and admired by all and sundry. Perhaps that is why UNESCO in the honour of Rumi has declared 2007 as the year of Rumi. Rumi further says that day dreaming leads us to our complete absence from the present world where we forget our very identity called 'I' and instead we find God in that place. Similar was the case with Jesus and Mansur-al-Hallaj Who denies their existence and says it is God inside them. Which is already discussed in this chapter where Mansur –al-Hallaj (c 858-922ad) uttered: "Ann I –Haqq", means I am truth or I am God. Therefore it is beyond the understanding of the common people who thought it was really a presumptuous and offensive claim for any human being to claim to be the divine. Further the claim was totally against sharia (Islamic law or Quar'an)t, and one was liable to be executed as a blasphemer. But if a person says that Ann-I-abd or" I am the servant of God" affirms two existences, his own and God's it was accepted, however if a person says Ann-I-haqq, "I am God" its Sufi implication was that the person has made himself non- existence and had given himself up to God thereby vanquishing his own identity. Indeed this when properly understood merely implied extreme of humility and self-abasement.

Therefore decades later Rumi was possessed with similar notions of oneness with the divine as Mansur-al-Hallaj possessed. As Rumi Spoke it through his poem "*The sunrise Rubby*" by answering a beloved's question in this way:

She ask, Do" you love me or yourself more?
Really, tell the absolute truth."
He says," There is nothing left of me.
I'am like a ruby held up to the sunrise.
Is it still a stone, or a word

> Made of redness? It has no resistance
> To sunlight." (Barks, *The Esst* 100)

The Sufis never possess other nor anybody possess them as they are the freemasonry. According to Abu-l-Hasan Nuri the Sufis are the one who has nothing in his possession nor is himself possessed by anything. Seyed-Gohrab in his *A Narration of Love*, asserts that if someone's self is annihilated it neither possesses nor is possessed (54). Instead it is an identification of the subject to become one with the other rather than the possession of either by the other. And this state of *fanaa* or love directs the Sufi in the path of goodness, beauty and truth. According to Ibn Sina, the Persian philosopher of the eleventh century, known in the West as Avicenna, asserts that everything that exists in the Universe desires to become assimilated to the Absolute Good (38). Therefore it is not about possessing the other rather it is an aspiration to possess a quality in the Other.

The above discussion does come to the conclusion that the beloved is taken or considered by the lover as the object of possession but the lover is in such a way in love with the object of love that he does not find any difference or separateness between them. Hence he becomes one with it. In that process a mutual bond creates between the two and the self of the lover expires in the end and remains only the beloved. Therefore in Sufism, the lover loss its 'self' in the love for the 'Other' to become the Other.

Such identification with God takes place when the Sufi reaches the stage of annihilation (*fanaa*) and exist nothing but God in them. Whoever is annihilated in God and attains to the reality of everything, 'as Bastami claims, he becomes all Truth, if he is not there, it is only God that sees Himself.'(Fatemi 163)

In the state of *fanaa*, the identification of self or I with the Other or Thou/He, transformation took place in such a way that the I-Thou relationship turns into I-I or Thou-Thou relation. Rumi gave an excellent example of such relationship in the following manner:

> There came one and knocked at the door of the Beloved. And a voice answered and said, 'Who is there? 'The lover replied, 'It is I.' 'Go hence,' returned the voice, there is no room within for thee and me.' Then came the lover a second time and knocked, and again the voice demanded, 'Who is there?' He answered, 'It is thou.' 'Enter,' said the voice, 'for I am within.'(Walker 206)

The constant urge to be unite with the ideal other makes the subject imagine the goodness in the other and hence becomes the other. It is worth remembering at this point that such Thou-Thou relationship comes as a result of the Sufi experiencing solitude, contemplation, and yearning to attain unity with the beloved. Such relationship is a sort of love that negates all multiplicity, duality, and I-Thou-ness: a state where the Sufi transcends 'the quality of making distinction between the things of this world', including any distinction (difference) between himself and the other. Thus is the Sufi 'completely annihilated from his selfhood and is united with God'. (Hanif 230)

Therefore the Sufis experience union with the ultimate Divine through his love for the idealised version of the earthly beloved, during the course of which the Sufi's 'I' is made one with the 'thou' and the self no longer has a place for self therefore the ego is lost. Rumi describes beautifully the state of annihilation in the following manner:

> A Cavalier of absence raised dust and galloped away
> He's gone
> Only his dust remain's
> When searching for God and truth
> Look straight ahead
> Not to the right or to the left
> His dust is always right here
> But he has gone to the land of absence. (Ergin, *The Rubais* 61)

And our real identity can only be gained after the removal of selfish self (nafs) then remains only the pure self to unite with the divine. The Sufis called this process as fanna and suggest the disciple to 'Die before you really die' which means to remove the veil of ego and to die mentally before to die physically. The main aim of the Sufis is to attain self-realisation or self-transformation which can be possible after we will remove all the veils between us and God. The greatest veil is to remove I from Me or I between 'you (God) and me'. So Rumi in the beginning could not understand the nature of his love for Shams and when he realised that he and Shams are no the different but the same he stopped looking for Shams. He even realised that his quest for Shams was actually the search for the divine union. And that connection of divine love he found in his face-to-face love for Shams, and also found that all that year he was looking for was not Shams but the divine in the form of human love. Because of this connection human being are always in pursuit of things one after another simultaneously in the hope of achieving complete happiness. But there is no end of it till they find the truth (God).

Rumi further says the lover must sacrifice themselves in order to get the divine as the duality cannot exist. In the poem *Drowned* he says: (Helminski & Rezwani *Loves's Rip* 92)

The life of lovers is in dying.
You will not win the Beloved's heart
Unless you sacrifice your own.
I am drowned in a love so deep
It swallowed my first love and my last. (*Mathnawi* 1757)

In this regard one of the famous Sufi saint Sa'id comments:

> Realise that you know nothing and you are nobody. It is no easy thing to attain this realisation. It doesn't come with teaching and instruction, nor it be sewn on with a needle, or tied with a thread. This is a gift from God and a question of whom He bestows it on and whom He causes to experience it. (Fardiman 244)

Therefore enlightment comes only to the chosen one whom God bestows that opportunity. Meditation for forty days was the ritual during the time of Prophet Muhammad to get divine knowledge on to be enlighten being. Once a follower asked Muhammad that he had been meditated for forty days but he could not receive any divine knowledge. In reply to his query Muhammad said that if someone worship God in desiring to get him or for something and in wrong direction cannot reach God but if someone would worship without any selfish motive he would surely become enlighten. When a drunkard asked God to take away his impurities by peeing off, the almighty replied that if his key is bent it cannot open the lock. Similarly if our direction and intension is wrong we can never reach the divine.

The Sufis believes that there is only one way to get God that is complete surrender, or removing of the veils by giving up all desire, lustre, gluttony, jealousy, hatred etc. Then only we can realise that the beloved, lover and love are the one. Mansur-al-Hallaj quotes in this way:

Between Me and You there lingers an "It is I"
Which torments me.
Ah! Lift through mercy this "it is I"
From between us both! (Fardiman 246)

And in this market of world one can get only what we give. If we will give up ourselves in the path of God, He will also give up

Himself to us. We never get anything extra, so if we will reveal ourselves to God, he will also reveal himself to us.

Don't come confused to the earth's bazaar,
And don't leave confused either.
In this business,
You can't get this
Until you've given that. (Ergin *The Rubais155*)

Rumi says we cannot get God if we will not come out from our comfort zone. To get him we must proceed towards the path of love which is not the easy and comfortable one. As love comes along with pain and suffering.

You can't get the taste of ecstasy
So long as you stay sobar
You can't know the soul
So long as you think you are only your body
You will never reach the truth
If you don't give up yourself. (Ibid 64)

Rumi further says that God warn us and tell us through his holy books that we must walk on the path to Him or the path towards annihilation as at the end there will be nothing but God. And the time will come when we will realise but there will be no time in our hand to regret.

God tells us:
O restless one
Abandon people
You are ours, our true one
Get used to us and acquire our habits
Because the time will come when there will be
No time
And you will have to stand completely alone. (Ibid 65)

Since the body is a dungeon for the us, Rumi suggest us to break free of this eggshell and fly to the eternity. If we will not walk on the path of enlightment we will remain in the dungeon of life and death but once we start walking on the path to our divine we may break free ourselves from this dungeon. Rumi explained it through his poem *The eggshell of the Body (Nevit & Johnson 133):*

You're like a bizarre bird
In the shell of the body's egg.
You can't fly because you're inside the egg.
But when this egg is crushed,
You'll fly free and save your soul.

Once we are free from this dungeon there will exist no enemy but friends everywhere. There will be no separation from our beloved both earthly and divine beloved. And in that moment of freedom divine beauty will show His face and will make us feel secure in his nest of blessings. Rumi says:

That beauty would show his face and say,
"I am the one who sees you, who loves you.
Since you are open to my blessings,
You need no longer be afraid of anything". (Ibid 134)

Rumi suggest not to observe his death as a sad one or a separation instead call it a union with the beloved and instead of mourning everyone must celebrate his union with the divine.

For the funeral:
Call the drammers, timbale beaters, and tambourine players.
March toward my grave dancing thus,
Happy guy intoxicated;
With hands clapping,
So that people would know that the friends of God
Go happy and smiling toward the place of meeting. (Fardiman 256)

Rumi's death is celebrated in 'Mevlana Moseleum' as 'Seb-i Arus' (Wedding Day). Rumi became the kind of lover who takes this world as a dungeon and wanted to move beyond it to reach the divine in order to unite with Him. At his death bed when his wife requested Rumi to stay little longer on this earth Rumi replies in this manner:

Am I a thief?
Have I stolen someone's
Goods?
Is this why you would confine
Me here and keep me from
Being rejoined with my love? (*Quote by Rumi* Web)

Rumi says when someone will understand the true meaning of death, will run towards it for it frees one's soul and unite with the divine. As he says through his poem *One Who Runs Away* (Helminski & Rezwani, 2008:100):

Anyone who truelyunderstands dying would flee
Towards death
As toward permament life, as toward a crown and
Royal robes.
When destiny decrees that so-and so
Will die while journeying,
Then so-and so, in fear of dying, flees on a journey.

Stop it, stop hunting what is not worth hunting,
For night's fancy and even night itself will flee the
Down. Diwani Shamsi Tabrizi 794

Rumi quotes Shams in his Divani shamsi Tabrizi 794 on the true concept of death in this way:

Anyone who truly understands dying would flee
Toward death
As toward permanent life, as toward a crown and
Royal robes. (Helminski *Love's Rip* 99)

According to both Shams and Rumi death is a beautiful journey towards union with the divine. And if someone would truly understand the meaning of death, will proceed eagerly towards it and will not run away from it.

In this stage of mind the sorrows and suffering Escape from sorrow, go toward the king;
Leave behind the rented house; go to your eternal
Abode! Divani Shamsi Tabrizi 2352 (Helminski 97)

could not touch him as he believed that all these comes from divine as a gift to learn through them. In pain there lies His favour and in His favour there lies pain. At this stage God himself is eager to embrace human soul.

The beloved is all, the lover only veils
Him.
The beloved is all that lives, the lover
A dead thing. (*Quote by Rumi* web)

Rumi suggest us to move beyond the narrow circle of the orthodox phase of religion and to reach back the state where there is no religion but only being (human) where no one is Christian, Jewish, Hindus and Muslims but only human being.

I grasp it, take it to my
Breast
And drag it into the
Whirling!
And when the bosom of
The motes
Is filled with the glow of
The sun, (Schimmel 203-204)

Through these lines Rumi talks about the meeting with the special person in his life Shams. He further says that his word are ashamed not to get proper word to explain about the description of his beloved. He quotes in his MathnawiI:

Whatever description
Or explanation I gave of
Love,
When I reach love I am
Ashamed of my
Exposition. (Nasr 113-116)

Shams wanted Rumi to get cooked so he left him twice ("Separation Cooks"). In other word he wanted Rumi to die before he would really die. Prophet Muhammad too suggest us to die before we really die.

You have suffered much agony, but you are
Still behind veil,
Because dying was the one thing needed,
And you haven't fulfilled it.
Your agony will not end until you die;
You cannot reach the roof without
Ascending the ladder. (Camelia &Helminsky 753)

Phophet Muhammad said that one must die before he dies. Which means one must die spiritually before the physical death. So that human being can repent their mistakes in their life time on earth. And in that process the wicked will get the opportunity to lessen their wickedness and get forgiveness from the lord. It is mentioned in Hadith (saying of Prophet Muhammad) that Muhammad himself asked for forgiveness seventy times in a day.

> He asked pardon of God seventy times every day. He likened genuflection and Prostration, the prescribed action in ritual prayer, to knocking the door ring of mystical attainment to the divine portal. Which inevitably opens to the persistant. (Renard: 129)

And it is through repentant and suffering one can remove the ego, desire, hatred and evils from oneself and can see the truth. It is said that before the revelation of Qur'an to Prophet Muhammad his heart has been cleaned by the angels. Rumi through his poem *The Kurd's lost Camel* describes that we have lost our true self (whole) or the truth from which we are apart or separated and it is nowhere but inside us and we just need to search that part within us to be unite and become the whole. In other words to be the whole we must seek within us for it exist within us. As Rumi asserts:

The Night of Power is in your soul;
Why do you not appreciate it?!
It stirs you each and every moment;
Why do you not stir it too?! (Helminsky *Love's Rip* 21-22)

The Sufis too follow the ritual of repentant, which literally mean to die before one dies physically. The Sufis live a life with society and family and with all the outer rituals. Rumi's Masnavi-vi reads (2611):

> There is no monkhood in Islam: the congregation is a mercy. He wanted to ensure the Mutual support and solidarity that monastic solitude did not afford, life in community Also provides two other benefits. It allows the believes to associate more forcely with People of proven holiness and to consult with them, thus minimize the false step one might take on one's own. (Renard, 121)

Therefore Islam too does not prefer monkhood among its believers. As it allows one to modify and complete ones behaviour in their mixing with their better half. And if someone would run away from all evils how would it teach him jihad (to fight the inner evils). However it is better to live among peoples in order to avoid unnecessary wrong path and to become a role model for the people to follow the right path which you have gathered or learned so far. In his *Mathnawi volume VI,* Rumi quotes prophet's hadith in this way:

> If anyone wishes to see a dead person walking this visible on the
> Earth, let him behold Abu Bakr, the devout (who) through being
> A true witnesss (siddique) became the prince of the Resurrected.
> (Renard 117-118)

Therefore according to prophet Muhammad if somebody wants to see the dead person on earth they must see the companion of Muhammad, Abu Bakr Siddique, who according to Islamic faith would be the prince of heaven. Abu Bakr and other companion of Prophet Muhammad were called the first Sufis in the Sufi history. As they were the one who though living a normal life with their family but inside were fully aware of the world and the next world after death.

So in order to repentant one must go through separation and suffering which indeed matures and prepare us for the next world. In the poem *I was dead and came to Life from the book Love's Ripening: Rumi on the Hearts Journey* Rumi says about his reaction on God's wretch or suffering in this way:

> You are the fountain of the rising sun; I am the shade
> Of the willow.
> You struck me on the head; I became humble and
> Melted.
> My heart found radiance from the soul; if opened up
> And cleaved.
> My heart wove new satin, and I become aloof to this
> Ragged garb. (Helminsky *Love's Rip* 68-69)

Rumi through these lines tried to express that if almighty gives us pain and suffering or hammer us on our head we become humble and all our proud goes away and we melt and realise our true self. Rumi believes that we are unaware of what God has planned for us and we mistook God's plan for us and we plan for ourselves and hence meet failure and disappointed. We should not forget it indeed we should surrender and trust God for his plan for us. As Rumi asserts in his Poem *What God's Plan:*

> Abandon your desire and take on the light of wisdom,
> For that desire would soon lead to disappointment.
> Be the king's game and don't hunt your own game,
> For your game will be swept up by the falcon of
> Doom. (Ibid 29-30)

As it is through the ritual and trust we can prefer God before everything and hence God would keep us before everything. Hence surrender is another important ritual and observation for the Sufis.

Hence after Shams departure Rumi could realise his true search for the divine. And could also realise that he and Shams are one. Rumi in his *Divani Shamsi Tabrizi* mentioned that we all are one in different body as he put this view in his poem entitled *We are Now One*:

> We stood together hand in hand in primordial time;
> Now at last, we are one again
> We are all of one soul struggling along one path,
> And all drunk with the same wine.
> From among the two worlds we chose love alone;
> Except for that love there's nothing we adore,
> What bitterness did our souls suffer from separation!
> At long last, we are free from separation. (Helminsky 41-42)

Through the poem *A Sip of Poverty,* Rumi says:

> The wine makes us all one and the same color;
> The small and the great become one and the same. (Ibid 96)

Rumi says that being in love of that real beauty he has forgotten everything and everyone. Evidently, the tenth century Iranian Sufi Sarrajin in his defends on Bistami's Bayazid and Hallaj *shatahât* or *blasphemous* statement states that it was made when they are in the state of ecstasy or *fanâ*. In this regard he brings the reference of the pre-Islamic love story of Majnum and Leili where Majnum was so crazy and into Leili's love that he cannot differentiate between Leili and any other thing around him. As Sarraj writes:

> "Majnum would say, when looking at a wild animal, "Leili," when looking at the mountains, "Leili," and when looking at other people, "Leili," to the point that when he was asked his name and condition, he said "Leili". (Michael 69)

Therefore by using this pre-Islamic love story of Majnun and Layla Sarraj puts an example of how being in love a lover is so filled with love that he speaks as if he himself is the beloved. Thus Sarraj in illustrating the example of Majnum and Leili describes clearly the mystical union where under the pressure of all consuming love they uttered such word.

Likewise, Rumi too summarized the same mystical condition whether the lover cannot differentiate between beloved and any other thing of the world. Hence he speaks in his poem *The Face of that Beauty*:

> We lost our colors in the light of your hue
> A million miles beyond the world of existence;
> The moment our souls become such idiots,
> Wasn't it for the face of that Beauty?
> (Helminski& Rezwani *Mathnawi VI* 103)

Rumi also realised this fact of oneness after his separation from Shams. Rumi further explains his brief realisation in this way:

> The first time I saw love
> I threw my heart and soul under its feet.
> Then I asked myself:
> Can the lover and the beloved really be two?
> They'are only one
> I must have been cross-eyes. (Ergin *The Rubais* 180)

Rumi exhorts us that the lovers do not need any teacher to be in love because love itself is a teacher. We are inspired by Rumi not because his sentimental consolation of love but the courage of dealing with the separation which lead him to realise his true search for the divine love. Rumi says after he realised the truth:

> I have lived on the lip
> Of insanity, wanting to know reasons,
> Knocking on a door. It opens.
> I've been knocking from the inside! (Barks *The Essential* 281)

Rumi says if we seek for something it also seeks us and when we are in search of divine love it also seeks us. God always put in us desire for several things then disappoints us resulting in pain and suffering. Which indeed melts, moulds and shape us. Rumi says:

First He pempered me with a hundred favours,
Then He metted me with the fires of sorrows.
After He sealed me with the seal of love,
I became Him.
Then, He threw my Self out of me. (Fardiman 250)

To be more convenient to this notion, Rumi says it does not matter whatever attracts us because behind all the attraction there is only one real attraction i.e. God. And that is why we can never get satisfied completely after we reach our desired goal. Infact there exist always a sense of incompleteness in us, which can only be completed by our divine whole. With the departure of Shams, the veil was removed from Rumi's heart and so he could peep inside his heart where lie in the ultimate truth that he and Shams are no two but one being in different forms or body.

I could reach great heights with your love,
And with longing for you
I will increase a hundred fold.
They ask, "why are you circling him?
O ignorance, I am circling myself."(Helminsky *MathnawiVI* 1138)

Our heart is an important place where we can find the secret of this universe. Rumi suggest us that instead of involving so much in this material world we must proceed on our heart's path where the divine dwells. As in his poem *The Path in the Heart* he says:

During the winter of lust,
How long will the garden of our heart
Stay imprisoned inside the fortress?
Look for the path in the heart,
O moonfaced soul. (Ergin139)

The very self of our rules all our desire, will etc. if we are conscious enough but if we are not conscious enough then our body rules our Self. In both Qur'an and Gita it is mentioned that if humans are ruled by their self then they are superior to angels but if they are ruled by their instinct then they are even inferior to animals. In Upanishads it is said that this self of ours is all in all in us which is the gods, five elements, all creatures and called as Prajna, Brahman or pure consciousness which guides us all and exist in all from minor creatures to great and those who realise this Self or divine soul in them would be free from this circle of life, death, sorrows and sufferings (Easwaran 274)

Those who realise Brahman live in joy
And go beyond death. Indeed
They go beyond death. (Ibid 275)

And this Self of ours is free from desire, from evil, free from fear (Easwaran, III). And this revelation as it can come to those who is conscious enough of the Self as the self cannot come to those who don't realise that they are self. In Upanishad it is mentioned in the following Manner:

> The truth of Self cannot come through one
> Who has not realised that he is the Self.
> The intellect cannot reveal the Self,
> Beyond its duality of subject
> And object. Those who see themselves in all
> And all in them help others through spiritual
> Osmosis to realise the Self themselves. (Easwaran 76)

And our soul is in love with the self and wants to return to its self for it needs wings to fly on for its next for the eternal rest.

> As an eagle, weary after soaring in the sky, folds its
> Wings and flies down to rest in its nest, so does the
> Shining self enters the state of dreamless sleep, where
> One is freed from all desires. (Easwaran III)

In Quar'an it is said that nothing can contain God but only the heart of the believer has room for Him. When Moses desired to see God, God said that he cannot bear the sight of God with his physical body as it is not possible to tolerate the light of God with his physical Self. Then out of query again he asked about the dwelling place of God. He said I dwell in the heart of those who are broken. Moses said that his heart is the most broken one then God said that he must be dwelling there in. So does God dwells too in the heart of Rumi when he was separated from shams. Rumi also says that God's mercy is just like water whose nature is to flow towards the lowest or the broken.

> God's Mercy is water; it flows to the lowest;
> I will become humble earth to be embraced by the merciful.
> No physician gives pills and remedies to the healthy;
> I will become all pain, if I must,
> To be given the remedy. (Helminski, *MathnawiVI* 56)

Rumi talks about his absence from his self through the poem *Submerged in Absence* in this manner:

> I have washed and cleaned the limber of being.
> I have nothing more to do with this world.
> My beloved keeps inviting me
> To sit with him for a while.
> I don't even pay him any attention,
> So submerged am I in absence.

What can you say to one
Who is not himself?
Crush my head a thousand times.
I couldn't care less. (Ergin *The Rubais137*)

Rumi says if someone will give money and his treasures in God's way he will return it back. And if someone will give their life on god's way will get the life back. He further says that a farmer would sow seeds, it might empty his barn but in the field it must be growing in double and if he would have left it in the barn it would have been eaten up by mice.

It suits the generous one to give money,
But truely the generosity of the lover
Is to surrender the soul
If you give bread for God's sake,
You will be given bread in return;
If you give your life for God's sake,
You will be given life in return. (Helminski & Rezwani 90)

He explains it very clearly that if someone starts divine journey would drown themselves more and more towards it. Because if we starts for a way the way appears. Fulfillment of material desire is also important in order to realise that there is nothing in it and then only proceeds towards the desire for the divine. And that journey towards our divine will make us desireless and we will find our self in the process of selflessness. We are well aware of the pangs of separation because once we were united. Similarly we know happiness because we have experienced sorrows. Rumi advise people to live their wanting which is the process of growing once feathers but one must be aware that it should be descent otherwise he has to fly without wings. In other words we must live a life of our desire because once we complete our desire we will no longer be crazy for them and will proceed further towards the truth. So, Rumi says that all the tags and pulls are bringing nearer to the ocean of truth.

Because the *nafs* or desires are the kind of energies which helps us proceed further for the divine union. Therefore this particular desire which arose one after another helps us moving towards the divine ocean. He further says that once we stop desiring or concerning the worldly affairs our heart stars seeing things which is beyond:

If you close your eyes to earthly concerns
Your heart will turn into an eye
And you will look out onto different worlds

As long as you don't become cocky
Everything you do will be admired. (Ergin & Johnson *The Rubais* 105)

In the poem *Open the Window,* Rumi suggest the lover of God to open the window of their heart to the innermost secret without any outward distraction. Then the beautiful face will appear to another beautiful face and then you will start thinking the other as your own. Probably that was the reason that all the Sufi saints including Mansur and Bayazid uttered the same that they are the same with the divine. (Helminski & Rezwani *Mathnawi* VI 95)

As you are made beautiful,

The beautiful one will become your own,

The intimate of your once lonely spirit. (Ibid 3097)

Hence we can say that God's mystery is important to hide from the human being because if it is too much revealed then we contemplate on it so much that it becomes quite impossible to comprehend and we mistook it in other sense.

Rumi says that if someone would question on God's answer to our prayer and we can make them remember the story of Jacob whose sight was returned just by the scent of Joseph.

How did Joseph's scent come to Jacob?
Huuuuu.
How did Jacob's sight return?
Huuuuu.
A little wind cleans the eyes.
Like this. (Barks *The Essnt* 137)

Rumi says by following outer religious rule we can only find the heaven but not the beloved. Through thoughts and signs we can only master some art but cannot get the beloved indeed we can get the beloved by being the lover which is possible only by love and complete devotion to it. Rumi says through his Rubais in this manner:

Thoughts and signs come from the mind
But the beloved comes only from love
Thoughts are like sullied water
But love is the pure water of life
You can ascend to the sky by following signs
But you won't find any trace of lovers there.
(Ergin& Johnson *The Rubais* 105)

Therefore we can say that Rumi's poetry speaks the language of love of God, separation fear, hope, joy and pain and union with the beloved. So it is his love and bereavement for the death of Shams found their expression in a sunge of music and dance and lyrics poem called '*Divani Shamsi Tabrizi*'. In fact Rumi views the true human as a reflection of this cosmic love matrix. Thus Rumi's poetry is greatly honoured by the people of all the cultures and traditions. And today Rumi's poetry speaks and nourishes the divine yearning of those who moved beyond the traditional notions of spirituality and embraces a sense of the sacred that transcends a singular religion, belief or text.

CHAPTER 3

The Mundane and Mystical in the Poetry of Shamsuddin Muhammad Hafiz

> Where does poetry live? In the overpowering felt splendour every Sane mind knows when it realises-our life dance is only for a magic Seconds, from the heart saying, shouting, "I am so damn alive!"
>
> Hafiz (Avery 13)

We find an interweaving of both the 'Mundane' (worldly) and 'Mystical' intoxicated love of God in Hafiz's poetry. The word "Ishaq" is an Arabic word which means love and is derived from the name of a plant called "Ashaqa" and it is a type of ivy which attaches trees and is its companion. According to mystical context love is nothing but of gathering perfections through God. It is an essence that is not effable and at the beginning, makes the lover totally annihilated so that no names and no effects of him is left and makes his existence disappeared. In the end, there is no lover and no beloved left and that is where love emerges in the form of a lover and sometimes as a beloved. When love gets its perfection, it annihilates the powers and disables the senses.

Hafiz is famous for his lyrics, ghazals and Divan. His poems mostly deals with the theme of love on both mystical and mundane level. Sant Kirpal Singh called Hafiz "a great mystic poet" and "a great saint". Mystical means beyond physical world, and mundane means related to our physical world. He used this traditional theme in such a way that there were no one in Persia to break his record. His expertness in mixing of two themes together i.e. the incongruous into a peaceful one made A.j Arberry termed him as "intellectual nihilism". (Arberry web)

Hafiz work is compiled with five hundred (500) poems which came in one title of *Divan. His* Ghazal followed the rhyme scheme of aabacada and is comprised of nine couplets followed by sixteen syllables. The couplets are called as beyt and line within it termed as 'mesraa'. William Jones in his translation on Hafiz's poem comments in the following manner:

> The wilderness and simplicity of this Persian song pleased me so much, that I have attempted to translate it in verse (...) I have endeavoured, as far as I was able to give my translation the easy turn of the original; and I have, as nearly as possible, imitated the cadence and accent of the Persian measure. (Jones 243)

> Jones in his translation of Hafiz's work tried to avoid beyts but expanded the nine beyts from the original ghazal with abcabc and octosyllabic lines. Hasan Javadi coments on Jones translation on Hafiz poem '*Song*' as, though it is not very faithful to the original, but it gives *a* favourable idea of the content and rhythm of Háfiz's poem to the reader. (Hasan Javedi,2005: 52)

Scholars are of the view that justice would not be done if we consider Hafiz work in translation rather than the original. A. J Arberry comments on this: 'It is a mistake to attempt to reproduce in English the mono-rhyme which is so characteristic a feature of the original.' (Hafiz eNotes) Richard Le Gallienne further comments in this regard in the following manner: So distasteful to English idea are the metrical devices and adornments pleasing in a Persian ear that the attempt to reproduce them in English can only result in the most tiresome literary antics, a mirthless, buffoonery of verse... Rhythms which in Persian, doubtless, make the sweetest chiming, fitted with English words, become mere vulgar and ludicrous jingle. (Ibid) A. J Arberry comments on Hafiz's work and calibrates in these following words: Hafiz is as highly esteemed by his countryman as Shakespeare by us, and deserves as serious consideration.' (Ibid))

J. Christoph Burgel asserts: The difficulty of understanding Hafiz correctly does not lie in his Lexicon or grammar (Ibid). He does not use rare or difficult words and his phraseology is simple and very clear. There is hardly any single verse of Hafiz posing a problem in itself. However, there is also hardly a ghazal not posing a problem of meaning and consequently, of interpretation. In other words, the obfuscation of meaning is created by the juxtaposition of verses that seem to contradict each other be it by their moral implications or by their belonging to different ontological layers.' (Glunz and Burge 20-33)

The main theme which encircles Persian literature specially ghazals are love, mysticism and hedonism, and it consist of eight to fifteen couplets (beyts), but each couplets represents and contains a different and complete meaning in it. Charles Reviczki in his letter to Jones on 24th February 1768 in London comments on Hafiz Ghazal in these manner:

> In each distich of the Gazel, the sense must be complete and finished. (Teignmouth 47)

The Origins of Ghazal is believed to have connection from two sources i.e. the lyric that was in Pre-Islamic era and also from the Arabic Qasida. Arthur Arberry asserts that the ghazal was originally referred to as 'a short love-poem' signifying 'the talk of youths and maidens' in Arabic and had a distinguished career in Arabic literature before the Persians took it over for the same purpose'. (Arverry, 1969, 113) The ghazal is the most important form of Persian literature among the other genres of Sufi literature, which is divided into prose (nasr), didactic and narrative poems (masnavi), quatrains (rubaiyat), and lyrical poems (ghazal). (Utas 207-9) It was in the ghazal that the Persian mystics found as their best medium to express the inexpressible mysticism of life. In this regard Bo Utas had put his comments as, it was through this specific literary genre that a great number of poets sang 'the perfection of the Beloved and expressed the inexpressible mystic experience'. (ibdi)

Arberry said, there are around twelve Sufi sects out of which two belongs to the heretical and the rest are the orthodox follower of Islam. The first category of heretical group of Sufis is called *Haloolia,* this category of Sufi believe that God has entered in them and the second group is called as *Ittahadia,* in this category the unionist help every enlightened being to get united with the divine essence (Naini 30). These two group of Sufis follow the Islamic rules but they also believed in complete libertinism. As for them the mosque is not the only place to worship God but it can be done anywhere including the wine house or tavern. Which is indeed a sin or infidelity for the other group of Sufis. And all the three Sufi poets of this particular thesis i.e Rumi, Hafiz and Bulleh Shah falls under this heretical group of Sufis.

Hafiz's soul enjoyed to express his inner feelings, thoughts, his philosophy into verse and he had chosen the medium of poetry. Our soul is sheer music, a music when we get lost in divine realization and tends to put on the form of poetry as Hafiz did. Hafiz was very good in encapsulating the worldly love with divine love in his poetry and that is why it become difficult for many to understand the depth of his writing. R.M Rehder, who is one of them who failed to comprehend Hafiz poetry, as he states:

> There is nothing in this poem to cause us to believe that this is a religious or Sufi poem, or that the beloved is in any way divine; rather it is a secular love lyric. (Rehder 67-73)

Though it is not easy for everyone to understand his poetry a gross still all are fascinated by its beauty, charm, rhythm and tune and it would be injustice if we consider his poetry as pertaining only to worldly affairs. As Javedi in his book "*Persian Literary Influence on English Literature*" states that it will be injustice not to consider his poem as mysticism. (Javedi 204) Throughout history of Sufi literature, the Sufi Mystical poetry has been a source of mockery and ridiculed by many orthodox critics.

Reading Hafiz poetry from starting to end is like a beautiful vision of inspiration which leading us to a mountain of faith where we can visualize our divine in sublimity. The most favourite form of Hafiz's work is his ghazal, which consist of words of conversation with God. It is believed that ghazals were the older form of poetry which were first used in the ancient Persian courts then those in later age became poetry. And some of these ghazals put in music form which become later day poetry.

The Ghazal or poetry of Hafiz were consist of fifteen couplets (beyts) or more. A beyt can be defined as the line consist of verse separated by two equal parts. And the couplets at their second line followed by a fixed rhyme. The very first couplet of each poetry has contained the main subject matter of the poem. The rest of the couplets are the changing perception from one point to another till it reached the objective of the poem. The objective line of the poem is called as "Maqta".

Hafiz like Rumi opted for same physical medium to reach the truth or divine love. For Rumi it was his friend Shams through whom he could perceive divine love and for Hafiz it is his love for Shakhi Nabat (Bunch of sugarcane), his lady love, the daughter of a rich businessman of Shiraz, who made him realize the divine love. It is said that Hafiz had hopelessly fallen in love with Nabat, but she was already engaged with a prince. It is Nabat's beauty which was the first thing that had a tremendous effect on Hafiz, so much so, that he became unconscious at her sight. He couldn't eat, sleep, etc. and therefore his love for her made him write his poems on love. But later in his life, when he realized the divine love in the form of

Nabat, he no longer wrote on Nabat but on God giving a physical form to his love. Hafiz was in great pain in his experience of mortal love hence he composed many poems and sang them every afternoon while passing Nabat's window. And the fire in his eyes continued to sparkle until it lit the lamp of Nabat's heart. Just like the Sufis heart burns till the cupbearer's (God's) heart burn for them in the same way.

Being disappointed in love Hafiz remembers the famous Sufi saint Baba Kuhi, who once promised people that whoever will be dedicated themselves for forty nights at his tomb he/she would be honoured with gift of poetry writing and would also receive his heart's desire. At the end of his forty nights at Baba Kuhi's grave, Gabriel came and informed him that he had been given the talent of poetry writing and offered him a cup of water of immortality, and then he was asked to express his heart's desire. However in this process Hafiz had experienced a different beauty or grace of Gabriel and had forgotten the mortal beauty of Nabat. The inner thought that was in Hafiz after Gabriel asked him his heart's desire: "If Gabriel the Angel of God is so beautiful, then how beautiful God must be". (Smith 9) After this realization he answered: "I want God". And then he was directed to another Sufi master Mahmud Attar, who was a God – realized man. Hafiz served him as his disciple for forty long years. But by then Hafiz took Nabat's beauty as the reflection of God's beauty. Which again does not means his love for Nabat was decreased; in fact, it grew more and more with the time.

Hafiz did not belief on any religious dogma like all other Sufis obout meeting God in the thereafter so he said that God is everywhere around us in the form of our friend and enemy that we meet, understand and learn from them for that is the meaning of our sojourn here on this earth. Therefore to love we have to accept and love everything that is both beautiful and rotten on this earth.

We often have different perception of beauty for the same object or person because it does not exist in the person or the object but with our own way of thinking. Therefore Hafiz through his poem aims to remove that veil of perception and learn to appreciate each and every aspect of beauty of the manifestation of God. Hafiz also wants to remove the stereotype ideology of humanity that God is the entity which can be found only in the hereafter or heaven and not in the Church, Mosque, Synagogue etc. He believes that whatever we desired for can be achieved here on this life itself if we can live an awakened life here on this earth. However his poetry not only influenced the Persian poet but also many Indian poets. One of them is Rabindranath Tagore who was greatly influenced by his poetry and depicted many more elements in his poetry. Therefore his influence in both East and West is notable. Many movement like Surrealism, Romanticism and Impressionism seems to have come from the influence of Hafiz as he was the spiritual master of many English writers like Ralph Waldo Emerson (1803-1882), French writer Hugo and Klingor, The British writer Moore, Algernon Charles Swinburne (1837-1909), Byron, Spaniard writer Federico Garcia Lorca (1898-1936), Russian Fet, Yesenin, Rushkin, German; Nitzsche, Goethe and Junger. His influence is incomparable when it comes to his contribution in art, poetry, and music of India and Middle East.

Moreover Hafiz like Rumi found the divine love after he has gone through the worldly love, Shaki Nabat. While searching for the worldly love he could find his inner desire for the union with God which existed in him prior to his birth. As Jones in his book '*On The Mystical Poetry of the Persians and Hindus*" Says:

> It has been made a question, whether the poems of Hafiz must be taken in a literal or in a figurative sense; but the question does admit of a general and direct answer, forever the most enthusiastic of his commentators, allow, that some of them are to be taken literally(...)Hafiz never pretended to more than human virtues and it is known that he had human propensities; for in his youth he was passionately in love with a girl surnamed Shaki Nabat(...) and the prince of Shiraz was his rival(...) (...)After his juvenile passions had subsided, we may suppose that his mind took that religious bent, which appears in most of his compositions. (Jones 452)

Hence he used both the mystical and mundane element in his poetry to show his divine love of God. Hafiz in his poem "*From First to Final day*" says that his love for the divine whole is not from the day he realized he is no different and separate from the divine but from the very day of the creation. He also had the same notion of God like Rumi that from the very beginning the desire for our beloved exists in us.

> For a long time that fire of desire for you is in this soul of ours,
> Because of longings that is deep in the hearts desolate hole of ours. (Smith 104)

In this poem Hafiz further asserts the belief that God has breathed into human frame and therefore we are part of the whole and He is the whole of ours. However this concept of Whole and part is already discussed in detail in the earlier chapters.

> Since I had heart that: "I blew my soul into him": in this matter
> I'm certain, that we're wholly yours and you're the whole of ours. (Ibid)

Again he declared that it is not easy to understand the mystery of love as it is only known to God or the supreme soul. It is better not to talk so much about it instead we must praise God for his shower of love.

> Love's mysteries are not manifested for every heart to understand:
> Knower of this spiritual mystery is the owner of the soul of ours.
> Praise of God, how long will you make explanation of the faiths.
> Be silent, in both worlds, Beloved's company is faith's goal of ours.
> Hafiz, until the final day give thanks forever for the favour that,
> From first Day, Beloved was conforming Guest of the soul of ours.
> (Smith 1040)

Hafiz showed his love for God through his mystical and mundane affairs of life. At the beginning of his life he wrote on mundane love through worldly symbols but later in his poetic career and after God-realization he wrote mostly on love of God rather than about his love for his earthly beloved. Hafiz best expressed his state of consciousness about God in the following lines:

> Praise be to God what wonderful wealth's given to me tonight;
> Because my Divine Beloved came to me, quite suddenly, tonight.
> The moment I saw Beloved's beautiful; face I bowed in praise;
> Thanks to be the grace of God, I'm fortunately happy tonight.
> The seed of my infinite patience has now blossomed this union;
> I'm harvesting fruit of my patience, Fortunes's with me tonight.
> (Smith 17)

Hafiz further comments on enlightenment in the following manner:

> What is true enlightenment? It is knowing that everything is raveworthy, but having the balance, the discernment, to withhold your applause at times, when there are young souls near...or people trying to sleep. (Synder, web)

In the Poem *Begging at the Winehouse Dor* Hafiz says once we accept the divine path to enlighten ourselves we have to surrender to the almighty first but dangerous are the one who is on the path of God but still has some selfish motive. Therefore once we are on the path to our divine we must completely surrender our worldly desires without being afraid of the suffering which may come the way to reach the divine.

> In the wine house where they drink wine to the memory of your sweet lips,
> Dangerous is the one who is still there drinking and thinking himself.
> It's wrong to solicit and beg at the wine house door;
> Throw the earnings of these thirsty dogs into the sea!
> He who is afraid of suffering can never be a lover:
> For these, submission or kissing is the only way. (Crowe 33)

In the Poem *The Great Forgetter* Hafiz says that the path of love is never a rosy one but a rocky one and whoever wants to walk on this path has to fall. The mystical divine often does that to us if we are not humble enough in possessing the love object which is called ego attachments. Hence God Snatches or separates us from that object of love to make us aware of the illusion that we had been possessing. Infact there should always be an emptiness in us so that the divine light could enter through it. That is why no matter whatever we possess we always feel an emptiness inside which is the urge in us for our divine whole. That is why more the person will be thirsty for love the more deprived he would be from it. Hence it is always suggestive that all of our emotions should be in limit rather than uncontrollable. Hafiz poem reads:

> O heart, the path of pride kicks up, all bubbles are burst,
>
> And the one who is thirsty will be told there's no more wine. (Ibid 32)

In Plato's words love can be defined as a human experience which relatively and virtually make us see the beauty in the world, and goes to the past experience of God Union and wish to fly towards it. And the feelings and affections that we possess for our earthly beloved are due to wishing for the 'God' meeting. He also says that it is through human love or relationship one can understand or comprehend the real absolute love for the divine which is also the prime goal of all beings. (Plato, 2002:15-19) Hafiz poems mostly deals with love and the lover and secondly their relationship is unique and ancient. Hafiz through his poem mentioned that it is the love for our earthly beloved which introduce us to the love of God, and love of God turns us towards our divine. Which also means that what is good in us gets better and better and turns into best. Hafiz poem reads like this:

> Without the Beloved's beauty inclination for the world, my
> ----soul hath not: O God, everyone who this hath not.
> That hath not (Hafiz 126)

According to Shaykh Shahab al-Din Suhrawardi humans can be symbolised as trees which have their roots in heaven and the love assumed to happen becomes the reason for human annihilation. According to the school of Aestheticism which was established in Iran with the combination of Greek philosophy and Eastern illumination by Abuhelman love is the only reason behind all the creations on earth. The Aesthetic school also believes that all the visible goodness and beauty are the manifestation of the divine. (Nilchian) Beauty in character or appearance is the source of love and love is divine attributes. The desire for beauty is given in the heart of the lover and beloved to reach the divine. The Aesthetic poet believes that the outer beauty is the source of love and love leads us to divine appreciation. God was a hidden treasure and he wanted to be known and hence he created human with a gift of soul, intellect, wisdom and love.

Hafiz too states that it is beauty and goodness in the beloved which attracts us to fall for them because that beauty and goodness are the emanation from the divine essence. Plato is also of the view that in realising or experiencing the absolute beauty one must free oneself from the limitation of acquiring only physical beauty but to take it as a ladder to reach the real beauty of divine. As Plato states:

> In perceiving beauty do not limit yourself to physical beauty O; rather take it as a ladder through which you go from the first step to second...eventually you will reach all the beauties. In this way you will find the beauty of the soul through the beauty of the body. In the end you will find the beauty of the almighty. (Plato 17)

In his poem *The Great Forgetter* Hafiz explained how God made him forget whatever he remembers of God's mystery as God liked to be kept and discovered as a hidden secret to mankind. It is believed by the follower of Islam that when Prophet Muhammad was on his Miraj (Mystical journey to Heaven and God). He had seen many of the mysteries of God but God again made him forget his mysteries. As it is already discussed in the earlier chapters that poets and philosophers of the world like Wordsworth believed that we as a soul know everything about God and His abode before we are born here on this earth but when we come down to earth we tend to forget everything obout God's mysteries and become blank to learn and experience.

> They call me "The Great Forgetter", and I'm afraid that now
> I'm stuck with this name.
> Hafiz says: come out from behind that veil!
> The only thing standing between yourself and the Beloved, is you.
>
> (Crowe 32)

To understand the concept of love one must understand the three perceptions of love i.e sensual love, imaginary love, and rational love. The beloved would also be categorized under this threefold categorization.

Love has to go through different stages, and the lover has to lose his heart in the first stage of love. In this stage the lover's main goal is to reach the beloved at any cost for his emotional, spiritual and physical satisfaction. For Hafiz that physical form of love was for his worldly beloved Shiek-e Nabat or Shaki Nabat and through her love he could recognise his true love for the truth (divine).Hafiz said in his poem *The Answer of the Rose* that it is not easy to reach the beloved as one has to come across many difficulties. As loves way is never easy.

> Should you desire the ruby wine from that jewelled cup,
> Many pearls pierced by point of your eyes lash is the way. (Smith 91)

And not everyone is lucky enough to experience that perfume of love as it would reach only those who strived hard in this path. Moreover lover's path are not the easy one.

> For an eternity love's perfume is never known to a one
> Whose heed hasn't swept the wine house threshold's clay. (Ibid)

Therefore a lover needs subtlety in character, experience the pangs of separation and should surrender to be alert or conscious in the path of love. And love need not to be understood as it is a spontaneous flow. The second stage of love is the virtual love where the lover enters in imaginary world and imagines the beloved. Another level of love is the 'luminous love' in which annihilation takes place and its the realization of eternity and immortality of the soul. In other word, the lover becomes free from self. In this stage, the worship of God converts into love of God. The lover plunged into love in such a way that he travels through a valley of consciousness, greatness and finally gets annihilated in the beauty and love of the beloved, that he himself becomes the hearing of the beloved and the eye through which the beloved sees: "I was her ear by which she was hearing and I was her eye by which she was watching...". (Nilchian 30-120)

Sadr al-Din Shirazi has categorized love in two ways one is virtual love and another is real love which is again subdivided into rational love. The true love is the love for divine and the virtual love is the worldly love which ends up in rational kind of love. And rational love happens in the people of insightful thought.

The word "love" was not in use for representing divine love in the works of early Islamic literature. Though it was mentioned in the holy *Quran* still they avoided the word as it could mean sensuality. Moreover, most of the mystics were not willing to accept the concept of love and affection between the creator and the creature. As it has been difficult to accept the concept of love and affection relationship between the creator and its creatures. Because God has been kept in such a high place like that of a king with power to rule our life or someone who should be feared rather be loved. It was not in use despite the fact that both the holy Qur'an and Prophet Muhammad himself has used the word "love" for God in his Hadidth he says: "When God likes a servant, God will make that servant to love Him and He will love him too". Then he quotes Qur'an in his hadidth: My servant! You are my lover and I also love you". And later the word "Habb" (affection) and "Ishq" has been started to use. Thus to bring to the notice that love is necessary in praying to our divine Hafiz through his poetry shares his intoxication with the magic and beauty of divine life that pulsates everywhere around us and within us. He brings attention to the fact that even the divine God gets intoxicated with our love. Through his poetry he invites us to awake awhile and listen to the delightful music of God's laughter. As he wrote in his poem *"I Heard God Laughing: Poems of Hope and Joy"*:

> What is these precious love and laughter
> Budding in our hearts?
> It is the glorious sound
> Of a soul waking up! (Ladinsky 88)

As Annemarie Schimmel in his book *"The genius of Shiraz: Sadi and Hafiz"* puts it: "Hammer advocated a plain 'worldly' interpretation of Hafiz while the great French orientalist Sylvestre de Sacy followed the line of mystically minded interpreters".

Mysticism is nothing but a personalised experience of interconnection between everyone and everything around us or the oneness of all existence. And this connection is also discussed in the seventh principle of Unitarian Universalism. According to Sufism we all are interdependent and interconnected. As when the Sufis mention about "love of God" they meant that interconnection and interdependence. And this particular love of God is the infinite interconnection with everything in this world. Hafiz states:

> The clear sky tried to prepare me for what it knew would someday happen; it began to show me ever deeper aspects of its splendour, and then one evening just asked, will you be to withstand your own magnificence? I thought I was just hearing things, until a spring orchard I was passing my days with at the height of its glory burst into song, about

our every human's destiny to burn with radiance. Still I felt my ears were playing tricks on me until the morning came when Go tore apart my chest...needing more room to bloom inside. I began to roll through the streets in ecstasy. Everyone thought I was crazy. I hope everyone someday knows how blessed I was. You will. (Snyder 8)

We must not be among those who are contended in sleep but be among those who wish to awake from the deep sleep and understands and stay 'awakened' connected to all of creation. Gurdjieff too declares the same thing that we are asleep and must be awake to fly (Perry web). The elements that can be found in Hafiz's poetry are the divine and human love, war and peace, youth and old age, God and its creation, illusion of existence, hypocrisy and sincerity, fear and joy, hope and hopelessness, greed, jealousy and envy, law of man and God, and joy of union, friendship, pain of losing the near and dear ones, the vanity and beauty of human life, praising God and master or Shiek, praising his lover, unity among all religions and last but not the least the mystical and mundane element in his poetry. He writes about the pointlessness of using our intellect to find God instead of our heart. He even discusses about the unity among all religion as the outer formalities of all faith. He wrote on the famous and not so famous personalities before and after his time including the saints, hypocrites, singers, painters, artist, thieves, soldiers, magicians, poets, kings, beggars, the intellects and the fools.

Hafiz is among the famous poets of Persia and of the world renowned for all time because of his sincere depiction of his time period be it deceit or hypocrisy or goodness in the people. The language that Hafiz used in his poetry amounts to a new language with its simple but precise word, colourful but fiery, rich but sparkling words. Hafiz not only had the talent to coalese the words together but also had the talent of creating his own exceptions and put it in his poetry, which was even the famous words used mostly by the Persian poets of all time. And it is not only the beautiful word that he is famous but also for his candid and precise meaning that he portrayed in his poem.

The process of 'fanaa' makes it difficult for the Sufi to convey their feeling in words. And therefore they have chosen poetry, lyric and ghazals and symbolism as their medium to express their feeling for their beloved. That is why for the Sufis Symbolism is a great medium to convey the inexpressible. As according to John Walbridge 'Symbolism' is a way to express the 'inexpressible' (Walbridge 9).

Charles Chadwick further categorized the use of symbolism in literature in two ways i.e human or wordly symbols to make understandable for the reader of general concept and secondly the transcendental or mystical symbols which related to the ideal world (Ellwood web). However the word symbol is derived from the Greek verb 'symballein' which means to 'throw together' and noun 'symbolon' which means 'mark' or 'sign'. Carlyle says, 'In the Symbol proper, what we call a symbol, there is ever more or less distinctly and directly, some embodiment and revelation of the Infinite; the Infinite is made to blend itself with the finite, to stand visible, and as it were, attainable there.' (Symons 3) Hence the Sufis used all worldly related symbols like the wine, the cup, the cup bearer, the rose and the nightingale, the sun, to express their mystical communion with the divine and also to reveal the truth which they received their dreams and visions. In Persian literature rose was symbolised God's silent beauty and nightingale is the beloved.

Hence the Sufis use symbolism as a means in order to express their indefinable thoughts or concepts. In other word, they become unable to express their message in words at their final stage called 'Fanaa' and so they use 'symbolism'. To understand Hafiz's poetry one has to understand the meaning of the symbolism that he gave to his poetry. For example when he says "the sky" he means fate, "the sun" means the truth or the beloved God, the moon implie the false beauty of the creation or the hand of the fate, " the wind" means the (agent or bringer of sad news) who brings misfortune, " the breeze" means the bringer of good news from God, 'the sea' symbolize the Ocean of difficulties that all lover must cross to reach their Beloved, the boat represents the master or guide who helps the Sufis for their God-realization, the pearl, means the God or truth and 'the pearl driver' means the lover of God, 'the shell' means the physical form of ours or illusions, "the desert" means the long duration that the lover must wait to reach their Beloved, "the hills and Valleys" means the hurdle that the lover experiences in love's path, the field symbolizes the world, 'the garden' symbolizes both the place in this world where the lovers meet on the inner realms where the lovers meet the beloved, "the Rose" means God, "Rosewater" means divine grace, the cypress symbolize the unchanged God, and the cypress cone means the heart of lover, the nightingale too symbolizes lover, "the Parrot" symbolizes the lover with the sweet word to convince the beloved to give love in return, "the Falcon" symbolizes the God or master who prays upon lover, the moth symbolizes the lover who extinguishes himself in the love (flame) of God (candle)., the path, the street, highway means both the inner journey to our real self or the physical journey to the wine house of the master who initiates us to the divine journey, "the winehouse" again symbolizes the inner self of the lover, again the wine symbolizes the love or truth or knowledge which changes our consciousness level and intoxicates us with the love of God, "the cup" symbolizes the heart of the lover, 'the wine bringer' symbolizes both the beloved or master and destiny which bring the cup (heart) to enlighten ourselves, 'the friend' symbolizes the God or the master, "the beloved's hair" symbolizes both God's grace that attracts humanity and the problems of the world in which we are trapped in, "the beloved's curl' symbolizes the beauties of God, "the beloved's eye means the power of God which annihilates us, the winemaker and wine seller means the great soul, the messenger, avatar etc., the painter symbolizes God, "the ruin" symbolizes the human physical body through mortal can find the way to the supreme soul, "the inn" symbolizes the world where we need to stay for a while to complete our gestation or learning. (Crowe xv)

> The meaning of this cup is the wine of eternity;
> The meaning of this wine, we understand, is selflessness. Saki-nama (32)

Further, A J Arberry, based on Muhsin Farid Kashani's (seventeenth century author) pamphlet named *Risala-yi Mishwaq*, has described the earthly terms which the Sufi mystic poet used in their poetry with its spiritual meaning. The main aim of Kashani was to defend and clear them of any kind of charges from the end of orthodox critics by the interpretation of the secret spiritual meaning behind the mundane discourses. As he says *Rukh* or face is the revelation of Divine Beauty in Attributes of Grace, e.g. the Gracious, the Clement, the Life-giving, the Guide, the Bountiful; Light; Divine Reality. *Khal* (mole): the point of Real Unity, which is concealed and is therefore represented as black. *Khatt* (down on the cheek): the manifestation of Reality in spiritual forms. *Lab* (lip): the life-giving property of God, and His keeping man in existence. *Sharab* (wine): ecstatic experience due to the revelation of the True Beloved, destroying the foundations of reason.*Saqi* (wine-bearer): Reality, as loving to manifest itself in every form that is revealed. *Jam* (cup): the revelations of (Divine) Acts. The whole seen and unseen world is like a *khumkhana* (vault) containing the wine of Being and the inborn love of god; each atom of the world, according to its receptivity and particular aptitude, is a *paimana* (goblet) of the wine of His love, and the goblet is full of this wine. *But* (idol): every object of worship other than God. Sometimes it is used to indicate a manifestation of the Divine Beauty, to worship which is the same as worshipping its Creator; sometimes it connotes a Perfect Man (*kamil*) or a Guide (*murshid*) who is the Pole (*qutb*) of his time. (Arberry 113-15)

Turk-e Shirazi ghazal of Hafiz is an example where he used such earthly terms to denote the spiritual meaning in it. Therefore Hafiz says that the earthly beloved's beauty is no less than the real beauty as it shows the face of the truth (God) and the mole (spot) on the beloved's face is the meeting point for union with the divine and the beloved's lip has the power of making alive the dead (lover).

Iraj Bashiri, too in his study and analysis of ghazal comments that in ghazal form a word may have different meaning from the modern understanding. (Bashiri) Hence, the same word may have both the mystical and mundane meaning in it.

However, The Symbol of wine, cub bearer, cup, was first used in the ninth century by the famous Sufi saint by Bayazid Bastami and gradually it was widely used among the Persian Sufi poets. Therefore all the symbols like the eyes, hair, neck, lips, of the beloved are the grace of God which attracts Hafiz for the union. And he also clarified in many occasions through is "*Divan*" that all these symbolism that he uses in his poetry are for the spiritual state and not the physical sense. He even says that the word "Human" itself means Hu (God) which means man and God in the form of a being where the spiritual union of the soul and the supreme soul takes place. Hafiz suggests us in his "*Wild Deer*" to give importance to our jewel (soul) inside us and to our outer shell (body):

> Pay regard to the jewel and leave the shell alone;
> By that way, a bad reputation is left to its own. (Smith 21)

Abn al Arabi comments in *Fatuhat II*, 326 that God loves us because He sees Himself in us as we are the mirror image of Him and hence if we love anybody for their beauty of body, mind and soul means we are loving none but God.

> And if you love a being for his beauty, you love none other than God, for He is the beautiful being. Thus in all aspects the object of love is God alone. Moreover, since God knows Himself and he came to know the world, he produced it, added extra of His image. Thus the world is for Him a mirror in which he sees His own image, and that is why God loves

> only Himself, so that if He declares: 'God will love you' it is in reality himself that He loves. (Ibid 18)

Scholars are in doubt regarding Hafiz use of physical symbolism. But Hafiz himself has mentioned in his *'Divan'* that his symbolism are spiritualized symbol which is only used for the beloved God. For example if he says wine which means love of God, and the friend, wine bearer, Beloved, Rose which means nothing but God; He even sometimes used the Beloveds physical description as eyes, neck, hair, lips, and praises them, which are also nothing but different stages of love for God which goes beyond the physical stage too go that we can find our divine love through the physical from of our earthly beloved which leads to divine union. For example if he says "O winebringer, fill my cup to the brim with your best wine, he means "O God, pour your divine love into my heart!" (Crowe xv). The Sufis wanted the Beloved's (God) heart to be filled up by their love and overflow for them but if it does not start flowing then they are in great pain. Among the different symbols in Hafiz poetry wine is the most important symbol as it represents love for the beloved. Therefore the cup of wine symbolize the heart of the lover which holds the elixir of life or the divine love, the consumption of which leads to union with the Divine beloved. In his poem *'Fair Maiden make our cups with wine"* Hafiz called the divine as the fair maiden and asking her to feel his heart which beats with the intoxicated love of the God. As he describes it in his poem *'Fair Maiden":*

> Fair maiden makes our bright cup with wine,
> Call for the singers,
> The world is on our side! (Nisarg 12)

Moreover, it the mystical and mundane elements which rule his poetry. According to him religion is man-made but God is above all religion and is the creator of everything. Hafiz states through his *Masnavi* collection, entitled "*The Wild Dear*":

> O God you are the remedy of those without remedy.
> You know the remedy for me...and for those like me. (Smith 22)

Hafiz finds God in every human and in every creation of God. As he believes we all are interconnected. He said he should be count in any particular religion as he is of everyone and everything. In his poetry he praises Muhammad, Ali, Moses, Jesus, Zoroaster, Noah, Abraham and many more saints of Persia of that time. The word "Interconnection" was nothing but "the love of God." And this love is infinite love between the divine and its creation. Hafiz, on pondering about what will happen after we die, he writes:

> The clear night sky tried to prepare me for what it knew would someday happen; it began to show me ever deeper aspects of its splendour, and then one evening just directly asked, Will you be able to withstand your own magnificence? I thought I was just hearing things, until a spring orchard I was passing my days with at the height of its glory burst into song, about our – every human's – destiny to burn with radiance. Still I felt my ears were playing tricks on me until the morning came when God tore apart my chest…needing more room to bloom inside. I began to roll through the streets in ecstasy. Everyone thought I was crazy. I hope everyone someday knows how blessed I was. "You will". "Interdependent web of all existence of which we are a part."(Hafiz and Sufi mystic 8)

Through their poetry the Sufis had took a bold step towards reaching the people with conservative Islamic law by using metaphors like wine and drunkenness. These are nothing but the Sufi's direct experience of divine which could not be described in simple words and hence took the help of poetry and its metaphors to describe their state of ecstasy. Hafiz utters in his poem *Plant the tree of Friendship:*

> O Beloved, my heart has fallen in love with your hair;
> Let them marry so all my restless will cease.
> O heart, after drinking a hundred gallons, you've fallen under the weight of all that wine. Go, and drink one more cup of wine, so tiredness will turn
> To collapse. (Crowe 22)

However, the uses of all the worldly images and metaphors like wine, cup bearer, love etc. is nothing but the representation of his divine love or state of intoxication. Hence, these are not really the real wine but the representation of his inner feelings and mystical experience which he represent through his poem. For example Majnum too in his letter to Leila, address himself as a 'bulbul' or the 'lone bird'. In his poem, '*A Persian Ode to Spring*', 'Majnum refers the poet as the nightingale (D'Israeli 29)

> Queen, hearest thou not through every bower
> The NIGHTINGALE, thy paramour?
> Oft has he lift each leaf and sighed,
> Lo! on his wild wing hear him chide! (D'Israeli 29)

Intoxication is that state of craziness which results after a Sufi surrenders to the overpowering love of the beloved God, where the Sufi seeks only fanaa (annihilation) in the baqa (subsistence) of the beloved God. Hence he does not see God as separate from the world, so he believes wherever there is love there is God. Inayat khan quotes:

> The mission of Hafiz was to express to a fanatical religious world that the presence of God is not to be found only in heaven, but also here on earth. (Ladinsky. 2006.87)

In fact, what is typical about Hafiz's poetry is his mixing of both the worldly and mystical themes. Hafiz therefore employed different symbols of the beloved at different levels. Sometimes the beloved comes in the form of the personal erotic beloved; the patron whom he directed his poem in the hopes of obtaining financial compensation for his art; and sometimes in the form of the mystical divine beloved God, who also intoxicated in the love of Hafiz. Sufi poetry is not just the experience of the Sufis and their relation of God but it is to make its reader to experience by themselves the bond that they have with their own divine.

> I needed to hang on to her curly ring,
> Help me please, let my affairs take wing.
> Said, release my hair, instead take my lips,
> Let go of long life, with good times swing. (Poem Hunter Web)

In the above mentioned lines from *Rubaiyyat 22* Hafiz clearly talks about his love of God in a worldly manner. For he talks, treats and sees his God in the image of worldly beloved. He further says that one must learn the courage from the warrior and wisdom from the sage and if one desire God's grace he must ride with the heavenly carriage or with the person whom God is satisfied. As Hafiz comments on it vividly in his *Rubaiyyat 23*:

> From warriors learn courage,
> And wisdom from the sage.
> If you truly seek God's grace,
> Ride with the heavenly Carriage.

Hafiz is sure that at dawn God's eye will surely watch and learn from the farthest planet Jupiter about his fantasies which would be going on at that time. And the ear of God might give Hafiz poem a privilege to be heard by God himself.

> At dawn your, eyes from Jupiter learn
> O God, may fantasies of my mind burn.
> The ear adorned with that elegant ring
> Gems of Hafiz's poems may earn. (*Rubaiyat* 25)

Hafiz describes his God's beauty in a beautiful manner through his *Rubaiyat* 26. Where he asserts that no one is as beautiful as our divine. Because once we start knowing and showing our gratitude to our divine then our divine will be so open to us that we would know He is like a hard rock on a clear lake.

One with such beauty none will make.
When her garments off we take
You can see her heart in her fragile breast,
Like a hard rock in a clear lake. (*Rubaiyat*, 26)

Hafiz urges us not to stop being in love with the worldly beloved as it is that love which teaches us mended us or break us at. It is this worldly love that makes us aware of everything around. It is our worldly love which is a bittersweet in taste i.e it gives both pleasure and pain because Hafiz said it is the lovers lips from where the cup sips:

Don't let go of the cup's lips
Till you receive your worldly lips.
Bittersweet is the worlds's cup
From lover's lips and the cup sips. (*Rubaiyat*, 28)

Hafiz also explained that all his life he was busy chasing the worldly dreams without knowing what the fate possessed for him. He also said that whomever he had showed his love they turned out to be his enemies.

I spent my life chasing my wishes
What benefits fate furnishes?
Whomever to I said I loved you,
Turned to my foe, why my luck ravishes? (Ibid)

Hafiz brought the symbolic language to perfection in his poetry. His poetry however remains ambiguous so it is difficult to guess in the above mentioned lines what he really means whether he was really referring to a fair maiden or was he really celebrating God, his true patron and beloved? Perhaps both. Because Hafiz in the ultimate analysis does not consider his divine as separate from this world. Even today scholars from the world over debate over the "true" meaning of his verses.

Nevertheless, he only celebrates the intoxicated love of God in his poetry but also condemns all the hypocrisy and mediocrity and urges us to rise above all and to fly on the wings of love. As Hafiz describes through the lines of his poem *"I Heard God Laughing"*:

You don't have to act crazy anymore-
We all know you were good at that.
Now retire, my dear,
From all that heard work you do
Of bringing pain to your sweet eyes and heart. (Ladinsky 3)

Hafiz was against the hypocritical way of worshiping God and violating the inner spirit of the law. Even in Luke's Gospel where on being asked about the coming of God's Kingdom, Jesus replied 'Within' or 'Among'. (Luke 17:21). Hence we can say that God is not outside but inside us. And all the religious rituals are nothing but connecting us nearer to God. All-Hallaj Mansur once said:

> "May God veil you from the exterior of the religious law, and may he reveal to you the reality of infidelity". (Dehelvi 96)

So what Mansur was really meant was to close our heart to the outward law and achieve 'manifest gnosis' which is possible only through the union with the divine God. Mansur spoke the above mentioned lines when he was going through a trial in Bagdad for proclaiming the word 'Ana I haqq' which means 'I am God". By the word 'Ana I haqq' what he really meant was that the beloved and the lover are one. As he uttered:

> I am He who I love, who I love is I
> We are two spirits dwelling in one body
> If though see me, though see us both
> And if though see Him, though see us both
> In that glory is no I or we or Though
> I, we, Though, He are all one thing. (Dehelvi 9)

Another great Sufi Bayazid Bistami (D.874AD) had a similar view asked his disciples to strike him if he made a similar claim that he was God. However when they tried to strike him with the sword, the sword instead of killing Bayazid turned towards them and wounded them. Then he told them under his garment there is nothing but God. Bayazid and Mansur had the same experience that is the perfect mystical state where love, lover and the beloved are the same, Keeping this in mind Bayazid said:

> 'O Lord' Remove the veil of mine and thine that exist between thee and me, that
> Have no existence separate from thy essence. (Dehelvi 87)

The Sufi thinker Ibn Arabi (1240) is of the view that we all have to go through the same step to reach God as there is no alternative way. Even the prophets, messengers and the faithful have to follow the same path to reach the divine. The Sufis follow certain step to reach divine are Islam, which means submission to Allah (God), iman; which mean faith on Allah and its Qur'an, ihsan; which is 'awareness of God as if you can see God while worshiping. As Hafiz states:

I wish I could show you,
When you are lonely or in darkness,
The Astonishing Light
Of your own being! (Ladinsky 1)

Hafiz through his poetry suggest on some of the preparations for the inner journey to unite with the divine. He urges us to denounce all our negative attitudes and unnecessary attachments that will lead us nowhere. In the poem *'And Applaud'* Hafiz wrote:

Your attachments! My dear,
Lets not speak of those,
For Hafiz understands the sufferings
Of your heart. (Ibid 4)

Hafiz through his poem urges us to broaden our understanding of true love both in human relationship and also in the relationship with God. He claimed not only that he was intoxicated in God's love but God himself was likewise lost, drunk in love of his beloved creature. As he explains it through his poem *'Several Times in the Last Week'* that God could not stop himself from meeting Hafiz seeking the address of his beloved creature. further it is said that if we go forward one step towards God, he comes down two steps towards us.

"God said, through the prophet, Man is my secret and I am his secret. The inner knowledge of the spiritual essence is a secret of My secrets. Only I put this into the heart of My good servant, and none may know his state other than Me." (Al-Jilani 17)

Love even transforms us and we start forgetting ourself and became one with the beloved. Thus sacred love is difficult and full of hardship as it involves of annihilation in the beloved God. Even the famous Sufi Mansur-all-Hallaj (C858-922) had to die after he achieved the stage of being annihilated with the divine and which leads him utter, "I am Truth or God". As the Persian scholar J. T. De Brujin in his book *"Persian Sufi poetry: An Introduction to the Mystical Use of Classical Poems"* said:

"The true follower of the path of love is equal to the qalander dervish which is eager to sacrifice his good name as a pious muslim for the sake of his total submission to the beloved"(1997:80)

In the poems, what strikes the reader is that Hafiz was genuinely concerned with the spiritual path as it was the only way to the realization of divine love. And also to release oneself from the distractions and turmoil of this world. Nevertheless, he only brought the spirituality in his poetry but also the problems and solutions of this physical world which can be called as the mundane affairs of day to day life. He was also a sensible person and so had written on the social problems and hence was at war with the hypocrites, kings, rulers, poets.

Hafiz uses quite a blasphemous language in his poetry in worshipping an earthly beloved as an idealised form of God. Sufism believes in the self-loss for the object of love and in loving the other becomes the other and forgets the self. Bastami's concept of fanaa became the example for Sufi self-loss in Persian literature. Lacanian concept on jouissance too resembles the Sufi notion of fanaa i.e self-loss or becoming the other by idealizing and keeping the other in one's own place resulting in annihilation of the self-identity.

Hafiz too like Rumi had followed the same Sufi path of love to return to its origin which comprised of the lover's desires for love object, followed by a sense of melancholy of inaccessibility of the love object; thirdly, the subject's start for a solitary journey; fourth is to remember the image of the absent beloved, then idealisation of beloved's image and imagines it as an absolute Other, longs to achieve it, then the lover has to meet separation from self to be unite with the absolute whole followed by death of the lover (annihilation) or die before the physical death.

Geoffrey Hartman in his *Romanticism and Anti-Self-Consciousness* shown two types of self 'the self-conscious self and that self within the self' (Hartmen, 2004:184). In order to find the second the Sufis are set for self-annihilation to overcome the former. In this concept of Self Gurdjieff says humans are born without a soul which means it is not aware of its Self and our soul can be acquired only through our consciuos effort. And our self has its two pole – one is to know our potentials, limitations and pretensions and another is to know the one supreme soul/Self which has its dependent on every existence on the Universe or which gives us an illusion of separateness but it lives in all our separate selves with an illusion of being independence. Thats why he used the word 'Know Thyself' (Perry web). In this context it is an urgent need to cite another concept of Self in the words of famous twelfth century Bokharan Sufi, Abdulhalik Gujduvani (Ibid):

> Be present at every breath. Do not let thy attention wander for the duration of a single breath. Remember thyself always and in all situations. Thy journey is towards the homeland. Remember that thou art travelling from the world of appearances to the world of reality.Solitude in crowd. In all thy outward activity remain inwardly free. Learn not to identify thyself with anything whatsoever. Remember thy friend (Allah/God). Let the invocation (dhikr) of thy tongue be the invocation of thy heart(qalb).

> Be constantly aware of the quality of the Divine Presence. Become used to recognising the presence of Allah in thy heart. (Ibid)

Gurdjieff further says human are not consciuos beings instead they are asleep with no true identity of their own. An in order to achieve consciousness one must die to what they are at present that is by voluntary suffering and also by being aware of the mess that one is in the present. After the recognition of the mess one must admit it then he can proceed for the next level towards the real Self. (Ibid) Therefore awareness of our Self or death before we die physically is a very important stage for the Sufis in the path of enlightenment.

Both divine or an earthly beloved awake in us a sense or desire to return to the origin. Hartman too talks obout the same notion of Romantic fantasy or a return to the imaginary state of non-separateness, a unity of being, they too like the Sufis believes in the loss of self through a process of loss of self in idealising the object of love which consequently leads to either symbolic or actual death. The Sufis die before they really die. Which means a symbolic death of the persona's self and rebirth of the enlightened self or 'Fanaa'. And the second type of death is the literal death which one die for the excessive grief or pain in the separation. Hafiz too desired for the symbolic death or 'fanaa' state after he crossed his literal death.

As earlier in chapter II it is discussed that the idealization of the earthly beloved in place of the truth is celebrated abundantly in Persian Sufi literature. Hafez, Sa'di, Maulavi, Nezami, Jami are the Sufi poets who used the example of beloved other who is self-sufficient, an unattainable, or a sheikh who is not even a perfect human. Therefore, the Sufis too believes that through the imagery or the idealization of the mundane beloved as an idealized substitute for the Divine 'Other' thereby the mystical divine could be found. In this process of union with the divine the self 'I' becomes 'thou'.

In this notion of self-loss the Romantics too speaks in a similar manner as Shelley in his *A Defence of Poetry* (written 1821, published 1840), refers to selflessness as a sort of compassion:

> The great secret of morals is Love; or a going out of our own nature, and an identification of ourselves with the beautiful which exists in thought, action, or person, not our own. A man, to be greatly good, must imagine intensely and comprehensively; he must put himself in the place of another and of many others [...] The great instrument of moral good is the imagination; and poetry administers to the effect by acting upon the cause. Poetry enlarges the circumference of the imagination [...].
>
> (Shelley, 1977:488)

Divine love substitutes all the earthly desire and once we start loving the divine through the earthly beloved all other needs become meaningless. The theme of divine love rules in Persian Sufi poetry in both the literal and the figurative way. The man-God relationship is used allegorically and is not unfamiliar in Sufi teachings. In the Old Testament too it is mentioned in *The Song of Solomon* about a dual theme of love where an intertwining of earthly and divine love could be seen which again resembles Hafiz work on the interweaving of the mundane and mystical elements in his Poetry. The theme of sublime love which manifests through the earthly love relationship and through several hardship in its achievement, is the lessen and step for the lover to love the divine. In other words its a training or lesson for the lover how to be unite with the Real/Truth. And the overflow of love and attraction for the earthly beloved is symbolically the attraction for the divine. The lover's existence is meaningless without the beloved. Profane and blasphemous images are used to describe the beauty of the beloved. In separation the lover choose the tavern to forget the pain of separation as intoxication soothes the lover. Horowitz writes:

> "The lost object is permitted to go its way, the de-cathected memory traces theirs, and thus the joy in having suffered love is sustained." (Horowitz 153)

Therefore according to Horowitz after the loss of the love object the lover becomes aware of its attachments and mourning for it, is a way of making memories in the absence and remembrance of the beloved. While Fraud says these memories are to let go the beloved whether, Horowitz argues that these memories are created in order to continue the love despite the absence or loss of the beloved.

Therefore in both the case the cause of mourning is same, transformation, but Freud's transformation is to move on to the new love object and Horowitz's transformation, is for awareness of the ego-attachments which come automatically after the love object is lost. The phenomenon of mourning is necessary as it shifts us driven by a hidden force and unconscious energies which acts as the cause of our transformation which is required to remember our origin/God where from we came and shift our love for the new love object or divine. We, the worldly lover or the virtual lover has to realize that whatever we possess is not really our own but our illusions which is the awareness of ego-attachments. which again teach us our separation from our beloved which once we thought our own and whose separation removes all our illusions for all our possessions. But all the obstacles in the path of love makes us realize our depth of love for our beloved which adds sweetness in our worldly relationship. In the Sufi path of love the worldly lover or the virtual lover has to exit and needs to start for the journey to be a real lover of the truth. Scott Peck asserts that the genuine love has to avoid self-deception or narcissism which only accepts the fact or the possessions at present. Because the soul cannot get healed until unless it accepts the opposite ideas which is contrast to the things at real.

Love's secret cannot be understood by anybody until unless someone experience it. Though it seems it is the lovers advances which wins the beloved's heart but the fact which we cannot deny that it is the beloved's attraction and attention which attracts the lover in love and become a lovesick. Shakespeare also had the same kind of notion on love's psychology as he said that though it seems like that the lover tries to convince the beloved but in reality it is the woman or beloved whose attraction and advances make the lover to be in love with the beloved. In Sufi path too it is the beloved's attraction which makes the lover get intoxicated in the love of beloved God. In this path of love and worship some attempts to get the beloved and some leaves it to their destiny.

The Sufis too followed the idea of mourning in separation of the earthly beloved to remember the past origin/ God or to shift the attention to the new love object i.e from the earthly beloved to the divine beloved. And both Hafiz and Rumi used the same technique to remember the Origin and shift the love through the earthly beloved to the divine beloved.

According to Suzanne Kirschner they approximated their own ideals of a return to the perfection of the primal yet unknown state of unity in order to have their spiritual requirements satisfied. (Kirschner 160-61)

Jane Gallop defines the word 'nostalgie' as an 'unsatisfied desire' and a 'melancholy regret (for something elapsed or for what one has not experienced)'. (Doniger 992) The melancholy regret suggests a sense of loss and a lament for what is lost or what is not experienced, i.e., an unsatisfied desire. In his essay '*Mourning and Melancholia' (1917*), Freud refers to melancholia as being caused by the introjection of a loved lost object. (Sayed-Gohrab 37) According to Jennifer Radden melancholia is 'a frame of mind characterized by a loss of something', 'a lack or want of something, or rather someone'. (Ibid)

Hafiz's Persona diverts his mind from mere an earthly beloved and elevate her in the image of divine. In his regard Freud's definition is applicable where the redirection of the drive is changed to a different object. Lacan too has his formula of sublimation which involves a mode that 'raises an object [...] to the dignity of the Thing'.57 In other words, the subject diverts his attention from the other as love object into an idealised image of the object.

Neoplatonism and Sufism, believed that unity of the universe and creations was of an undifferentiated unity interrupted by material creation which resulted in the separation of humanity [...] from God'. (Nasr and Leaman 374-433) Kirschner again urges, man's division from God is not merely a separation between the subject and 'the object of his perception', but also 'an inner division in man's selfhood'. (Kirschner 161) And this, separateness can be removed from the process of self-loss and become the other. This transformation into the beloved brings pleasure to the lover's melancholic state caused at the un-attainability of the other. As Rosalind Minsky states, gives 'rise to pleasure'. (Freud 37)

As it has already been discussed in Chapter one and two in detail on the origin of our true Self and the Sufi-Neoplatonist's believes in the return of the self to its origin, God. Since it is already qouted Christopher J Murray in the previous chapter where he says, "the Romantic Neoplatonic philosophy was based on the principle that 'all creation originally existed in a harmonious unity (the One), then fragmented (the Many), and now longs to return to a state of unity' (Murray 1129). And it is already discussed in chapter I that we are separated from our origin /God, and thats why we all possess qualities of the original and this original 'One' within ourselves is already present in us and all other things. This original One leads us to 'sense the cosmos within ourselves' and provokes in us 'the divine impulse for reunification of the cosmos'. (Murray, 1129) In chapter Two it is already discussed on the quality of the soul and its desire to return to its origin, in a poem entitled *The Song of the Reed* (or '*Ney-naame*') from *Masnavi-ye Ma'navi*, by Maulana Jalal ed-Din Rumi, known as Maulavi. (Jones, 1799: 458-60). This poem is an allegorical account of the separation of the lover, the reed (*ney*), from its native land, the reed-bed (*neyestaan*), where it had belonged. It is already been quoted Jones in chapter two who brought different references on our true existence from different Sufi theology:

> In eternity without beginning, a ray of thy beauty began to gleam; when Love sprang into being, and cast flames over all nature; On that day thy cheek sparkled even under thy veil, and all this beautiful imagery appeared on the mirror of our fancies. From the moment, when I heard the divine sentence, *I have breathed into man a portion of my spirit*, I was assured, that we were His, and He ours. Where are the glad tidings of union with thee, that I may abandon all desire of life? I am a bird of holiness, and would fain escape from the net of this world. (Jones 453-54.)

However, this going back or return to the origin, as mentioned earlier in chapter two, is a kind of condition or the self-made negotiation with the cost of self-extinction which in Sufi term called as 'fanaa' (*al-fana' fi 'l-tauhid*), and this self-extinction is required for the union with the Origin. Before this 'fanaa' occurs to the Sufi get intoxicated in the divine presence where he sees the divine in everything and this state is known as 'Baqaa'. And it also mentioned in chapter two that, Bayazid Bastami, was among the first Sufis who declared the state of *fanaa* publicly. According to Junayd-e Baqdadi. *Tasawwuf*, 'is summed up thus: the Real or, 'the Truth', i.e. God makes you die to yourself, and causes you to come alive again through Him'.

The imagined beloved must be without fault as it is an epitome of the whole and the part gets dissolve in it, so the whole must be perfect and without fault. But the perfect other can be a divine beloved or an earthly beloved because even the earthly beloved is being idealised as the ultimate real. Idealisation is very important for the Sufis in order to get the ultimate divine. During the mundane love the Sufi has to be obsessed with the lost love object in such a way that it transforms the mundane love object into the divine. And this feeling of imagination comes again in us with the divine and heavenly spell or naturally from the divine realm. Lacanian theory would suggest that the idealisation of the other makes the subject forgetting the self and which again helps the Sufis to unite with the divine which can only be possible with the non-existence of the 'self' or 'ego'. (Nilchian)

Lacan has given the term 'sublimation' to the subject's idealisation of the beloved. And the object of love is placed in the place of the absolute truth. It is the lover which puts the beloved in the place of the supreme God and the lover is sublime and great because of inaccessible nature of it. As it is said if we do not get the thing we desire for it becomes more and more important in our life so similarly if we don't get our love object we start thinking about it more and more and hence the love grows with its inaccessible nature. Hence Lacan is of the view that the Other is not perfect and therefore it needs to be idealised for the absolute Real. But Hafiz in his poetry expressed that the Other is as perfect as the divine other for the subject. Because even the imperfectness of the other looks completely perfect in the eyes of the lover. And therefore there is no harm in exalting the earthly beloved as the Sublime.

To Hafiz even the bitter words from the beloved's lip is sweet. As he states:

> If you curse me or malign me,
> I will still pray for you,
> For bitter word is what befits
> Sweet ruby-coloured lips. (Ibid)

The completeness and beauty of the Other attracts the Subject for its completeness to become the Whole from the part. The important of idealisation of the earthly beloved is that by idealising the beloved as sublime the subjects go for submission to the Other. And the idealised beloved is a self-sufficient beloved whom the subject desired for.

Philip Shaw states in his *The Sublime*, that the infinite, proves to be inaccessible and unknowable. Shaw asserts that the lost love object becomes sublime because it is inaccessible. An even in our mundane love affairs we know the intensity of our love object when it became inaccessible or lost. Shaw also believes that the love object becomes sublime because of its exaltation to the place of inaccessible. (Shaw)

As earlier discussed in chapter II about the love station which a Sufi has to go through for the union with the divine. Bashiri too shares the five stages of love (eshq). The first state that the lover has to attain is the loss of heart, second state is the regret for the lost love object, third state is the Ecstasy, in this stage of mind the lover could see the presence and absence of flashes of light, the fourth state is the loss of patience, the fifth state is the Ardour of love where the lover loss his senses. (Bashri web)

Bashiri further compares this five stage of Sufi love with one of the ghazal of Hafiz in a chart but in order to complete the meaning of the ghazal he added two more stages in it which are loss of mind and annihilation. In the chart the first beyt is *dil* (heart), *beyt*, which means loss of heart, the second beyt is *luilyan-i shukh shirin kar-i shahr ashub* which means vivacious, beguiling, commotion-inspiring gypsies, the third one is *wajd* (ecstasy, the fourth one is *khwan-i yaghma* (festal board), impatience, fifth beyt is *yusif*, or loss of consciousness, sixth and eight beyt is Zulaikha or the sacrifice of the Sufi (Self-loss), the seventh and ninth beyt is Hafiz which means annihilation. (Bashri web) Therefore one must consider that the Sufi poetry or Hafiz poetry has got both the mystical meaning in the mundane frame of words.

It is already discussed in chapter II that the Sufis goes to the extent of idealising the earthly beloved to the place of divine Being. Hafiz too did the same in idealising his earthly beloved Shaki Nabat in the place of divine being. Hafez's idealisation of such an earthly love object and exalt it to the higher and self-sufficient and contended place is noteworthy.

However Hafez's Sufism is different from the orthodox group of Sufis as it aims at liberation of the soul and to get away from the restrains of laws and tradition. In this stage his love for the beloved goes and reach as a certain point where there is no veil between the lover and the beloved accept their own existence. Hence the lover desires complete self-annihilation and wants union with the beloved. Hafez's falls under the category of Sufis like Bayazid Bastami and Mansur Hallaj, who too idealises the earthly beloved as the self-sufficient being.

Hafiz found out the secret of the world by idealisation of the earthly beloved with the help of wine or love of God, poetry and then by intoxicating in divine love. In order to understand the concept of idealisation of the other one have to understand Lacan's and Freud's formulation of the self and the other. A better insight into the notion of the idealisation of the earthly beloved, the following section provides an analysis with special reference to the formulations of self and Other by Lacan and Freud.

As a bird of Paradise, to parting I did agree
Fell in the trap of life and worldly tragedy.
I was an angel, I resided in the heavens;
Renovation of the world – the mission given to me.

(*Ghazal* 317: 2-3)

In order to justify his excessive love and desire for submission to the love object Hafez too had substitute his worldly beloved in place of God by assigning her divinely characters of perfection, beauty and self-sufficiency. But to get the divine, one has to sacrifice or leave hold on the worldly desires after being learn to desire for the sublime.

Just like discussed in the previous chapter where Zulaika leaves her desire for Yusuf and Majnoun for Leili or their worldly beloved to get the divine, Hafiz too while in search of Nabat or the veiled maid in Alastor, realized that his real love is not for the worldly beloved but for his divine and hence he too starts for the journey of divine love and written several of his poetry on God by using his worldly beloved as the divine. Therefore the denunciation of the worldly love object leads us to the spiritual reality or perfection.

As earlier discussed in chapter two that critics like Burke believes and says in his *A Philosophical Enquiry into the Origin of Our Ideas of the Sublime and Beautiful (1757),* that the beloved is an weaker entity whose submission to the lover makes him fall for her. But Jones in the *Mystical Poetry of the Persians and Hindus* says that the beloved itself is so complete, beautiful and perfect that makes the lover fall for it, which is already discussed in detail in the previous chapter. However, Jones's persona in his '*Song*', does not only desire to possess the love object but to become it or transform into it. In Hafez's poetry too the lover's desire in the same way to become one with the beloved. Jones's stanza reads:

> O! when these fair, perfidious maids,
> Whose eyes our secret haunts infest,
> Their dear destructive charms display,
> Each glance my tender breast invades,
> And robs my wounded soul of rest,
> As Tartars seize their destin'd prey.

Hafiz was not so good looking and as an orphan worked in a bakery. One day while delivering bread he happen to meet a girl named Nabat and fell in love with her. But he got disappointed knowing that the girl was already engaged to be married. When asked for advice from his master he advised him to climb the mountain and lit a candle for fourty days. After Nabat came to know about the depth of Hafiz's love for her, she decides to marry him and asked him to stop that the final climb to the hill but he decided to obey his master. Interesting thing happened in him when he was coming down from the hill. A realization came in him on pondering upon the beauty of God created angel Gabriel and his earthly beloved, Nabat, therefore how beautiful the creator of this creatures would be. From this time he became the lover of the truth and served his master for fourty long years to be united with that real love and whatever he wrote it became a divinely flavoured. It is already discussed in chapter two that when the lover actually gets the love object he refuses for it as the realization for the true love for the divine came down in him. Just like Mujnoon did when he saw Leili and refuses her and Zuleikha did to Yusuf (Joseph). However, for Majnoun it took around thirty long years to understand the divine love through the worldly love. In all the versions true love is represented as chaste. Therefore the worldly beloved like Leili in both Jami and Nezami took the image of divine light where Majnoun gets dissolved in. In D'Israeli's '*Leili and Majnoun*' the beloved plays a role of a perfect earthly beloved and had failed to produce them as a divinely or chaste. But the fact that Majnoun was a true lover and the union between them is of chaste desire.

It is said that humans are never satishfied no matter what they do and achieve in their life as we are always in search of the divine whole. Hence no matter how happy we are in our life we stay in melancholic state of mind. Rumi's quote from his *Fihi-ma-Fihi* (Discourses) in the English translation of Arasteh's book *Rumi, the Persian, the Sufi.*

> Even if a man possesses a hundred thousand worlds he would find no rest.
> When he engages in the arts and crafts, holds a diversity of offices, studies the sciences, medicine and astrology, when he pursues pleasures he is only climbing the transitory rungs of the ladder where there is no abiding station.

According to Rumi this melancholy is brought to the lover by the inaccessibility and self-sufficiency of the beloved. And the melancholy is reduced through the help of intoxicated wine and music. It is believed that the melancholic feeling which creates in the lovers heart is nothing but the reminder that the real beloved God puts in us to have the desire for the truth.

In Hafiz's ghazal and poem he uses the term '*Jaam-e Jam*' (cup of wine) or the 'cup of Jamshid' (wine). A mythical king of Persia, named as Jamshid is believed to possess a cup or '*jaam*' where he could see the reflection of the divine reality. Seyyed Hossein Nasr puts an analysis on this famous cup of Persia in Sufi's perspective:

> In Sufism it has become the symbol of the heart of the Gnostic in which all realities are reflected, the eye of the heart (*'ayn al-galb* in Arabic or *chasm-i dil* in Persian) with which the mystic 'sees' the supernal realities. (Nasr, 1973: 33)

> We can compare this with this translation by Jones from another ghazal of Hafez: Bring the wine, my dear companions, bring the wine! [...] Reach the liquor, that sparkles like a flaming ruby. [...] O thou who art in love,

> drink wine with eagerness; and you, who are endued with wisdom, offer your vows to Heaven. Imitate *Hafez*, and drink kisses, sweet as wine, from the cheek of a damsel, fair as a nymph of paradise. (Jones 322)

Hafez was also got influenced by the mythical cup of wine into which he could see the reality. Seeking of wine (Mey) for Hafiz is not something worldly but of divinely love where he could see the secret of life. For Arberry which is an impossible task for human understanding level to comprehend the secret of life, as he states: powerless to fathom the mystery of life (Arberry 705-709) It is also for him to seek or attain the state of fanaa. Hafiz is quite moderate in his esoteric feeling as he did not forget the reality of life. His ghazal, *Beyt eight* reads:

> Come, sing of wine and minstrels – seek less the secrets of life; none has solved 'nor can 'this enigma with the logical mind. (Ordoubadian, 2006:82)

However, Hafiz mentioning about wine in his poetry is also symbolize his desire to break free of all the formal and sobar life inorder to know or forget the secret and mystery of life. Arberry observes, 'symbolizes his rejection of all formal, sober/ life, whether it be the life of the cloistered Sufi, the orthodox theologian, or the philosopher'. (Arberry, 1946:706)

Arberry did not like Jones translation of Hafiz poetry as he things that Jones was a mere decorator or jeweller who can go any extend to make the looks in a perfect shape and hence he too like other translator misinterpret Hafiz's work. As he said Arberry goes on to claim that Hafez was 'misrepresented' by Jones who confessed himself 'a casual, careless jeweller of words'. (Arberry, 706-708)

However, Hafiz had taken art or poetry to reduce his sense of melancholy for the unattainability and inaccessibility of the beloved. The benefits of idealising the earthly beloved for the sublime is the acceptance of the persona to the beloved as a non-possessive one. In Isaac D'Israeli's Mejnoun and Leil, the excessive grief for the unattainability of the beloved made the Persona, Majnoun to idealize and elevate the beloved for the divine and wrote many more ghazals to reduce his melancholic state of mind:

> From the pain of grief and fire of love
> He did not rest unless on that mount
> He clapped the hands while roaming up there
> Tumbling and uprising like the sots
> He warbled on and ran here
> And there in rapture. (Nilchian 123)

Hafiz's poems are the expression of his growing understanding of love. And it can be seen that he followed all the Sufi steps in love from the earthly to the divine beloved for union. As his series of love poem starts with the game of love, followed by the praising of beloved's beauty, the next level poems are about the desire of longing, the grief and pain of waiting, the last level of poems were of joy for union. He explored in his writing the different forms of love be it his affection for his wife or his tender feelings or the grief for their death or separation. Sometimes he depicts in his poetry the depth of his relationship with both his teacher and his lady love Shaki Nabat and his adoration of God. In his poem he tries to show his true feelings for the beauty of divine which is present around and within us. He suggest us to enjoy every small occasions in our life with love in our heart for everyone and everything around us and also to arise a bit in the path of awakening. As already mention that he wants us to be awake n feel God's presence in us and listen to his laughter: "What is this precious love and laughter budding in our hearts? It is the glorious sound of a soul waking up!" (Hafiz, The Gift)

Hafiz used the earthly symbols to present and compare his divinely beloved. For example the blackness of the beloved's locks with the darkness of the night: 'The blackness of thy locks is darker than the hue of night.'64 According to the Persian poetry the imagery of the beloved's locks is used to represent two attributes of night as mysterious and long. In the '*Persian Song of Hafez*' Hafiz showed that the beauty of the earthly beloved attracts the Persona as it is so beautiful and perfect. Hence all the poet here desired for the sight of sweet maid's charm and beauty.

Saints choose the easy escape from the material or false world and take shelter for their prayer in the forest or cave but Hafiz had undertaken the difficult road to be among the people and make them understand the life's secret through both mystical and mundane element in his poetry. As uses of only mystical element may not serve the proper medium for general people to understand. And hence Hafiz used mundane way to make us understand in a better way and also because of the worldly beauty we can assume the beauty of the truth as the world is the manifestation of the divine.

With the splendour that in the mirror, the beauty of Thy face fell,

Made, this entire picture into the mirror of fancy
All this reflection of wine and varied picture that have

> Appeared is a splendour of the face of the said that, into cup fell
>
> (Ghazvini & Ghani 111)

However, Hafiz is of the view that without going through the love and beauty of the world one cannot reach or achieve the beauty of the truth or divine beauty. And to see the beauty one must go through love because love makes us see things beautiful. Hafiz's medium of divine love was his love for Nabat through whom he could feel and see his divine. The Sufis believe that there is no other way to reach our divine except the way of love. By loving the earthly beloved's beauty Hafiz prepared himself to perceive and understand the eternal beauty of God. As Hafiz states:

> The Universe was not aware of love's passion and rapture, the whole seditious of the world was based on the Almighty God's coquetry.
>
> (Ghazvini & Ghani: 210)

God himself is a hidden beauty and hence whatever he creates it comes beautiful. In Sura As-Sajdah it is mentioned as: "He who has made everything which He has created most good" (Quaran).Which probably means whatever he has created is good because of his attribute is goodness. Further it is mentioned clearly in Qur'an Surah al-Baqarah that wheresoever we will turn our face there is the face of Him. As God is beautiful and good and hence his creatures too are beautiful and good.

The flow of beauty and glory can be summarized in Qur'an Surah Al-Lail where it describes about the beauty of day which is in image of God. As it states: 'By the Day as it appears in glory (God).' In Islam it is believed that God has created or shaped human face with his own hand and hence it is special. And not only in Islam but in many other faith it is believed that human are created in divine image or beauty.

> Here the face is the manifestation of the divine goodness; the main
> – intension of the sign is indicating the Holy essence of God.
> Out of his goodness, he drew an image; indicating that
> – Comeless is in us. (Shabestary 494)

Human face is the sign of divine beauty and so to be in love with our earthly beloved is a kind of training for us to understand the beauty of our divine in us. Therefore Hafiz's poetry makes us think beyond the boundaries of our old believes, understanding and takes us to the world of imagery and metaphor. Sometimes the same poem does not make any sense to us but at certain point of life that particular poem makes a tremendous effect and understanding. For Hafiz religion is about experiencing God rather worshiping. He also suggest us through his love poem of God that the world and its all related works are "nothing into nothing" and love is the only bridge to divine and its creatures and is the only worthy thing in this world. Gertrud Bell states on Hafiz Poetry in his translation of *Poems from Divan of Hafiz* in the following manner:

> It is as if his mental eye, endowed with wonderful acuteness of vision, had penetrate into those provinces of thought which we of a later age were destined to inhabit. (Bell, 1897)

When Hafiz at last reach the final station of union he described his condition through his poem *The Night of Union* in this way:

> Praise be to God what wonderful wealth's given to me tonight;
> Because my divine beloved came to me, quite suddenly, tonight.
> The moment I saw Beloved's beautiful face I bowed in praise;
> Thanks be to the Grace of God, I'm fortunately happy tonight.
> The seed of my infinite patience has now blossomed this union;
> I'm harvesting fruit of my patience, fortunes with me tonight. (Smith 185)

Hafiz here tries to explain that we must be patient enough in the path of God to union because one day we must harvest what we have sown. Hafiz explained that to live a life with love is far more better than a life with knowledge and wisdom as Aristotle too died just like an old beggar man. Our death should not be a dead of ours instead everyone should remember us forever for our love for each other.

> Do not boast of wisdom: Aristotle must give up life
> Like the miserable old beggar, when death has its day.
> Go for a way you pious fanatic, and don't criticize us,
> For the work of God is no small thing...in any way.
> Don't pass your whole life in such a way in this world
> That when you are dead, "He is dead", they will say. (Smith 190)

Our mind is generally overpowered by the divine of our heart which contains love and once we start living our life with just love we will realize the reason of us being on earth. Hafiz suggest us through his poem "*New Ways Design*" to forget our past and start for a new journey of life. We should also be generous to ourselves as well as to others then paradise will no longer be somewhere else but be here on this earth. We must also be humble enough with our adventurous and daring self. (Smith 288) Hafiz also comments that whatever role we got in our live that is nothing but from our own destiny and therefore without questioning we must live it and play our roles.

> Whether I am the thorn or rose, its due to Gardener's hand
> That reared and gave to me nourishment, to grow day by day. (Smith 289)

Hafiz though a mystic he did not forget the reality of life hence he used the mundane affairs in his poetry to make people understand the depth of love that he possessed for the divine God. However the loss of Self or Fanaa which is mentioned is the most important part in Sufism. The *Alastor* poet too experienced the same kind of impulse to return to its Origin which all other Sufis felt. When the notion of union with the worldly Other and the Subject's desire to return to the lost object becomes impossible the both the figurative and literal death occurs to the Subject. The appearance of the ideal maid, at the end who stands beside him (Persona), surpasses all the worldly beauty:

> Two starry eyes, hung in the gloom of thought,
> And seemed with their serene and azure smiles
> To beckon him. (*Alastor*, ll. 479-80,483, 490-92)

It is at this very moment that the light shines within the Poet's soul. However, Hafiz's desire of union with God could be seen and felt through his poem. He is found telling God through his poem that since the divine has already promised union and therefore he is not worried for anything. Hafiz also says that there is nothing to be wonder about His lovers being sit and cry infront of his threshold as the ants are always near the sugar. And there is no point giving pain and suffering to the lover who not even scared of the sword as his life is already taken by the divine.

> Since you have promised me union,
> What is there left here for me to do?
> No wonder your lovers sit on your threshold and cry;
> Around sugar there are always plenty of ants,
> What use is a sword to me now that you have already taken my life?
> As your lover, all I've ever asked for is a glance. (Crowe 30)

Therefore, Hafiz is a known figure to one and all whoever interested in Persian literature. His greatness lies in his unique portrayal of depth of thought and uses of symbolism. Because it is not a cup of tea of everyone to express their thought precisely as does by Hafiz. It wasn't easy for anyone to discuss the life its inner law, God, soul, secret of the universe its manifestation but Hafiz had the courage to take up such difficult task to accomplish his great aim of bringing a sense of unity among God and its creation and creation to creation.

Though like Rumi Hafiz had started his love journey through the worldly beloved he did not end up disillusioned in the worldly Other but realized that his love for his worldly love Shaki or Shiek-e-Nabat is not the real love but it's a way to the real love for our divine whole. Hafiz is a moderate kind of lover who used all the mundane symbols to represent his love of God. And his wine not the wine in worldly sense but it symbolise love of God. And the wine house is the place where all the Sufis make Dhikr of Allah (God) in order to get united/annihilated with God. In his poem *I've Said It Before and I'll Say It Again* translated by Thomas Rain Crowe, states that there dwells a jewel inside him and for whom his heart goes wild:

> O friend don't blame me for this broken heart;
> Inside me there is a great jewel and it's the jeweler's shop I go.
> Even though, to the pious, drinking wine is a sin,
> Don't judge me; I use it as a bleach to wash the color of hypocrisy away.
> (17)

Unlike Rumi's lover in his poetry we cannot see Hafiz Persona gets united with the divine but we can only see the desire for union in the lover. Hence we can say that Hafiz although he tried his best to be united with the divine but there is no evident that actually annihilated in God in his life's journey on earth. As from his last word we can guess on his mental and spiritual status that the desire of union was still left:

> Open my grave when I am dead, and thou shalt see a cloud of smoke raising out from it; then shalt thou know that the fire still burns in my dead-heart-yea, it has set my every winding-sheet alight. (Bell 36)

> Here he gives the worldly expression on the same:
> If the scent of her hair were to blow across my dust when I had been dead a hundred years, my mouldering bones would rise and come dancing out of the tomb. (Ibid)

To conclude in the words of Molavi, Jalal-al-din Muhammad Balkhi (Rumi's father) in his *Masnavi I* where he asserts: Where love be form this (earthly) side or form that (heavenly) side, in the end it leads us yonder (Soroush 111). Which means that whether the love is for the worldly beloved or the divine both leads us to the same Truth. Therefore through both mundane and mystical elements Hafiz showed his ecstatic love for the Divine in an artistic way.

CHAPTER 4

The Radical Unorthodoxy in the Poetry of Bulleh Shah

Due to foreign invasions Sufism could not grow in India in the manner as it grew in other Middle Eastern countries. In India Sufism was generally established it khankas in the rural areas due to political and geographical issues. Hence it could not develop in the way it was expected to. One of the important characteristics of Sufi Punjabi poetry is its uses of simple language unike the bomb bursting languages in other Urdu Poem. Though the Persian language is the most attractive language for poetry and ghazal Punjabi language is no lagging behind among Indians and other south Asian countries. It is also famous for its uses of mysticism than materialism in the Punjabi Sufi Poetry.

The verse form are being used enormously in Punjabi Sufi Poetry are – 'Kaf'i or 'Kafiya', which is the term used in Persia meaning rhyme, 'Bara Mah' means the twelveth month of the year. In this kind of verse the poet describe the pangs of separation from the beloved or divine and at the union which occurs at the very end of the twelve month. Another verse form that are being used in Sufi poetry is 'Athvara'. It is the waiting time that the disciple awaits for the beloved or divine union at the end of the eight's day. 'Siharfi' is another form of verse which is a collection of short poems of praising the beloved. In this type of poem the first line will begin with the Arabic word first word 'Alif'.

Another form of verse is 'Qissa' (Story). It is a poem in a form of love story where the lover and the beloved love each other madly but the society acts as a barrier of villain in their union.Therefore resulted in their tragic end. Such type of Poetry includes the story of 'Laila-Majnum', 'Shree-Farhad', 'Sohni-Mahiwal' etc.

'Dohra' is another form of verse which is the favourite verse form among the Punjabi folks by Hashim, the famous poet of

Punjab. The real meaning of 'Dohra' is 'chand' or 'moon'. The next form of verse is the 'Var' which is being used in all Punjabi religious poem. 'Var' means 'dirge' which is used in song form which consist of praising of the beloved God. The stanzas in this kind of poem are called as 'pauris'. The last but not the list form of verse in Punjabi Sufi Poetry is the 'Bait' which is a couplet poem and without much more rules to follow.

The people of Indus valley had been tolerant and broadminded. When harsh policies had been adopted by few officers of Mughal ruler against the non-muslim it was the Punjabis who revolted against it. Bulleh Shah was born in the turbulent times when the Sikhs were fighting against the Mughal Empire and the caste system was at the inhuman stage among the lower caste by upper caste Hindus. However Bulleh Shah's poetry was the embodiment of the reaction against all these inequalities in the society. According to Lajwanti Raffia Krishna Bulleh Shah as a Punjabi Sufi poet is one of the greatest Sufis of the world and his thought equals that of Jalal-ud-din Rumi and Shams Tabrez of Persia. (Maisam)

Bulleh Shah wanted to create an heaven on earth to live in with peace, harmony and tolerance, by removing all kind of discrimination. The change that he wanted to bring among the people was by spreading the notion among people that the same God is the source of all in the universe and through love of all creatures on earth one reach God. In other word, he suggests people to see each other as the reflection of one God through Ishq (love). In his last message to Humanity through Prophet Muhammad Allah (God) has given the hints about his existence and nearness to humanity in his Holy Qur'an in the following manner:

> As also in your own
> Selves: will yet not then see?
> Where Human beings see Almighty Allah as omnipotent over all universe, man can realize (feel) His existence in his own body and testifies.
>
> (Quran 51:21)
>
> For we are nearer to him.
> Than (his) jugular vein. (*The Quran* 50:16)

According to Bulleh Shah it is important to impart the knowledge of God to humanity through love of God. As it is the only way to bring change in human heart which is very essential for unity among them.

> Instruct them in Scripture and Wisdom.
> The movement of Sufism (mysticism) was initiated and promoted to

> impart certain knowledge of this reality to mankind. This movement kept going in almost all religions of this world with a slight difference.
> (The Quar'an 2:129)

The saints are sent here as a guide to mankind and hence all the Sufi saints who came to the subcontinent played a mojor role in spreading tolerance and love among people. They don't even spread the message of Islam (peace) but also showed people that we all are equal in God's realm hence we should treat equally even to our slaves. They have even opted the Bhakti movement and created a different of Sufism in Punjab for the Punjabis. Infact Sufism in Punjab was the mixture of Sabar, and Takwa, Sontokh and Riazat, Takkawal and Toba, Raza and Prem. (Maisam) The people of subcontinent embraced Islam not because of the sword but because of the impressive tolerance, love and equality of the Sufi Saints with all their practical demonstration on life situation. Abdul Majeed Sindhi comments on the influence of the Sufi saints in his word:

> The training of commendable attributes of Muslims was made possible only because of these saints and chosen people. They created brotherhood, equality, tolerance, love of peace among different societies as well as sects. A healthy society with peaceful tolerance came into being. (Sindhi 30)

However, Bulleh Shah was much ahead of his time and also one of them who tried to bring peace and harmony in that time turbulent Punjab. According to him divine love is the only solution to all the discrimination, racism, sectarianism, hatred, terrorism, classicism etc. Therefore Bulleh Shah too like Rumi and Hafiz emphasized on the love of God to spread peace and harmony among the people. He also fought against all kind of racism, sectarianism and lingualism in order to make this world a better place to live in.

He had a close relationship with the ninth Guru of the Sikhs, Guru Tegh Bahadur, whom he dissuade from taking revenge upon those Mughal officers but later he himself was beheaded by them and Bulleh Shah hailed him as a 'holy warrior'. No doubt Bulleh Shah had been brought up and educated on completely Muhammadan ways as it was done in those days in the Saiyid family. But in his poetry one can see his rejection of orthodox hold of mullahs over Islam. It is his teacher, Khwaja Ghulam Murtaza, who trained him as a rebellious personality including Waris Shah, author of Punjab's greatest romance in verse 'Heer'. Nonetheless, not all the Mughals are same, Akhbar, emperor of Hindustan showed his liberal attitude towards the people of his country by restricting cow slaughter in order to show his respect to the sentiment of Hindu community. Prophet Muhammad too showed his great tolerance among the people. It is believed that one day a lady was trying to run away from the village of Muhammad as she believed that Muhammad was a magician and would convert her soon into Islam. But co-incidentally on her way she meet Muhammad but could not recognise and starting complaining and saying against Muhammad but instead of scolding her Muhammad took her luggage to help that old lady to reach her destiny. At the end of her journey when enquired about the name of the person who helped her carrying her luggage and after knowing the name she could not stop herself from Embracing Islam.

The Holy *Qur'an* says we should not criticise any other religion as God knows better what is right and wrong. And prophet Muhammad was the living Qur'an (Allah's word) and hence showed all the mercy towards the people. As when the Arab world was fully occupied by the Muslim community they decided to show inequalities towards the non-believer but Prophet Muhammad had proclaimed that if anybody would harm the minorities he would be the first person to witnessed against that person in the resurrection or judgement day infront of God. (*Bukhari*)

> Once a Muslim was a Muslim was killed by the Sikhs and inorder to take revenge on it the Muslims too assassinated a Sikh. Bulleh Shah raised his voice for this kind of violence as he believed that violence is not the answer for another violence. He asserts on the teachings of religious tolerance and non-violence. (Translated)

> O Bullah! you must not hurt or harm even to the slaves of Muslims and Hindus. Both are the creature of God and worship or pray to him. Leave it to God. (Akhtar 167)

Indeed he had a strong disregard for violence and extremism. Being a Muslim it was a matter of courage for him to speak against his own people. He also suggest that if somebody questions on our religious believe or deed we must not fight for it instead we must agree with it because people are sometimes helpless to follow in whatever they are programmed in.

> A lover of God?
> They'll make much fuss;
> They'll call you a kafir (non-believer)
> You should say – yes, yes. (Maisam)

According to him if someone would understand the philosophy of Isaq (divine love) with pious intention then all other philosophy of Ram, Rahim, Allah, or God will be easy and acceptable. For this today's world of religious violence he suggests through his poetry that why we create such problem for us by separating and holding each one of us as separate entity instead the same or one with God as God himself said he is nearer to us than our jugular vein. He says that all our sense of separateness come with the term of rich, and poor, good and evil, right and wrong, master and slave, friendship and enmity, love and hatred etc. Once we remove this veil of our excuses we cannot stop ourselves but to love each other as everyone possessed the colour of One God. As Bulleh Shah says somewhere you exist in the color of Negroes and somewhere as the whiteness of Roomi, somewhere you exist as Ranjha and somewhere as Yusaf (Joseph), somewhere as a Europian, and somewhere as a sikh. (Akhtar 124). Inother word he sees God in all of them. As He states through his poem:

> Ranjha has come in the garp of a recluse,
> What a disguise my love had to choose.
> His hawklike eyes are haunting;
> They relieve pain, they are enchanting.
> Ranjha has come in the garb of a recluse.
> Rings in ears and locket round his neck of a swan,
> He is another Yusaf carved out of man.
> Ranjha has come in the garb of a recluse. (Duggal 63)

He says that all our dispute of our differences will come to an end when we could remove this duality of caste, creed, sect, religion, color etc. as these are nothing but our egos of identity. All these act as a thief under our soul's garment.

According to Khawaja Ghulam Fareed the creator of every human being is one and the same, and all creations reflect the same (one mighty existence). So, One existence must be recognized through all. Similarly, the truth is well known and evident, so we must not recognize what is untrue. As long as white or black, beautiful or ugly is concerned, you must make it sure that it (appearance and colour) is just a deception. Otherwise Allah's light is present in every appearance. He describes the philosophy of human regard and dignity in these words. (Hashmi 226)

At a very young age Bulleh Shah's family had to move from Uch to Kasur, todays, Firozpur India-pakistan border. He belong to a pious Syeds family and hence was trained in a Islamic orthodox way.

Bulleh Shah's poetic verse is in Standard Punjabi language called 'Maanjhi'. And are in 'Kafi' form. The Kafi is nothing but refrains of the first or the second line or both lines at a time, generally used in Punjabi Poetry and are sung by Qawwaals (group of singers).

> Kafi is often chanted like a song. At the end of a stanza the singers sing the refrain repeatedly... (to) build a particular mood or atmosphere.... The kafi is generally sung by qawwaals, a group of singers. They get so deeply involved in the singing that they become a part of the chorus. The word kafi is derived from the Arabic kafa, which means a group. (Puri and Shangari,1978).

His poetry seems modern with loosely followed prosodic structure. According to Khaled Ahmad the popularity of Bulleh Shah's poetry is because of his use of modern language, as he remarks "is his relatively modern vocabulary."(Puri 135) The theme of his poetry consist of everyday life situations like prayer talk, love, relationship, good and bad circumstances that were going on at that time, orthodox believers and rigidity etc. T.S. Eliot's states that "the poetry of a people takes its life from the people's speech, and in return gives life to it". Eliot also observed that "no poetry, of course, is ever exactly the same speech that the poet talks and hears; but it has to be in such a relation to the speech of his time that the listener or reader can say, 'That is how I should talk if I could talk poetry". (Puri 135) The line of his poetry is non-poetic but only in terms of rhythm. It follows exclamatory technique with a non-rhythmic tone followed by a use of proper noun 'Bullah'. He is credited to have authored around fifty to one hundred and fifty Kafi. He is quite unique among other Punjabi Sufi poet because of his piousness in character which also represents the piousness of the Punjabis. However his composition of poetry were called as the 'Pinannacle of Sufi literature'. (Naqvi) He tried to reach the divine within him through the love of humanity. Like Rumi he too had gone through the earthly beloved, his master, Innayat Shah to realize the divine love. His life itself speaks the secret of the path that he took and it serves other seeker of truth to realize their goal.

The word 'radical' is derived from the Latin word 'radix' which means 'root' or the change of the root of old or societal believe system which come in the way of fundamental right of equality. In other word 'radicalism' means to change social structure through revolutionary means. In Sufism radicalism means to overcome all the rules and regulations of religious law which a Sufi achieves after the Sufi rejects the self and becomes the Other (fanaa).Which already described in detail in the previous chapters. Bulleh Shah's 'radicalism' was his voice against the inequalities that were going on in his time. His poem *Better Be Quiet* reads:

> Better be quiet!
> The truth nobody tolerates.
> Tell the truth and they would swear.
> They sit not near the truthful.
> Truth is sweet only to the lover dear.
> The truth of the Code is a disaster.
> The truth is joy at the lover's end.
> The truth creates a new world.
> The place the Code has with the disciplined.
> Love cannot remain quiet.
> He who has enjoyed the scent of truth.
> He who has woven the chord of union.
> He would quit the world, false, uncouth.
> Better be quiet! (Duggal 201)

The irony is that because of his unorthodox view he was denied to be buried in the community graveyard but in today's world the same person got worldwide recognition and respect for his humanitarian philosophy. Bulleh Shah wanted a straight bond between the man and his creator. By discarding the rituals and the ceremonials prescribed by all the religions. He proclaimed that good deeds were the only way to unite with the divine. That is why he has chosen the path of love like other Sufis as it is the only way to bring change in the heart of people by removing all kinds of veil from their heart to reach God. As Bulleh Shah explained it in his poetry:

> Burn the prayer mat, break the water pot;
> Quit the rosary, throw away the staff.
> Lovers say at the top of their voices,
> Leave the Kosher and eat the shot.
> Love is ever new and fresh. (Duggal 73)

Bulleh shah was considered one of the greatest Sufi saint of the land of Punjab because of his uncompromising truth which made him expose the deceits of the cruel and the righteous clerics. He was a person who called a spade a spade. He was a person who could voice against the authority of orthodox society and all the evils that were going on in his time. He always tried to be the bridge between the Muslims and Hindus. But the tension arose with the ideology of the rulers life Shiek Ahmed and Sarhand who had a believe that "The glory of Islam lies in ridiculing the non-muslims. Those who give quarter to Kafirs disgrace Islam..." (Maisam). At this time of social crises Bulleh Shah stood as a hero to deal with the injustice. It is said that the beauty of any community or ruler lies in heart which means if our heart is clean we will look beautiful. In the book *The Fourty Rules of Love,* the mystic teacher of Rumi, Shams was happened to say to one of the judge who was boasting about the beauty of their city, Bagdad, that once the beauty of the heart is corrupt by the outer world or selfishness it will take away the beauty of everything around. Perhaps that was the case with the Mughal emperor and the Brahmin caste who became corrupt in their heart and misused their power. Hence the downfall came in the demolition of their empire which were overtaken by the Jatts. Bulleh Shah had an eye to see the future and hence said in his poem *Strange Are The Times*:

Those in tatters have turned into
Kings,
The kings have taken to begging
O bulleh, that which is His
Command
Who can alter His decree. (Duggal 102-122)

The Mughal empire was declining because of the disorders in their rules and regulation. As God's world runs with certain rules and regulation so must be with its people otherwise destruction is a must to teach a lesson. The 18th century was the time when the Sikh movement was at its pick to bring downfall of the Mughals. Whom Bulleh called as 'Bhurian' or the one who wear blanket, as he says 'Bhurian wale raje Keete' (Where is the king with blankets). (Naqvi) Though the poorest section of Sikhs 'the Jatts' who were the revolutionaries at that time could not capture the state power Bulleh's sharp eyes could make out what would happen in future. As he utters through his poem:

The Iraqis are despised
While the donkey are prized.
Strange are the times!
....
Crows swoop on hawks
Sparrow do eagles stalk
Strange are the times. (Duggal 100-122)

The very line of the poem represents the upside down of the natural orders of the life of the rulers from being a predator to the prey. Bulleh Shah was very much aware of the political, religious and ethical change of his time. He also says there were very less respect for each other in the family. As he says;

There is no accord between fathers
And sons,
Nor any between mothers and
Daughters
The truth ones are being pushed
About,
The tricksters are seated close by. (Naqvi web)

Hence he was also observing the moral degeneration, the corruption, anarchy and injustice that was prevalent at that time. Through the last stanga of the poem he suggest us that despite all the bad times in our life we must keep faith in our God. Who can substitute and end our days of trouble with the days of happiness. He says God has the ultimate power to sort out everything and anything in our life so we must seek forgiveness only from him.

Strange are the times!
Says Bulleh, kill your ego
And throw away your pride.
You need to forget yourself
To find Him by your side. (Duggal 100-205)

Therefore God gives us bad time too in order to Shake us and clean us from all the dirts of our heart. Hence if we our time is bad we should not lose hope on the Almighty instead we must observe what it wants to teach us.

In his poem *Remove Duality and do away with all Disputes* says remove all kind of duality that exist among us for each on religious dogma. As it is the illusion to think that the God of Hindus is different than the God of Muslim. Because no matter in what form or formless we call on Him he remains the same God, the only difference is with the different name by which we call on Him.

Remove duality and do away with all disputes;
The Hindus and Muslims are not other than He.
Deem everyone virtuous, there are no thieves.
For, within everybody He himself resides.
How the Trickster has put on a mask! (Smith 199)

After his realization of the truth the concept of right, wrong, good, evil disappeared from him. All the illusions of duality gone away from him and he could see the divine in all the creatures of God. And there exist in him nothing but love, compassion and forgiveness for all inplace of caste, creed, religion color etc.

Therefore if we scold or speak bad about others God we are eventually scolding our own Creator. Hence it is better not to consider oneself represent oneself from a particular religion rather than as a human being. It is believed that in one occasion Bulleh Shah and his disciples were eating food during the Ramazan (fasting month during daytime for the Muslim community) and a group of people passing by had asked about their religion and on their declaration as Muslim they were beaten up but when they asked Bulleh Shah about his religion he replied that he belonged to non and he was saved. "They said, Who are you?" They replied we are Muslims. Don't Muslims feel hungry? Then they were beaten up. But when they went inside and saw Bulleh Shah in meditation they asked him to the same question but he did not say anything then they left. Then on complaining about beating by the traveller Bulleh Shah asked them "What did the ask you?" The disciples replied, "They ask us who we were, and we said we were Muslims." Bulleh retorted, "That's why you were beaten. You became something and you suffered. I don't become anything, and they said nothing to me." (Smith 200)

Therefore from the incident of Bulleh Shah's life one can conclude that we are our own judge. As for whatever deeds of ours we would judge and regard ourselves we would get the same kind of reward or punishment that we think we deserve. Our soul is eternal and it has no religion or caste, creed, community etc.

Understand the One and forget the rest,
Shake off your ways of a non-believer
Leading to the grave and to hell, in quest. (Maisam)

He suggest us to forget all the barriers to reach God and only to remember the truth (God). He also says that after he found God within him, he forgot every rules of life. He even compared the Mullahs and the Brahmins to dogs who were faithful to their masters. So according to him there is no difference between them and dog. He blames them for they mislead people by scaring them in the name of God. Thus he wanted to do something better so that on the judgement day he could stand up as a better person than those merchants of religion. As Bulleh Shah writes in his poem "*Dogs are better than You*":

Staying awake and praying at night
The dogs are also awake, superior to you
They never stop barking
And go and sleep on a pile of rubbish, superior to you
They never leave their master's door
Even when beaten with shoes, superior to you
Bulleh Shah you'd achieve something
Or the dogs will win this contest, superior to you. (Rafat 51)

In ancient India the evil of cast system was prevalent and hence the people from lower caste did not get proper respect and right in the society. At that time the Sufi saint Kwaja Mainuddin Chisti came to India and spread the message of brotherhood and equality among the people of India. Bulleh Shah also tried the same by showing disregard for the inequalities that was prevalent in his time. Even though he was from a Syed family he had chosen Shah Innayat an Aryan (lower Social strata) as his murshid or teacher. In the "Song of the Saints of India" (*Bang-i-Auliya-i-Hind*) the following reference are mentioned:

From the tribe of gardeners was brother Shah Inayat,
He received honor from Shah Raza Wali Allah.
He earned his living in the small town of Qasur Pathana.
The ruler Husein Khan of this town was his arch enemy.
From there Inayat Shah came to the city of Lahore;
Two miles to the south of the city he made his habitation.
It is at this place that we find his tomb.
In 1141 he departed from this world. (Chopra 5-7)

In the beginning of his life even Bulleh Shah was too influenced by the caste system and later through his master Innayat Shah understood the emptiness that lies in all these outer differences among humanity. As he states in his poem on the vainness that lies in all the caste system:

The low-cast and high-caste
Are created by God who cares not for family;
He disregard the beautiful
And cherishes the not-so-comedy.
If you wish to enjoy the glory of the Garden,
Go and serve the Araeen.
Why bother about Bulleh's caste?
Obey the command that comes from the Saeen. (Duggal 97)

According to Bulleh Shah whoever suggest for all the rules and restrictions of religion, caste creed except love of God and humanity are the real hypocrites, deceivers and are doing it against the nature of God. No doubt he was a follower of religion Islam and its prophet Muhammad but he did not like grouping or sectarianism or any kind of division among humanity.

He was quite an unique figure in the Muslim world and could boldly ask the people to destroy the mosque, temple (literally means Impure heart) and could also say that he was tired of reading the Qur'an and Vedas because it is the human heart where God dwells and not the great monuments and buildings like the mosque and temple. He describes this in his poem:

> Tired of reading the Vedas and Qur'an,
> Kneeling and prostrating my forehead sorn,
> At Mathura or Mecca He does not dwell. (Duggal 73)

It is believed that Bulleh Shah's Sufism had been started with the following of Shariat but the Shariat has relevance as long as duality persists, when the duality disappears one is liberated from all bounds. That is exactly what happened to Bulleh Shah so even though he had been qualified as tariqat he became a liberated person and could see the divine in every human being. Even though he was quite critical of religion he never denounce it completely. As he states in his poem:

> I see him in every face;
> And yet people notice him not
> Here and there it's all his grace
> My love has made me forget
> Prayers, fast and going on pilgrimages. (Duggal 65)

While Bulleh Shah in his writing he never questions the Islamic religious orthodox. But sometimes he used metaphors to express his frustration towards the rigidity of the Mughal officers and the upper class Brahmins. Though his poetry he spread the message of universal brotherhood. He believed in spreading the knowledge of mysticism as it is required for religious tolerance in the society. This was because according to Sufism the prime duty of every human being on earth is to regard and treat all equally.

> Remove duality and do away with all disputes,
> The Hindus and Muslims are not other than He.
> Deem everyone virtuous, there are no thieves.
> For within everybody He himself resides.
> How the trickster has put on his mask! (Puri 8)

Khawaja Ghulam Fareed says:

> My heart always reminds me that if you find someone even in the shape of an idol do not call bad names because it may be a form of the same Almighty existence. (Hashmi 225)

Bullah Shah believes that if someone would desire of the garden of love then he must get involved in the path of mysticism. He says that this path is the better one as there is no one who is higher or lower in this path, hence there is no discrimination. As Bulleh Shah states (translated):

> The mystic secret is the real divine love. The person finding it gets free from all discriminations of lingualism, regions, and sectarianism. (Akhtar 143)

And to this path of mysticism only a knower of this path (Sufi saints) can lead us. Hence we must always take the help of the spiritual master to know the path of God. The Qur'an too says the same that if you do not know then take the help of them who knows:

> And ask those who know if you know not. (16:43)
> And follow the path of him who turns unto me. (31:15)

Therefore Bulleh Shah too took the help of his master Shah Innayat Khan for his guidance to the path of mysticism. As in Sufism there are four main stages that the Sufis has to cross i.e Shariat, Tariqat, Marufat and Haqiqat and when the Sufi reach the final who stage i.e Marufat (mysticism) and Haqiqat (Truth) there exist no rules and regulation of religion but only truth (God). Therefore Bulleh Shah too reach that stage where he did not find religious laws important as it were for him. Hence in several occasions on being questioned about his religious belief, he replied that he was neither a believer nor a non-believer. Neither was the virtuous nor a sinner. Neither was he Moses nor the Pharaoh. He makes it clear that he was neither a Muslim nor a Hindu. As he declared it through his poem, "*Neither Hindu nor Muslim*":

> Neither am I a believer in Mosque
> Neither am I an Infidel
> Neither amongst the virtuous nor among the sinners
> Neither am I Moses northe Pharaoh
> Bulleh, who knows who I am. (Rafat 82)

Indeed his poetry comes to us through Qavvals or the singers of our time. In his poem *Come to Our Abode* Bulleh Shah showed his disregard for the orthodoxy religious view of his day. At a time when the influence of the religious doctrine was so powerful that Islam had become a fundamental part for the life of Punjabis. And if somebody happens to speak against it, he would be regarded as the revolutionary against once own society. Bulleh Shah stood firmly against all the religious orthodoxy and was known as a severe critic of both Islamic and Brahminic clergy. He went so far as to ridicule the clerics for misleading and exploiting the people with their false promises. He goes to the extent of calling them thugs (Cheaters). He writes in his poem "*I'm Harbouring a Thief*":

The Muhhah and Qazi show me the way,
Their Maze of dharma that is in sway.
They are the confirmed thieves of time,
They spread their net of saintly crime. (Rafat 97)

Since he was a voice against all of injustice in the society he did not give any room for hypocrisy. Through his poem *I am Emancipated* he says that he could liberate himself from all the rules of religious orthodoxy.

I am emancipated, emancipated I am,
I am no prisoner of being born a Syed,
All the fourteen heavens are my territory,
I am slave to none.
Only they shout loud while calling others to
Prayer
Whose hearts are not pure.
Those who go to Mecca on pilgrimage
Have little else to occupy them here. (Maisam)

He said that going for religious pilgrimage is not the ultimate place for purification to reach God. To be a pure human one must remove all kinds of ego, hatred for each other, pride of one's self and selfishness. In other word, we have to be clean from our inner core of heart then only we will be able to liberate ourself and can called as a pure being. Hence we must not only listen to the orthodox clerics who tell us to go for pilgrimage for the purification of our heart. The holy Qur'an also says about the purification of our heart in Sura *Al-Furqan (The Criterion)*.The 11th century saint Abdul Qadir Jilani quotes on the importance of self-purification:

A Jihad fought against self-will is far
Superior to that waged by the sword. (Gibbons and Jones 31)

Therefore Bulleh Shah through his poem showed his strong rejection of the orthodox hold of all the religious clergies and the nexus between them and the rulers which had created a huge gap between man and God. He possessed similar view about acquiring self-knowledge like Rumi and Hafiz as which is the only way for the mystical union with God. As Sufism itself is a journey of acquiring the self-knowledge which leads to the truth. Bulleh Shah was in search for a spiritual guide for his enlightenment then an angel appeared and directed him for Shah Innayat. As Bulleh Shah also after acquiring self-knowledge under the guidance of is murshid Innayat Khan could not remember anything accept remembering God. He even forgot his own self as according to Sufism only after death of the self the divine can enter. It is believed that a Sufi cannot be called a Sufi until he reached the stage where he will utter "there is no being but God" and "there is nothing but God God". So we can see that even Bulleh Shah had been gone through the same stage where he vanishes his own self just like Rumi denied his self-existence for Shams and Hafiz for the God as he says, by uttering the word Ranjha I became Ranjha myself and Ranjha is in me and I am in Ranjha, no other thought there is, I do not exist, He himself exist, He amuses himself (Gibbon 4). Though Bulleh Shah did not write much, but whatever he wrote all are of great inspiring to the people all over the world.

Damn prayer, throw mud on religious fasting
Black out the kalma with ink!
I found my Love when I turned within
People search clueless. *(Puri 134)*

Bulleh Shah's non-acceptance of all the religious rules, restrictions of classicism could be seen in his poetry with the flexibility of his kafi. According to him there is no use going for all the our rituals if we are not pure inside. The essential tenets that Bulleh Shah followed in his life time were: the first one is to free our mind of any kind of delusion in order to find the truth within us, the second one is our pointless searching for our divine in the temple or mosque, the third one is the importance of withdrawing of the soul to the inner world and to look to the inward path. The fourth one is a way of finding bliss trough the love of murshid. The fifth one is the concept of word which has the power to create the universe. The sixth is the concept of birth and death. Which takes place in our life repetitive way until unless we are aware of our true self.

The mullah and the torch-bearer
Are of a kind in this,
They offer light to others,
Themselves in darkness. (Puri 134)

He further describes that without a proper master one cannot know the path to our heart where we can find our true love. He also states on the meaningless of all our outer purification which we try to do by going to all worshiping place. As his poem reads:

They say, Go pray
in the mosque.
What profits prayer
In the mosque
If prayer is not said In the heart?

What profits washing
If prayer does not wash in the heart?
Without a Perfect Master
Your prayer is no prayer (Duggal 55-70)

Through these lines of his poem he criticizes the religious scholars for reading so many books and guiding so many people but inside them they are ignorant about the truth. He also says that no doubt these scholars have gone to many mosque and temples but they did not yet visit their soul. Instead of asking purification and perfection from the divine they must clean all the ill intensions from their heart. As Dr. Allahma Muhammad Iqbal states in his poem (translation):

The talk is not of prostrations, but purity f intension.
Often people come back with empty hand, after every prayer.
(Ahmed web)

His master was from lowar strata of life and he still love and respect his master which is another revolution for him to show people that classicism is nothing but an ego concept of our mind.

It is believed that Bulleh Shah like Rumi reached the divine love through the love of their master. And it is Shah Innayat who introduced him with the truth through mysticism. Bullah has fallen in love with his master and has devoted his life in his path of union. His Lord and Master is Shah Inayat. According to Innayat Shah t he secret of spiritual progress lies in detaching one's mind from the world outside and attaching it to God within. (Gibbons and Jones 32) Bulleh Shah says that it is master who has captivated his heart. Shah Inayat wrote "Dasdtur al-Amal" where he mentioned and showed about his knowledge and skill on the various methods on the attainment of salvation in Hinduism. He utters that this knowledge of salvation was adopted by the Greeks during Alexander's invasion to India, then from the Greeks it might be adopted by the Iranians then by the Sufi mystics. One of the famous Sufi scholar, Muhammad Ali Raza comments on Shah Innayat is the following manner:

Shah Inayat "migrated to Lahore where he established an institution of his own. In this institution came men of education for advanced learning in philosophy, Sufism and other spiritual sciences of the time." Shah Inayat wrote considerably on Sufism and its developments. His writings were mostly in Persian. He was an erudite scholar whom Bulleh Shah made his Hadi or Guru."(Chopra 5)

The meeting between Bulleh Shah and Innayat Shah had started in testing each other's spiritual knowledge which mean Bulleh Shah had already acquired little spiritual knowledge prior to meeting Innayat Shah. As on reaching the orchard of Innayat Shah Bulleh inorder to test his master he invoked the name God to pluck the unripe mangoes without touching it. Shah Innayat too came to know the mischief of Bulleh Shah and asked him, Well, young man, why have you brought down the unripe fruit from the trees?" And Bulleh Shah was wishing to hear from his future master so that he could get chance to talk to him. He said, "Sir, I Neither climbed up the trees, nor did I through any stone at the fruit, how could I tear it from the trees?" Then his master gave a glance at him and said, "O, you are not only a thief, you are also being clever!" But Innayat's glance was so intense that Bulleh Shah could not stop but fell at his feet. On Innayat Shah's enquire about his name and intension to come to him Bulleh replied, "Sir, my name is Bulleh and I wish to know how I can realize God." Innayat Shah said, "Why do you look down? Get up and look at me." When Bulleh looked at him he gain give another glance at him and said, "O Bulleh what problem is there in finding God? It only needs to be uprooted from here and planted there." From that time he became a murid of him in his search for the Divine. According to Bulleh Shah the 'mystic' is someone who follow his master and God alone, and with a singularly defined purpose. One's will is that of God. (Gibbons and Jones 39)

Just like Rumi and Hafiz in Bulleh Shah's life too became a tragedy after his master Innayat Shah went against his critical comments on Islamic tradition and culture. However the reason for their separation is not so clear but. There was a long separation among them and this pain and pangs of separation matures Bulleh Shah and showed him the truth of all existence. It is said that his master knowingly did that to him for his spiritual development.

Bulleh Shah's mysticism unveils the formality of all the religion and found out that God dwells nowhere but in every beings of God. Hence one can make a direct contact with their divine. As the Sufi ideology circles around the concept that God is our whole and we are the lost part which always desires to be united with the whole. His love of God can be seen in the following verses of his poem:

How many knots should I tie for my wedding?
My learned friend, advice!

> The marriage party must come on the
> Prescribed date,
> Will forty knots be wise? (Maisam)

He also suggest that coming to earth means to learn some skills, so better we should not waste our time in idle pursuit or fighting with each other. Just like every mother tells her daughter to learn something and prepare herself to fit-in her in laws house. She also tells her that she is not a permanent member of their house and must go to her other house, so better prepare herself and learn some skill for the next house to live in. Through the mother daughter discussion Bulleh Shah tries to tell us that we are also the temporary dwellers or visitors of earth so better we must ponder and work for our next life.

> Living with parents is just four days,
> You must not squander in foolish play.
> Waste not time, you must work,
> You'll come to grief if work you shirk.
> Attend to your spinning, maid! (Duggal 171)

In his poem *All in One Contained* he speaks on the oneness of God. Therefore he too like his master believes that the reunion with God is possible only when we would detach ourselves from the outer world and attach ourselves to our inward world or God.

> Pour not on prayers, forget the fasts.
> Wipe off Kalma from the sight.
> Bulleh has found his lover within,
> Others grope in the pitch-dark night.

He says that it is futile to search or somewhere in the sky or outside as it exist within us. We are not separated from our divine. Infact our body is the living temple for our divine. Hence everyone of us is special and divinely. The only thing that we have to do is to recognise it within us and which lies in our goodness and in loving and serving others selflessly. The Quar'an says "Man is the top of all creation. God's own light shines in him; he should not waste his time in frivolity. He must know himself. "However he recognises the hidden secret behind all religion and found out that "God dwells in the human soul".

> In vain, you rub your forehead on the ground and you display a long visible mark on it. By prostrating during the prayer, the forehead gets rubbed and gets a mark, Bulleh Shah says, "Why do you show this mark as a mark of your piety?" (Naqvi)

Therefore he suggest us that it is better not to show off people that we are religious or pray to god but to try connect within our own 'self'. He also says through this poem *All in One contained* that we should worry too much for our finance but to look at the bird which go out everyday for food and trust God but on the other hand we are not trusting our divine and are worried about storing all comfort for our living. But when you are truely in love with the divine you really don't desire for any material happiness except union with Him.

What use is it bowing one's head?
To what avail has prostrating led?
Reading Kalma you make them
Laugh
Absorbing not a word while the
Qur'an you quaff
The truth must be here and there
Sustained
It's all in One contained. (Naqvi)

Through this poem he also suggest to us to remove all the concept regarding the fear to get heaven and hell instead clean our heart without fearing punishment and reward. And if we want to make God happy with us we must go forward to help each other with good intension as God dwells in everyone of us. He also suggest us that if some someone needs help, it is better to help then to go and offer rituals in the mosque or temple. After he lost his ego he could find the love of God. As he utters in his poem *Loss of Ego*:

I have got lost in the city of love,
I am trying to know myself.
I cannot lay my hands on the substance,
I have rid myself of ego,
And discovered my true self.
All indeed has ended well.
O Bulleh, I find the Lord pervades both worlds,
None now appears a stranger to me. (Gibbons and Jones 55)

However in this present day of racial hatred his poem can bring hope and great change in the heart of people to show the divine light within them which is capable of loving all the creatures. He said that in the city of love we get what we sow and our God is the light and the world is its veil. (Gibbon and Jones 43) and all our veils of ego and hatred must be removed from our heart so that we can find peace with our lords. And if our soul will be in darkness the final door to God will not open to us.

CHAPTER 5

Conclusion

The different elements in the poetry of these three Sufi poets highlights the liberalism behind the religious doctrine and brings out the hidden meaning behind all the religions, which develops in us a sense of unity. Farid-ud-din Attar through his poem "*Perfume of the Desert*" translated by Andrew Harvey and Eryk Hanut has described about the relevance of the Sufi thought to the contradictory world. As he said:

> In the dead of night, a Sufi began to weep.
> He said, "This world is like a closed coffin, in
> Which
> We are shut and in which, through our ignorance,
> We spend our lives in folly and desolation.
> When death comes and opens the lid of the coffin,
> Each one who has wings will fly off to eternity,
> But those without will remain locked in the coffin,.
> So my friends before the lid of this coffin is taken
> Off,
> Do all you can to become a bird of the way to God;
> Do all you can to develop your wings and your
> Feathers." (16)

Therefore the Sufis are there as facilitators to help mankind make the transition from the world to the eternal life. However the stage of 'fanna' or 'annihilation' is a kind of state of mind where the Sufi is ready to loss the Self and put the other in place of the Self. It is through this state (Abvaal) and stage (maqaam) the Sufi understands love for the other. According to al-Qushairi 'States are the gifts, the stations are earnings. (Arberry 75) It is said that feeling of separation leads to suffering and that suffering leads us to the realization of God which seems to be expressed in the writing of these three Sufi poets. With the departure of Rumi's friend Shams, Rumi perhaps realized his own real self and also the divine God. Perhaps Hafiz too realized the same through his worldly love Shiek-e Nabat and so speaks about love and suffering through his poem "*Come, Fair Maiden*":

> I enjoy the divine company of my beloved,
> Even though my beloved
> Has taken away all my peace of mind. (Nisarg 9)

Bulleh Shah too like Rumi and Hafiz tried to express divine love through the ordinary lovers of the world. To represent the intensity of the divine love both Rumi and Hafiz and Bulleh shah have used the example of the love and longing of Zuleikha for Joseph which is indeed the aspect of divine love that we should possess for our God. Rumi in his collection of poems entitled *The Essential Rumi* translated by Coleman Barks mentioned about the dept of love that Zuleikha possed for Joseph:

> Zuleikha let everything be the name of Joseph, from clergy seed
> To aloes wood. She loved him so much she concealed his name
> In many different phrases, the inner meanings
> Known only to her. (108)

Similarly Hafiz also gives us an example of divine love through his poem "*If the Shirazi Turk would only Grant my Hearts desire*":

> My beloved is as beautiful as Joseph,
> My Beloved's love is strong enough to enchant Zuleikha. (Nisarg 6)

Just like Rumi, Hafiz also used the worldly ordinary language to represent the divine love as well. He uses the symbol of wine as love and the cup as the heart of the lover and the fair maiden serving it as the beloved. Similarly Bulleh Shah in his poetry consider him as Heer and God as Ranjha. He believes that love of God can be attained only through love of man. As he asserts through his poem "*God has Come down as Man*":

> Ranjha has come in the garb of a recluse,
> What disguise my love had to choose. (Duggal 17)

Bulleh Shah too had shown his love of God through his mundane love of his Master Innayat Khan. As he states:

> I've discovered something that now
> Is...
> By my true Master, God manifested
> Is!
> Somewhere, the One true friend is
> Is,
> The One...also Majnun and Layla,
> Is. (Smith 79)

Unlike Bulleh Shah, Rumi was a strict follower of the *Shariat.* That he was a follower of the *Shariat* is explicated in the following lines of his *Mathnawi III Quatrain no. 1173*:

I am the servant of the Qur'an as long as I have life.
I am the dust on the path of Muhammad, the chosen one.
If anyone quotes anything except this from my sayings,
I am quit of him and outraged by these words. (Helminski & Rizwani)

One can see that Rumi had mastered the essence of the *Shariat* from the following lines of Rumi quoted by John Moyne in his book "*Rumi and the Sufi Tradition: Essays on the Mowlavi order and Mysticism Quotes*" (70):

We have caused much uproar,
We have picked the essence of the Qur'an.
Throwing away the skin to the dogs.

Moyne further clarifies about him in this regard that Rumi was a devout Muslim who frequently expressed utmost reverence for the prophet and who had memorized the Qur'an and frequently quoted from it. Although Bulleh Shah was not a strict follower of *Shariat* in his later life but is rooted in Islam. He recognised the common themes that run below the surface of all religion. He accepts the external difference between them, but he acknowledges the universal core that pervades the mystic sides of all religions. Bulleh Shah believes that the great truth that all teachings agree upon is that 'God dwells in the human soul'. In *Srimad Bhagavad Gita* chapter thirteen verses eighteen says(590):

He is the supreme source of all
lights and is beyond darkness.
He is Knowledge, the object
Of knowledge, and the goal of
knowledge. He is situated in
everyone's heart.

In Chapter II, it is already discussed about Prophet Moses who asked God about his dwelling then God replied that He dwells in the heart of those whose heart is broken and in pain. One of the first and famous female Sufi Rabia-al-Basra utters in her poem *In My soul*:

In
my soul
there is a temple, a shrine, a mosque,
a church,
that dissolve, that
dissolve in
God. (Basri web)

Perhaps the greatest contribution of Bulleh Shah was the amalgamation of Bhakti and Sufi elements in his poetry. Bhakti movement was for those downtrodden Hindus who were practically slaves in the hands of the upper class Hindu Brahmins. They even had to go through the upper class Brahmins to worship gods. Therefore Bhakti movement was the protest against this kind of authority. But he was not only against the caste system but also with his own muslim ruler those who were somehow arrogant towards the people of other faith. Through his poetry he tried to criticize those injustice that were going on in his life. Bulleh Shah was among those who tried to bring unity among the people of all the religions. Though he belonged to a Saiyid family he became a murid of Shah Inayat who belonged to an Aryan (Low) tribe. When he was questioned about the fact that, why being a descendant of prophet, he became a disciple of Shah Inayat who belonged to a lower social strata. In a satirical manner he replied to them through these verses:

> Aryans and Syeds (noble ones) are born everywhere.
> God could not care less who is who. In fact he hugs
> The ugly ones and shuns away the beautiful ones.
> Who so ever calls me Syed shall receive the punishment of hell
> Whosoever calls me an Aryan Shall sway on the wings of heaven.
>
> (*Dawn web*)

Therefore Bulleh Shah was the first Sufi saint who raised his voice against the injustice in his time. And through his poetry he tries to depict the social orthodoxy that was prevalent in that time in India. Despite their differences in view both Rumi and Bulleh Shah had opted for the medium of dance and music to reach God. The Punjabi Sufi mystic Bulleh Shah was no less popular than these two Sufi poet. Indeed he is known for his radical nature.

Hafiz was also greatly admired by the scholars, for his ability to mix both the worldly and the mystical element in his poetry which can also be found in both Rumi and Bulleh Shah. Several commentaries have been written on his poems from both mystical and mundane point of view. As Reza Saberi in his translation of "*The Down of Hafiz*" stated that:

> Even the non-mystical poems of Hafiz have some subtleties and imagery which can be Interpreted mystically and spiritually. It will not be far from truth if we state that for Hafiz, As for all Persian mystics, The whole world with all its diverse forms and phenomena is but A manifestation of God. (Saberi x)

There have been several other interpretations of Hafiz poetry, which celebrate the delightful ambiguity of his verse. Serious writers like Daniel Ladinsky were sometimes found to argue over Hafiz about the fact whether he was a spokesman for the proletariat or was he a forerunner of the Islamic revolution of 1979. Therefore from the extent to which his poetry has been recited and appreciated by Sufis, both in solitary reading and in ritual performance, we may qualify him as a Sufi poet who impact the world.

Rumi's poetry brings us the universal message. The message is perceived by every individual in a way that it utters the same kind of truth which mankind can easily relate with their dream for a healthy, rational and harmonious living. It is easy to comprehend his message as it is of love, peace, harmony and unity rather than of religion, nationality, culture. Rumi asserts that he neither belongs to any religion nor nationality but of Humanity:

> What is to be done, O Moslems? for I do not recognize myself. I am neither Christian, nor Jew, nor Gabr, nor Moslem. I am not of the East, nor of the West, nor of the land, nor of the sea; I am not of Nature's mint, nor of the circling heavens. I am not of earth, nor of water, nor of air, nor of fire; I am not of the empyrean, nor of the dust, nor of existence, nor of entity. I am not of India, nor of China, nor of Bulgaria, nor of Saqsin; I am not of the kingdom of 'Iraqain, nor of the country of Khorasan. I am not of this world, nor of the next, nor of paradise, nor of Hell; I am not of Adam, nor of Eve, nor of Eden and Rizwan. My place is the placeless, my trace is the Traceless; 'Tis neither body nor soul, for I belong to the soul of the Beloved. *(Divan-i Shamsi Tabriz 125)*

Rumi had given equal emphasis to all the religion of the world and believed in the unity of all being on earth. According to Leonard Lewisohn Rumi had crossed the limitation of individual religion. Rumi was against the notion of God being found and can be worshiped only in the mosque, temple, churches, and synagogues. Instead he affirms like Hafiz that God can be found even in the tavern (wine store) which is forbidden in Islam. Rumi in his message tries to make us hope for a better and a tolerant world. In this world of spiritual and moral crisis one need to ponder on the much advance thought of Rumi who possessed liberal mind and was above all kind of prejudice for other religion, nation etc. The *Qur'an*, *Sura Bakara* (The Cow) says on the intolerance of the people for the other religion:

> And the Jews say the Christians follow nothing (true) and the Christians say the Jews follow nothing (true); ye both are readers of the scriptures.

> Even thus speak those who know not. Allah will judge between them on the Day of Resurrection concerning that wherein they differ. (2:113)

Therefore if God is not differentiating among us then we should not also possess all kind of hatred, anger, prejudice for each other. Rumi too believes in kindness, tolerance and forgiving nature of human being.

The similarities that one can find among these three Sufi poets is their uses of mystical romantic love themes in their poetry. A brief study of these Sufi poets is enough for one to understand the reasons of their formulation of such kind of poem. Love has the power to change a religious man like Rumi, Hafiz and Bulleh Shah into a great passionate lover of both earthly and divinely beloved which turn them into mystical poet. Rumi's poetry basically mystical in tone for his earthly beloved through whom he got involved in divine love. On the other hand, Hafiz and Bulleh Shah too through their earthly beloved understood the love of God and therefore they tried to seek the divine love through different manifestation.

> The day the lesson of love i learned
> Into river of my divine desire i plunged:
> I was swept up...confounded.
> Then Shah Innayat me across rowed!
> O my friend. enough of learning! (Smith70)

Therefore love enabled these Sufi poets to express their inner intense and deep feelings of love through their poetry. Love has enabled us to enjoy every moment of our life. It is nothing but a kind of intense feeling of affection for someone with an ecstatic emotions. For the Sufis love is something which makes them sacrifice the worldly good for others and accepting patiently all the bad and harmful things that comes from others. They all believe that love is the essence of our existence and hence we must choose the way of love.

Hafiz and Rumi exchanged the same kind of concept on divine love, as they believe that those who has the courage to sacrifice themselves in the path of love can attain and achieve the divine presence or eternity. Rumi's *Divan of Shams Tabrizi*, is an Ode where he described the different qualities of love:

> Love takes back rest and tranquility of its owner and is compared to a black bloodthirsty lion; it breaks thousands glasses and tears thousands shirts; nobody can flee from love's trap
> I ran towards him suddenly. His lover shouted: hey!

> Do you know he is a bloodthirsty? How dare a man like you go towards him?
> O heart! Do not twist in his tress-like noose; for there you see served heads, crimeless, guiltless.
>
> (Hafiz, Ode 94).

In Rumi's poetry the lover is a helpless and powerless person in the presence of the beloved, but in Hafiz's poetry the lover is a moderate person and could see and observe things rationally and hence he did not lose his power of thinking on the path of love. According to Hafiz the person who can handle both his worldly duties along with the path of Shariat (Islamic law/Qur'an) and Tariqat (ways of Sufism) can be called as the perfect man and not the one who leaves their worldly duties for the love of beloved. Hafiz does not present his lover as a restless lover for his earthy and divinely beloved instead he is a moderate kind of lover who could control his emotions in a moderate way. As Hafiz asserts:

> "They ask what love is. Tell them Leaving the discretion. He who is not free from discretion is not a free man". I have said many a time, and I'll say it once again though I move upon this path, another one maintains my path (Hafiz, Ode 380)

Infact the lover in both Hafiz and Rumi's poetry, is completely free from all his negativity and hence the veil between him and the beloved does not exist:

> O lovers! If they ask who are you o dancers! Say we are the heart of hearts. There is no veil between the lover and the beloved. O Hafiz! You are your own veil; get out of the way. (Hafiz, Ode 266)

The lover at a certain point annihilates himself that he becomes one with the beloved. Hence there exist no duality but unity between lover and the beloved. In Rumi's Odes, too the lover reaches at a point where annihilation takes place. According to him at this very stage of annihilation the lover is happy, gay and in playful mood as he knows he is free from all the veils which once existed between him and the beloved. Rumi's Ode goes like these:

> He who I am the soil of his door, he is beating my ceiling and door.
> He who I am attached to, he is whirling round my head (Rumi, Ode 2093)
> Similarly, Hafiz Ode too goes like these:
> O Saqi, we are waiting on the shore by the sea of annihilation.
> Regard it, for the space between lip and mouth is nothing.
>
> (*Smith Hafiz Ode* 74)

Rumi and Hafiz, suggest the lover to be patient enough to endure all the pains in the path of love that might come their way to reach their destiny. They said whoever will be in this path should not leave half way because of the hindrance that may come across in that path but to continue with great patience and enthusiasm to meet their goal. Rumi and Hafiz have their unique way of portraying their experience on love through their poetry. Rumi's lover in his poetry seems to be free and frank in his love affair but Hafiz poetry is circled in the human level.

Rumi was aware of the difficult road of love still happily accepts it but Hafiz when he entered the difficult road of love expressed those in his poetry. Hafiz stated on the lover's painful condition through his poem *True love*, *The Cure for Blindness* respectively:

> Those who are truely in love are easy to spot:
>
> With yellow face strained with grief, they stand out in the crowd.
> (Crowe 56)
>
> O Beloved, is there no cure for our blindness?
> Give us back our eyes so that we may see Your face.
>
> (ibid 59)

Likewise Rumi too had explained on the difficult roads of love:

> 'Why is Love murderous from the first, so that he who is an outsider runs away'(Rumi, 3rd Vl.6999). Likewise Bulleh Shah had also expressed his pain and grief that he felt and experienced in his love's journey in the following manner:
>
> All the taunts have wounded me
> Agonising pain has captured me,
> Beloved should come to hold me:
> Heart is longing for the Beloved,
> Heart is longing for the Beloved! (Smith71)

Rumi himself is the symbol of lover who speaks with all frankness on his love affairs. Rumi's poetry deals with the lover whose love affair is mutual not one sided and he did not find any difference between the love and the beloved. Hence Rumi's love is a mutual affair between the lover and the beloved which is the true love between the creator and the creatures. But Hafiz, has put his the beloved in such a high position that the beloved becomes perfect as he puts her in the image of the perfect divine.

Bulleh Shah was radical for the inequality of his time, Rumi too were against the clergy. Qonya was very shocked that a person like Rumi who was the famous maulana of that time raised his voice against authority and fought for pursuing mystical ways which Shams had brought to him. Rumi comments in the *Critique of Rules* that if the authority would be in the hands of profligates Dhu'l Nun (Mystic of Egypt) is inevitably in prison. He also said that the authority and pen was in the hands of the traitor and that is why Mansur-al-Hallaj was criticised. In chapter II it is already discussed that in his later life after he crossed the stage of Sharia and specially after his meeting of Shams Rumi started losing his interest in the outer laws, obligations etc. and got involved into mysticism which Shams had gifted him. Instead, Rumi then started following all the Sufi ways to proceed towards mysticism like Dhikr (invocation of the names of Allah), Raabita (establishing a mutual bond), Muracjcjabah (watching and being vigilant to receive the light of truth) attending even Sama Mehfils (spiritual music concerts). For this change in Maulana his disciples were at raged because they did not want an outsider (Shams) to interfere and change their masters way from a strict follower of Shariat to a mystic. Later Shams disappeared in 1247 from the life of Rumi and had never happend to return.

Hafiz too had found hard to tolerate the hypocrisy of the society, authority, people, saints who wore the blue cloak to show that they are like the sky desire heaven but inside the clour of their heart was black. Hafiz asserts:

> I am the servant of all who scatter dregs of the cup and are clothed in one colour (Sincerity), but not of those whose bodies are clad in blue while black is the colour of their hearts. (Naini 8)

He also just like Bulleh Shah did not submit himself to any rule of orthodoxy and liberates him from all the rigid orthodoxy by the teaching of his master, Attar. There were many critics who accused Hafiz for his unorthodoxy attitude in his poetry including Shah Shuja, who being the minor poet was jealous and leaved no chance to criticise Hafiz. And in one occasion Shah Shuja keeping in mind to defeat Hafiz in a wit trial said that Hafiz poetry were unorthodox and a mixer of wine, love, God, Sufism, etc.

The ideology of all religion is based on love of God, which was also same for Hafiz who expressed it all and again in his 'Divan'. Hafiz says that love is the only element for which God has created his cosmos. And can only be found in human heart and through nothing but with love of God and his creations we can reach him. Hafiz had a similar notion with the other two Sufi poet on the outer religious norms:

> We are not in pursuit of formalities or fake religious laws, for through the stairway of existence we have come to God's Door. We are people who

> need to love, because love is the soul's life; love is simply creation's greatest joy. Through the stairway of existence, O, through the stairway of existence, Hafiz, have you now come, have we all now come to the Beloved's Door. (*Power Quotes on Love* web)

The similarities that we can find in these three Sufi poet is that all of them has an exemplary relationship with their master or friend or shiek. As Rumi with his friend cum master Shams, Hafiz with Muhammad Attar, Bulleh Shah with his master Innayat Khan, another great Sufi saint. All these three masters were responsible to initiate them into the Sufi path or God-realization. Another similarities between Hafiz and Bulleh Shah was that both revolted against the hypocrites of their time. Hafiz like Rumi uses the concept of friendship through which he could visualize God in them.

> "O breeze, if you reach the land over these of the friend
> Bring a scent of musky air from fragrant hair of the friend. Hafiz

Through this poems he expresses his inner urge for the union with God who he addresses as a friend and asking the wind to bring the scent of God as he could not see or visit God. Even though he can't see his friend God on the earth but desired to see him after his death. He also desires to remain a faithful servant to his friend or God. Hafiz too like Bulleh Shah tries to break the orthodox religious rules and embrace freely the truth. Hafez's ghazal read:

> Last night from the Masjed towards the wine tavern our Pir came:
> O friends of the Path! after this, what is our plan?
> How may we, disciples, turn to the Ka'ba, when
> Our Pir hath his face towards the house of the Vintner. (Homayoun 22)

The Sufi is indeed opposing all the rules and restrictions of the religious order to break free themselves from this dungeon of life. Hafiz too exchanged Similar notion with Rumi on the theme of separation between lover and the beloved/God. In his poem "*Grief of Separation*" Hafiz exchanged the similar notion on separation with Rumi. As he explained how separation is a feeling of grief which cannot be expressed in word but can only be felt in heart. And the stories of terror, the judgement described by the preacher is nothing but the pain of separation that everyone of us experience in our life time on earth. He also says it is pointless to ask anyone the whereabouts of the beloved friend as others may misguide us. Hafiz also urges us through this poem to come and join the old wine and winemaker (spiritual guide) and love of God which can lead us get forgiveness from our God. Hafiz also suggest us not to ask questions on this and that accepts God's sovereignty calmly.

> I heard a saying that by the old man of Canaan they say is said:
> "Grief of separation from the friend is such, it in no way is said".
> The tales of terror that the preachers tell about Judgement Day,
> Are only a hint of all the suffering when good-bye's day is said.
>
> (Smith 90)

God tried His best to bring peace and harmony among its creatures in every age. Christian mystic and theologian, Thomas Aquinas says that when he asked God to let him love God, God replied which part? He replied all of his part. Then God repeated his question and asked whether he would be able to love a small portion of cruelty and hatred of His world

> I said to God, let me love you. And he replied, which part? All of you, all of you. "I said. Dear Thomas, 'God spoke, you are as mouse wanting to impregnate a tiger who is not even in heat. I Said to God again, Beloved I need to love you-every aspect, every pore". God said, "There is a hidden blemish on my body, though it is an infinitesimal part of my Being – could you kiss that if it were revealed? ' I will try. Lord, I will try', God said. That blemish is all the hatred and cruelty in this world". (*Power Quotes on Love*, web.)

> For just as the body is one and has many members, and all the members of the body, though many, are one body, so it is with Christ. For in one spirit we were all baptized into one body – Jews or Greeks, slaves or free – and all were made to drink of one spirit. For the body does not consist of one member but of many. If the foot should say because I am not a hand, I do not belong to the body', that would not make it any less a part of the body. And if the ear should say, Because I am not an eye, I do not belong to the body', that would not make it any less a part of the body. If the whole body were an eye, where would be the sense of hearing? If the whole body were an ear, where would be the sense of smell? But as is it, God arranged the members in the body, each of them as he chose. If all were a single member, where would the body be? As it is, there are many parts, yet one body. The eye cannot say to the hand, 'I have no need of you,' On the contrary, the parts of the body that seem to be weaker are indispensable, and on those parts of the body that we think less honourable we bestow the greater honor, and our unrepresentable parts are treated with greater modesty, which our more presentable parts do not require. But God has so composed the body, giving greater honor to the part that lacked it, that there may be one division in the body, but that the members may have the same care for one another. If one members suffers, all suffer together; if one members is honored, all rejoice together.! Corinthians 12:12-26 (*Power Quotes on Love*, web)

Jack Hyles further comments on love in the following manner:

> You will never really love until you love someone who hates you. (ibid)

In *Bible* Mathew chapter five verses fourty four says:

> But love your enemies, do good to them, and lend to them without expecting to get anything back. Then your reward will be great... Luke, 6:27

All the religion believe in heaven and hell, angels (Al-Malaika) and devils, but by different names. In Islam, Christianity Judaism and Hinduism the different angels are bestowed with different responsibilities like in Islam angel Michael is assigned for Rain, and overseas the cultivation of crops. In Hinduism it is called Parjana Dev (angel) who was assigned for the same, Where Israil in Islam, Azrail in Christianity and Yama in Hinduism is assigned by the supreme soul/Allah/ God/ Brahman, for the purpose of claiming soul from the creatures of God. Jibril in Islam, Gabriel in Christianity and Narad Moni in Hinduism are the angels of communication between God and its creatures. In Qur'an it is mentioned that to every nation and people God has sent around 1,24000 prophets(messenger) but only twenty five names are mentioned in Qur'an. (Hadith, 266) Before Prophet Muhammad whoever was sent were for their people and nation but Muhammad was sent for all humanity and creatures of God. 'We sent you not, but As a mercy for all creatures'. (Qur'an, 21:107) To make it more clear we can quote *Hadith* from *Sahih Bukhari*:

> Allah's Messenger said every prophet used to be sent to his nation only but I have been sent to whole of humankind. (*Bukhari* 429).

To every nation and people God always send a Warner or informer about the right and wrong so in Qur'an too speaks about sending of guide or messenger/prophet to every nation and community according to their need and understanding level. And the followers/Ummah will be judged between them. As the *Qur'an* says:

> To every people (was sent) a Messenger when their messenger comes (before them), the matter will be judged between them with justice, and they will not be wronged.

> (*The Qur'an* 10:47) Say (O believer): we believe in Allah (God) and that which is revealed unto us and that which was revealed unto Abraham, and Ishmael, and Isaac, and Jacob, and the tribes, and that which Moses and Jesus received, and that which the prophets received from their lord. We make no distinction between any of them, and unto Him we have surrendered. (2:136)

In Hinduism those messengers are called as 'Avatar' which comes from the word 'Av' and 'Tr' means descend down or come down which means some special soul with special connection with divine comes down to earth for some special cause. In Christianity they are called as messenger and in Islam they are called as Prophets. 'Let no man in the world live in delusion. Without a Guru none can cross over to the other shore' (Guru Nanak web).In the Holy *Guru Grant Sahib* it is mentioned clearly that without a Guru (Messenger or Mediator) and inner purification (free from ego, hatred etc.) one cannot walk towards the divine path:

> False is friendship with false and greedy. False is its foundation. O mullah, no one knows where death shall strike. Without spiritual wisdom, the people worship ignorance. Without the Guru, there is no spiritual wisdom; without Dharma (righteous duty), there is no meditation. Without truth, there is no credit; without capital there is no balance. (web)

Here it says that without Dharma (rituals) one cannot communicate or meditate upon the divine. Therefore without a religious base one cannot be called as an enlightened being.

The angels or gods and goddess are the individual souls, like the human being but they unlike human has no earthly body but the soul body which is the body of the light and according to Hinduism, Christianity and Islam consciousness already exist in them without its beginning or ending. And these beings are purely genderless creature which is believed in both Qur'an, Bible, and the Vedas. Whenever they are strong and powerful we consider them as male, and female when gentle and compassionate but in reality they are neutral gender. For example Lakshmi and Saraswati are not regarded as wives of god Vishnu and Brahma but are the personified genderless deities extend abundance and learning.

> For Rumi humans are like water in the jug completely wrapped in the earthenware or surrounded by the worldly pleasure. To break the jug to flow, it needs to break first of all rules of religion, caste, creed, community, gender etc. He even called God by different names just like Hafiz and Bulleh Shah, sometimes as a cupbearer of wine, carrier of water bag or heart, and the moon etc.

God Sometimes gives us pain, shakes us and brought out all the nonsense inside us, all the erroneous notions of truth which dwells is us and makes us realize the truth of life. Through his poem *Tired of Speaking Sweetly,* Hafiz found to speak on our days of sorrows when we feel like God has forsaken us completely but in reality he wants to bring out the best in us by shaking us well with all the pains and sorrows:

> The beloved sometimes wants
> To do us a great favour;
> Hold us upside down
> And shake all the nonsense out.
> But when we hear
> He is in such a playful drunken mood. (Poems from Hafiz web)

The setup of so called rules in our life may hinder our spiritual growth. God does not belong to one community or religion, so if He himself does not categorize his creatures who we are to do so. The Sufis are also called as the heresy as they goes above the obstacles of religion and community, rules and regulations. In order to emerged into the truth that we have come from the same source of truth we must free oneself from that jug (rules).

For the Sufis God is more important than religion and so despite being known the fact to go astray follow the path of a rule free life. Among the three Sufi Poets, Rumi and Hafiz were the follower of Shariat till the end of their life on earth but Bulleh Shah though at the beginning was the follower of Shariat later broke free himself from all rules and regulation in the love of God. Religious rules and regulations are as necessary as the religion itself as it is the one which makes aware of our own identity with God. But those should not be an obstacle for our growth. As Religion is only necessary for an orderly and disciplined life. The Sufis also believe that religious rituals are necessary as it acts as knocking at God's door to call Him. Rumi in his poem *Everyone is welcome to this School* showed his liberal thought on all religious faith:

> The fly of the soul has fallen into
> This buttermilk forever.
> Muslim, Christian, Jew, and Zoroastrian:
> All are welcome here. (Ergin *The Rubais* 157)

Beyond everything and every rule of the world there is invisible way to explore. Therefore to explore the invisible which is the secret of God's essence one must move above all the prescribed norms of the world. Instead of judging and fighting with each other's faith one must follow the path towards the union. Rumi asserts:

> There is a better way for you to use your wings.
> High above the dome of the sky
> There is a new and invisible way for you to play. (Ibid 158)

Rumi through his poem suggest us not to be victim of the material world but to be agent of the spiritual world for development and raise of humanity.

> O heat, listen to the song of the nightingale,
> Not the braying of the donkey.
> O heart, go and loot the rose garden.
> The thorns can't hurt you.

One of the most influential recent proponent of core pluralism, Hutson Smith (b.1919) is of the view that all religion which follows some common core are same religion. He also asserts that the "absolute Truth", "The True Reality" or the 'God' is the celestial plane and he is nothing but our personal God. It is the source of all our desires, and the core of truth that exist within our self. Human 'spirit' is the highest self which lies under an ordinary self of ours. He also believes that our soul is the source of supreme soul called 'Atman' or 'Brahman", and it can be visible only when we surrender our finite selves: My istigkeit (is-ness) which---we see in God's is-ness. (Smith 3-4) And that is why Gurdjieff emphasize on the development or transformation of the 'Self'. Gaining knowledge on self is important as it is an esoteric change that one has to undergo. But the main concentration on the Self is no gain until unless we apply it on our 'Self'. We have to make effort on our Self by observation on how and why we behave and act in particular way. (Patterson web)

William Patrick Patterson in his journal on *Gurdjieff, Sifism & Muhammad* quotes Gurdief in his vision of Christianity, where he said that Christianity or the worship of one God exist before the birth of the Christ as he said: 'There were Christians long before the advent of Christianity' (Patterson web).Ouspensky too found reporting Gurdjieff in the similar manner:

> It will seem strange to many people when I say that this prehistoric Egypt was Christian many thousands of years before the birth of Christ, that is to say, that its religion was composed of the same principles and ideas that constitute true Christianity – the Christian church, the Christian form of worship, was not invented by the fathers of the church. It was all taken in a ready-made form from Egypt, only not from the Egypt we know but from one which we do not know. This Egypt was in the same place as the other but it existed much earlier. (Ibid)

In the poem *The Moment you are With yourself* Rumi comments if we will think about ourselves we will suffer of disappointment but if we will start thinking and doing things selflessly we will be happy forever. He asserts:

> The moment that you are with yourself,
> You are under the clouds of sorrows;
> And the moment that you are selfless,
> The moon will come to your side. (Helinski & Rezwani 11)

Hence non-existence is the real existence or truth. As Rumi asserts:

> The lack of any sign or evidence whatsoever
> Is the sign and evidence of this beloved.
> (Ergin & Johnson *The Rubais* 92)

> In order to be admitted into the asylum of love
> I went completely crazy and lost my mind. (ibid 93)

In Veda it is said that we should love our neighbour as we love ourselves. But a question arises that we feel both pain and happiness only in ourselves and not in our neighbour so why should one love to their neighbour. In reply it is mentioned that the veil between our neighbour and ourselves is a mere illusion and not a reality. In Gita it says:

> He who know himself in everything and everything in himself, will not injure himself by himself. This is the sum and tenor of all morality, and this is the standpoint of a man knowing himself a Brahman. (Bell,2015:42)

Bulleh Shah through his poem shows that our soul do not possess any religion, Caste creed, nationality etc. but it is eternal neither it has a beginning nor an ending which is also the truth/divine. Instead he only talks God and his relationship with His creatures:

> I take myself to be the beginning and the end;
> I do not recognize aught except the One. (Smith 201)

After he realized the truth he had devoted his life in the path of humanity and truth by delivering his message of oneness of God among the people though his poetry. And all of our try to be restfulness makes us restless. Rumi says we must be so hard working that rest will search us. Because if we search for something we will never get that, so it's better to be empty and selfless then only all the objects of our desire will turn towards us as a gift from God.

> All of our displeasure is due
> To your seeking pleasure.
> Abandon pleasures, and austerity

Would become a pleasure to you.
All of your frustrations are due
To you seeking your wishes
If you didn't all wishes would
Come to you like offerings. (Rezwani 12)

Therefore once we learn to deal with our desire we would no longer desire anything and hence would attain all those desired for.

Mikael Stenmark, the Swedish Philosopher is of the view that the three religion Judaism, Christianity and Islam is originated from the same core faith or these are the different version of the same monotheism or Abrahamic monotheism. He also says that "some are equally right view" which means all the faith are right in the same degree. (Stenmark 2009) The pluralism Hiduism asserts the slogan that "all religions are true". (Sharma, 1999:ch.6) Which means nothing but all religion are directing us towards the same 'Absolute Truth' or God. According to Raja Ram Mohun Roy Hinduism, Christianity and Islam if understood from their real origin, all teach the same truth of the same Divine and mankind. In his lifetime he did not even liked to be called himself as a Hindu or a Brahmin. (Sharma ch. 2)

According to Peter Byrne (2004: 201-10) all major religions are equal in that they refer to and facilitate cognitive contact with a single, transcendent reality, each offers a similar moral – and eternal – oriented "cure" and each includes revisable and incomplete accounts of this transcendent reality.

The Sufis followed the Shariat (Islamic law) where the ritual of Salah (Five times prayer) was included. It is said that all our rituals is a stepping stone towards our divine. And Salah is nothing but expressing the reverence to God for his boundless compassion and mercy towards humanity. It is also a way of submission and devotion to God. As there are several ways of worshipping God and Salah is one of them. Some pray to an imagined form of God my making idol or statue some see him in light and some search it in the formless. Some pray in silent and some with music and dance. Therefore no matter whatever is the way of expressing their devotion towards God the objective is the same to attain the divine connection or His approval of us.

No doubt God is omnipotent, omniscient and omnipresent and can understand the intension of the devotees no matter whatever way they call him. Mass prayer existed in almost all the religion including Christianity, Islam and Hinduism.

> Set up regular prayers, for such prayers are enjoined
> On believers at stated times. (*The Qur'an* 4:103)

The muslims go for mass prayer five times in a day and Christians and Hindus and Buddhist too goes to their respective prayer house to offer prayer to God. Therefore this mass prayer is a concept of showing equality as there will be no one superior or inferior in the house of God. The most important thing about this rituals are to eradicate all the evils from us. That is why the Sufis too followed Shariat or Salah (Namaz) which helps them removes all the dirt from their heart. Salah consist of four sections which includes recitation of verses of Quar'an, which are nothing but the praises of God and a way to show faith in his instructions.

Recite what is sent of the book (Qur'an) by inspiration to thee and establish regular

> prayer: For prayer restrains from shameful and evil deeds; and remembrance of Allah (God) is the greatest (thing in life). (The Qur'an 29:45)Therefore remember Me, I will remember you, Give thanks to Me, reject not Me. (2:152)

The chanting and prayer verses are the praise and remembrance of God and same in meaning in almost all the religion as they all chant the divine name or praise Him to guide us in the right path. In every religion and faith the way of worshiping God might be different but the words or verses that they utter during the prayer is more or less same in meaning. The *Upanishad* says:

> May we hear only what is good for all
> May we see only what is good for all.
> May we serve you, lord of love, all our life.
> May we be used to spread your peace
> On earth. (Easwaran 224)

In Surah *Al-Fatihah* (The Opening) *The Quar'an* says:

> Guide us to the Straightway
> The Way of those on whom you have bestowed your Grace,
> not (the way) of those who earned Your Anger,
> nor of those who went astray. (*The* Quar'an 1:6-7)

The *Bible* too says the same in verses thirteen of chapter six of the Gospel of Mathew:

> And lead us not into temptation, but deliver us from evil:
> For thine is the kingdom, and the power, and the glory, forever. Amen.
> (Mathew 6:13)

Similar concept can be found in the Sikhs meditation as they also believe in chanting divine names and charity just like the Sufis. Which can be seen in the three most important teaching of GuruNanak:

(i) Chanting the Holy Name and thus remembering God at all times.

(ii) Making a living honestly, without exploitation or fraud.

(iii) Sharing with others, helping those with less who are in need.

The Holy *Quar'an, Surah Bakara* (cow) says: Eastablish worship, pay the poor due, and low your heads with those who bow (worship). (2:43) It also says, Say: call upon Allah (God), or call upon Rahman (Attributes to Allah, the most Gracious): By whatever name you call upon Him (it is well): For to Him belong The Most Beautiful Names (Attributes). (*The Qur'an* 17:110) Even in Hinduism if there are different gods those are nothing but the different attributes of the Absolute God. Gita Chapter seven verses twenty three says: man of small knowledge who worship the demi gods goes to the planet of demi gods but those who worship me would come to my seven planet. Again in Chapter thirteen verses fourteen says:

> Super soul is a light. All things comes from the divine source.
> I am the beginning, middle, and end of creation.
> Of all the sciences I am the science of Self-
> Knowledge, and I am logic in those who debate.
> Among letters I am A; among grammatical
> Compounds I am the dvandva. I am infinite time,
> And the sustainer whose face is seen everywhere. (Easwaran 188)

Hence every religion is a blend or a mixture or an amalgamation of the other. The famous Jewish Scholar and author, Hugh Schonfied asserts that the sufis in the beginning had its root in Zoroastrian Magi and had established many of its schools in the Middle East, in Mosul and the later joined by Jewish refugees from Egypt which were the victim of Roman percecution. As Schonfied states:

> There were religious fusions and amalgamations, and the emergence of spiritual hybrids. Zoroastrianism and Mithraism lent their characteristics to Jewish Essence teaching, and found a Greek expression in the Hermetic and Christian Gnostic. The coverage of the Roman empire right round the Mediterrean carried the cults with it, and opened the way of new blendings. (Schonfield 166)

That is how Sufism was continuously invigorating by many other believes. And during the time of prophet Muhammad the entire Arab civilization was in danger because of war, earthquake, global pestilence, gender inequalities by the Byzantine Christianity the Sufis change their adherence from Zoroastrianism to Islam as Islam was becoming the source of providing with safety, security, justice for humanity. In this way the Persian teaching, wisdom had transformed to the Muslim culture and gradually spread all over the world through the great Sufi saints.

Therefore the Hindus, Muslims, Christians and Jews must pick up the holy book of each other so that everyone despite mere prejudice can understand each other's beliefs. Therefore before judging we must understand each other's faith then only unity among us could be possible. If we can bring back that unity in diversity we are successful in some extent.

Hence every religion has different image of their God, as some believe it's a light, for some its formless, some see him in a form or body or image as no one could see God in reality but can feel His existence all around. One can say that our divine is the same but our way to Him is different. Therefore nobody is wrong in their perception on God. Rumi says if we look at others as other and not we then we are multiple and not one and if we start judging good or bad the trouble starts there and we will never grow until unless we free ourselves from all this boundaries. As he utters in his *Rubais*:

> Since we start seeing others
> We're no longer one
> We've become multiple. (Ergin& Johnson *The Rubais* 68)

It is better not to explain all the secret between you and your divine to everyone. As the secret may vary from individual to individual to comprehend it properly. There is a saying that if we understand and experience too much of anything we can't explain it properly until unless the person himself experience the same. Different people have different way and concept of their divine so it is better not to talk and criticise beyond one's faith. Rumi argues that it is better to make them understand the same through their own faith. In other word it is better not to force your faith on them which could be termed as Intolerance. As Rumi through his *Rubais* States:

> Don't reveal secrets to those who don't believe
> don't tell the beloved's story to an outcast
> don't speak to stranger who can't understand
> Don't talk to a thorn-eating camel about anything but thorns. (Ibid 87)

Despite having different views all these three Sufi poet tried to bring peace and unity among the people of all religion. In order to bring peace and unity among the people of all religion Rumi happened to say in an unpublished manuscript "*The Quatrains of Rumi*' translated by Ibrahim Gamard and Ravan Farhadi, that he was neither a Muslim nor a Christian neither he belongs to East nor West. Similar words were uttered by Bulleh Shah after decades through his poem "Neither Hindu nor Muslim". In bringing oneness among people Hafiz was also not lagging behind. As he also uttered through his poem *Strive* (Smith 184*)* that there needs no mosque if your heart is unclean or impure:

> Kaaba and house of idols are not one when there is no purity:
> All is not well when in house of the heart, purity is not.

Hafiz like Bulleh Shah too came out from an orthodox family believed and opted the liberal thoughts where he did not put any limitation in his thought and believe. In his poem *I Have Learned So Much,* describes how he has learned so much from God that he does not even consider himself as a Christian, Hindu, Muslim, Buddhist or a Jew, neither a man nor a woman. And he also says that his love for God freed himself by burning every aspect of him into ashes and thus he become free of every concept and believe, that his mind was holding since long. As he utters:

> The Truth has shared so much of itself
> With me
> That I can no longer call myself
> A man, a woman, an angel,
> Or even pure
> Soul. (Poems of Hafiz, web)

One can find Hafiz says that every person we meet we expect them to love us unconditionally but we do not dare to speak that out aloud but we want to be understood, we want to be loved, then why do we not start loving and understanding each other. As Hafiz spoke through his poem *With That Moon Language*:

> Admit something:
> Everyone you see, you say to them,
> "Love me"
> Of course you do not do this out loud;
> Otherwise,
> Someone would call the cops.
> Still though, think about this,
> This great pull in us
> To connect. (Ibid)

Just like Rumi and Hafiz, Bulleh Shah's poems were also not only admired in his time but also adopted by both street singers and renowned singers of both Indian and Pakistani film industry. Therefore the three Sufi poets through their poetry tried to bring oneness in the world; a sense of unity in diversity. P B Shelley asserts that 'those who love not their fellow-beings, live unfruitful lives'. (*Powers Qoutes,* 70)

Therefore we all are one and are mutually supporting each other on this cosmos of God. Gurdjieff's notion of 'world-creation' is derived from 'an old Sumerian manuscript' discovered by a philosopher named as Kurdish which says in this way: 'Everything that exist maintains and is maintained by other existence.' Which says that our universe is like a web where everyone and everything supports each other beautifully and passionately (Lepage).

Works Cited

Primary Sources

Hafiz, Shamsuddin Muhammad. *Divan of Hafiz*. Translated by Paul Smith. Vol.2, Melbourne: New Humanity Books, 1986,Print.

..........*Divan*, edited by Muhammad Ghazvini and Ghasem Qani, Tehran 2004.Print.

..........*Drunk on the Wine of the Beloved: 100 Poems of Hafiz*. Translated by Thomas Rain croowe, Boston & London, shambhala,2001. Print.

.... Hafiz: The Oracle. Translated with introduction and interpretations by Paul Smith. New Humanity Books; Book Heaven Book sellers and Publishers, 2012, Print.

.... *The Garden of Heaven: Poems of Hafiz*.Translated by Daniel Ladinsky. New York:Dover publication Inc., 2003

.... The Garden of Heaven: Poems of Hafiz. Translated by Getrude Bell. Dover Publications. 2017, Print.

.... *Fifty Poems of Hafiz*. Translated by Arthur, J.Arberry. Reprint, Richmond Surrey.Uk: Curzon Press,1993.Print.

.... *Persian Lyrics or Scattered Poems from the Divan-i-Hafiz: With Paraphrases in Verses and Prose*. Translated by John Haddon Hindley. Manchester: Oriental Press, 1799.Print.

.... *Teaching of Hafiz*. Translated by Gertrude, Lowthian Bell. Reprint, With a Preface by E. Densison Ross and Introduction by Idrish Shah, London: Octagon Press, 1979, Print.

.... The Teachings of Hafiz. Translated by Gertrude Lowthian Bell. Pinnacle Press, an imprint of Creative Media Partners, 2017, Print.

.... *The Tangled Braid: Ninety-nine Poems by Hafiz of Shiraz*. Translated by Jeffrey Einboden & John Slater. Fons Vitae, 2009, Print.

.... *The Gift*. Translated by Daniel, Ladinsky. London: Penguin, 1999. Print.

.... *Ghazal of Hafez Shirazi in Persian with English Translation*, compiled and corrected by Behrouz Homayoun Far, 2001, Print.

.... *I Heard God Laughing: Poems of Hope and Joy*.Trans. Daniel, Ladinsky. New York: Penguin, 2006, Print.

..........*The Rubais of Hafiz*. Translated by Sayed Abdullah Majid. FB & C Ltd. Dalton House.2015.

.... *The Rubaiyat of Hafiz*. Translated by Syed Abdul Majid, LL. D.Rendered in English by L. Cranmer – Byng. E.P. Dutton and Company. 1915. Print.

.... *The subject Tonight is Love: 60 wild and Sweet Poems Of Hafiz*. Trans. Daniel, Ladinsky. U S: Penguin Book, 2003. Print.

.... *The Poems of Hafez*, Translated by Reza Ordoubadian, Ibex Publishers, 2006, Print.

.... *Poems From The Divan of Hafiz*. Translated by Gertrude Lowthian Bell. William Heinemann.1897. Print

Rumi, Jalal-ud-din. Rumi, *Divan-i Shamsi Tabriz*. Edited by Badi'uzzaman Furuzanfar. vols.10, IJ of Tehran Publication, 1957-67.

.... *Love's Ripening: Rumi on the Heart's Journey*. Translated by Kabir Helminski And Ahmad Rezwani. Shambhala Publication.2010.Print.

.... *Selected Poems from the Divmi Shamsi Tabriz*. Trans. R.A. Nicholson. Cambridge UP, 1977.

.... *Sign of The Unseen*: The Discourses of Jala-ud-din Rumi. Trans. W.M. Thackston, J.R. Putney. Vermont: Threshold Books, 1994. Print.

.... *The Analysis and Interpretation of Masnavi-ye Sharif*. Edited by Abdul-baqi Golpinarli. vols.3, The Publication Press of the Ministry of Culture and Islamic Guidance, 1995, Print.

.... *The Essential Rumi. Trans.* Coleman Barks. New York: Harper Collins, 2004.Print.

.... *Kulliyat-e Shams*, edited by Forouzanfar Badi-uz-zaman, Tehran, 1988. Ode 190.

.... *The soul of Rumi: New Collection of Ecstatic Poems*. Trans. Coleman Barks. New York: Harper Collins., 2001.Print.

.... *The Sufi Path of Love*: The Spiritual Teaching of Rumi. Trans. William C. Chittik. Albany: State University of New York Press, 1983, Print.

.... *The Forbidden Rumi*. Translated by Nevit O. Ergin, and Will Johnson. New Delhi: Inner Traditions India, 2006, Print.

.... *The Illuminated Rumi*. Translated by Coleman Barks and Michel Green. New Yprk: Broadway,1999,Print.

.... *Selected Poems of Rumi*. Translated by R. A., Nicolson. Mineola: Dove, 2001, Print.

.... *The Pocket Rumi*. Translated by Kabir Helminski. Shambhala Publication, 2000. Print.

.... *The Purity of Desire*: 100 Poems of Rumi. Translated by, Ladinsky, Daniel and Nancy, Owen, Barton, US: Penguin Books, 2012, Print.

.... *The Rubais of Rumi:Insane with Love*.Translated by Nevit O. Ergin and Will Johnson.Inner Traditions. 2007. Print.

.... *Teaching of Rumi*: *The Masnavi*. Translated by. E.H, Whinfield. Octagon Press. 1994. Print.

.... *Mathnawi-I.*Translated by R. A Nicholson. Ed. *The Mathnawi of Jalaluddin Rumi.* Luzac, 1925. Print.

.... *Mathnawi-I.* Translated by S.H. Nasr.ed. *Rumi Lament of the Reed.* Asr Media, 2000, Print.

.... *Mathnawi-III.* Translated by Camelia Helminski and Kabir Helminski. Shambhala Publication, 2000, Print.

.... *Me and Rumi: The autobiography of Shams-i-Tabriz.* Translated by William C. Chittick. Fons Vitae, 2004, Print.

.... *Mystical Poems of Rumi.* Translated by A. J., Arberry. Boulder: West View Press. 1979. Print.

.... *Dar-Al-Masnavi*: Mathnawi III. Translated by Helminski, Kabir and Ahmad Rezwani. 1998. Print.

Shah, Bulleh. *Baba Bulleh Shah: The Pearl of Punjab.*Translated by Parvez Iqbal Anjum. Printed in The US, 2017, Print.

.... *Bulleh Shah:Selected Poems.* Translated by Paul Smith. New Delhi: Book Heaven. Booksellers & Publishers. 2006. Print.

.... *Bulleh Shah: A Selection.*Trans. Taufiq, Rafat. London: Oxford University Press, 2014, Print.

.... Bulleh Shah: Sufi Lyrics. Translated and edited by Christopher Shackle. Harvard university Press, 2015, Print.

.... *Sain, Bulleh Shah: The Mystical Muse.* Trans. K.S. Duggal. New Delhi: Hind Pocket Pvt.ltd. 2010. Print.

.... *The Book of bulleh Shah.* Translated by Paul Smith. Book Humanity Books, Booksellers & Publishers, 2015, Print.

Secondary Sources

Abrams, M.H. *Natural Supernaturalism: Tradition and Revolution in Romantic Literature.* WW Norton & Co.1973, Print.

Ad-Dimashqi Imam Imaduddin Abdul-Fida Ismail Ibn Kathir. *Stories of The Prophets. Darussalam*, 2003, Print.

Ahmad, Ishtiaq. *Studying Bulleh Shah's Select Poetry in the Perspective of Sufism.* Open Publishing GmbH.2017, Print.

Al-Jilani, Abdul al-Qadir. *The Endowment of Divine Grace and the spread of Divine Mercy.vo.1.* Philadelphia: Pearl Publishing House, 1990. Print.

---.*The Secret of Secrets.* Enterpreted by Shaykh Tosun Bayrak. Cambridge: Islamic Text Society, 1992.Print.

.... *The Book of the Secret of the Secrets and The Manifestation of Lights.* Kitab Bhavan, 2011, Print.

Arberry, A. J. *An Account Of The Mystical Of Islam.* New Delhi: Cosmos Publication, 2003. Print.

.... *Sufism: An Account of the Mystics*. Translated by Arthur J. Arberry. London: Dover Publication, 2001.Print.

.... *Arabic Poetry*. Cambridge university Press.1965.Print.

.... *Introduction to the History of Islam*. London: Longman, 1943. Print.

.... *The Kuran* Interpreted, London: Oxford University Press.1964.Print.

As-Sufi Abdal-Quadir. *The Way of Muhammad*. Diwan Press. 1975. Print.

Attar, Fariduddin. *Muslim Saints and Mystics*. Translated by Arthur J. Arberry. London: Arkana, 1990.Print.

.... *Perfume of the Desert: Inspirations from Sufi Wisdom*. Translated by Andrew Harvey and Eryk Hanut. USA: Quest Books, 1999. Print.

.... *The Conference of Birds*. Translated with an Introduction by Afkham Darbandi and Dick Davis. Published by Penguin Group, 2011, Print.

Baba, Meher. *The Everything and the Nothing*. Beacon Hill: Meher House Publications, 1989. Print.

Bal, Rabisankar. *A Mirrored Life: The Rumi Novel*. Translated by Sinha, Arunava. Penguin Random House.2015. Print.

Barks, Coleman. *Rumi Soul Fury: Rumi and Shams on Friendship*. US: Harper Collins Publisher. 2013. Print.

Browne, E.G.*A Literary Hostory of Persia*. Vol.3.London: Cambridge University Press. 1920. Print.

Bruijn, J.T.P. De. Persian *Sufi Poetry: An Introduction to the Mystical Use of Classical Poems*. Richmond: Curson Press, 1997. Print.

Byrne, Peter. "It is not Reasonable to Belief that Only the One Religion is True". *Contemporary Debates in Philosophy of Religion*. Ed. Michael Peterson and Raymond Van Arrogon. Malden, MA: Blackwell, 2004. Print.

Byron, George Gordon. *Lord Byron: Selected Poetry*, edited by Jerome J. McGann, Oxford University Press, 1998, Print.

Chittik, W.C. *Sufism-A Short Introduction*. Oxford: One World, 2000. Print.

Dehlvi, Sadia. *Sufism: the Heart of Islam*. New Delhi: Harper Collins Publisher India, 2009. Print.

.... *The Sufi Path of Love: The Spiritual Teachings of Rumi*. New York Press, 1983. Print.

Chopra, R. M. *Great Sufi Poet of Punjab*. Iran Society. 1999. Print.

Danner, Victor. Trans. *The Book Of Wisdom*. (19978). N J: Paulist Press.1988. Print.

.... *The Islamic Tradition: an Introduction*. N J: Sophia Perennis, 2005. Print.

Encychopaedia Brittanica. 14th.ed., 1968, Print.

Dabashi, Hamid. *Ayn al-Qudat Hamadani and the Intellectual Climate of his Times, in History of Islamic Philosophy*, edited. by Seyyed Hossein Nasr and Oliver Leaman, vol. 2 Routledge, 2002, Print.

Easwaran, Eknath. *The Upanishad*. Jaico Publication House. 2017. Print.

.... *The Bhagavad Gita.* Jaico Publishing House,2017, Print.

.... *Conquering The Mind.*Jaico Publishing House. 2017.Print.

Ernst, Carl W. *Sufism: An Introduction to the Mystical Tradition of Islam.* Boston: Shambala, 1997. Print.

Evan, Maurice. *Elizabethan Sonnets.* Phoenix Press, 1994, Print.

Freud, Sigmund. *Psychoanalysis and Gender: An Introductory Reader*, edited by Rosalind Minsky, Routledge, 1996, Print.

Ghazal is a lyric form common to Arabic, Persian, Turkish, and Urdu literature, typically concerned with earthly or mystical love and in couplets. *Encyclopedia of Literature in Canada*, edited by William Herbert New, University of Toronto Press, 2002.

Ghosh, Aurobindo. *Pondicherry Savitri*: Sri Aurobindo Ashram, 1973. Print.

Gibbon, Bob and Sian Pritchand Jones. *Bulleh Shah: A Sufi Mystic of the Punjab.* India: Pilgrims Publishing, 2008. Print.

Gillani, Khursheed Ahmad, Syed. *Spirit of Mysticism*, Fareed Book Stall, Lahore, 1981,Print.

Glunz, Michael and J. Christoph Burgel. Editors. *Amguity: A Study in the use of Religious Terminology in the Poetry of Hafiz.* Peter Lang.Inc.1991. Print.

Gurdjieff, G.I. *Meeting With Remarkable Man.* London: Routhledge & Kegan Paul. 1971. Print.

Golpinarali. *Introduction to Aflaki.* 1959. Print.

Hashmi, Prof. Hameed Ullah. *You are my Divine Love.* Explanation by Khawaja Ghulam Fareed, Maktaba Daniyal, 2001.

Helminski, Camilla & Kabir Helminski. Editors. *Mascetti, Manual Dunn. Rumi: The Path of Love.*1999, Print.

Horowitz, Gregg M., *Sustaining Loss: Art and Mournful Life,* Stanford University Press, 2001, Print.

Higginbotham, Blake. *We Are One: In Fullness of Time..* the consummation of all things. A.K. A. Publication, 2016, Print.

Hujwiri, *Ali bin Uthman. kashf Al Mahjub*, translated by R. A Nicholson, Adam Publisher, Delhi, 2006, Print.

Isaac, D'Israeli Romances, London: printed for Cadell and Davies, Strand; Murray and Highley, Fleet-Street; J. Harding, St. James's-Street; and J. Wright, 1799.

Javadi, Hasan. *Persian Literary Influence on English Literature, with Special Reference to the Nineteenth Century*, Mazda Publishers, 2005 p. 52.

Jones, William. *The Works of Sir William Jones.* vol. 6, London. G G nd J. Robinson.1799. Print.

Keats, John. *John Keats: Selected Poetry,* edited by Elizabeth Cook, Oxford University Press, 1998. Print.

Khan, Inayat. *The Sufi Message of Inayat Khan*, Vol.x. London: Barrie and Jenkins. 1964. Print.

Kipling, Rudyard. *Kim*. Macmillan & Co.ltd.1901. Print.

Kirschner, R. Suzanne. *The Religious and Romantic Origins of Psychoanalysis: Individuation and Integration in Post-Freudian Theory*. Cambridge University Press, 1996, Print.

Lacan, Jacques. *God and the Jouissance of The Woman, in Feminine Sexuality: Jacques Lacan and the École Freudienne,* edited by Juliet Mitchell and Jacqueline Rose, translated by J. Rose, Macmillan Press, 1992, Print.

Lessing, Doris. *The Four Gated City*. New York: Knopf, 2009. Print.

Lewis, Franklin D. *Rumi: Past and Present, East and West: The Life, Teaching and Poetry of Jalâl al-Din Rumi*. Oneworld, 2001. Print

Lewisohn, Leonard. Interview with Shusha Guppy. "*Heart and Soul*." BBC World 25 Nov. 2008.

Mannani, Manijeh. *Divine Deviants: The Dialectics of Devotion in Donne and Rumi*. Peter Lang Publishing, 2007. Print.

Murray, Christopher John, *Encyclopedia of the Romantic Era, vol. 2,* Fitzroy Dearborn, 2004. Print.

Hartman Geoffrey H., *The Geoffrey Hartman Reader*, edited by Geoffrey H. Hartman and Daniel T. O'Hara, Edinburgh University Press, 2004, Print.

Moyne, John A. *Rumi and the Sufi Tradition: Essays on the Mowlavi order and Mysticism Quotes*, Binghamton University: Global Publication, IGCS, 1998, Print.

Naini, Majid M. *Mysteries of the Universe and Rumi's Discoveries on the Mystic Path of Love*. US: Universal Vision Research,2002, Print.

Naik, Zakir. *Concept of God in Major Religions*. Adam Publishers and distributors. 2007, Print.

Nasr, Seyyed Hossein. *Sufi Essays,* State University of New York Press, 1973, Print.

.... *Sufi Essays*. 2nd ed., State University of New York Press, 1991. Print.

Nicholson, R.A. *The Mystics of Islam*. London.: Arkana,1989, Print.

.... *Rumi: Poet and Mystic*. Unwins Paperbacks, 1978. Print.

.... *Studies in Islamic Mysticism*. Jayed Press,1976.Print.

.... *The Mathnawi of Jalalu'ddin Rumi*. vol. 8. Cambridge UP, 1940.

Nurbaksh, Javad. *Traditions of the Prophet: Ahadith*. New York: Khaniqahi-Nima-Tullahi Publicatios, 1981, Print.

Ouseley, William. *Persian Miscellanies: An Essay to Facilitate the Reading of Persian Manuscripts; with Engraved Specimens, Philological Observations, and Notes Critical and Historical*, London: Printed for Richard White, 1795.

Ouspensky, P.D. *In Search of the Meraculous: Fragments of an Unkown Teaching*. New York: Harcourt, Brace & World. 1949, Print.

Puri, J.R. *Bulleh Shah (1680-1758): The Love Intoxicated Iconclast*. Translated by T.R., Shangari. India: Radhasoami Satsang Beas.1986, Print.

Rehdar, R. M. *The Unity of the Ghazals of Hafiz*. Der Islam.1974. Print.

Saberi, Reza. *The Divan of Hafiz: bilingual Text Persian-English*. U S: University Press of America, 2002, Print.

Sahih Al-Bukhari. Vol 1, Vol 2, Vol 3, Vol 4, vol 5, vol 6, Vol 7, Vol 8. Translated by Dr Muhammad Muhsin Khan. Darussala Publisher and Distributors. Riyadh-Saudi Arabia.1997. Print.

Salzmann, Jeanne. *The Reality of Being*. Boston: Shambhala, 2010, Print.

Sattari, Jalal. *Haalaat-e Eshq-e Majnoun*. Tous, 2006, Print.

Seyed-Gohrab, Ali Asghar. *A Narration of Love: An Analysis of the Twelfth Century Persian Poet Nizami's Layli and Majnun*, Universiteit Leiden, 2001, Print.

Schimmel, Annamarie. *A Two – Colored Brocade: The Imagery of Persian Poetry*. Chapel Hill: The University of North Carolina Press, 1992, Print.

………. *Deciphering the Signs of God: A Phenomenological Approach to Islam*. SUNY Press, 1994, Print.

………. *The Genius of Shiraz: Sa'di and Hafiz*.albany: Bibliotheca Persica.1988.Print.

………. *Love is a Stranger.: Selected Lyric Poetry of Jalaluddin Rumi*. Shambhala Publications, 2000, Print.

………. *Mystical Dimension of Islam*. Chapel Hill: University of North California Press, 1975, Print.

………. Rumi's World: The Life and Work of the Great Sufi Poet.Shambhala.2001. Print.

Schonfield, J. Hugh. *The Essence Odyssey*. Element Book, 1984. Print.

Scott, Ernest. *People of the Secret*. London: Octagon Press.1983. Print.

Smith, Hutston. *Beyond the Postmodern Mind: The Place of Meaning in a Global Civilization, Updated and Revised*. Wheaton, Illinois: Quest books, 2003.

Smith, Paul. *Bulleh Shah: Life and Poems: Introduction to Sufi Poets Series Book 11*. India: New Humanity Books, 2014, Print.

Shah, Idries. *The Sufis*. New York: Doubleeday, 2006,Print.

………, *The Sufis*. New York: Anchor Books,1971.Print.

………,. A Perfumed Scorpion. London: Octagon Press, 1983.Print.

Shafak, Alif. *The Forty Rules of Love*. Penguin Random House. 2015. Print.

Sharma, Arvind. *The Concept of Universal Religion in Modern Hindu thought*. New York: St. Martins's Press, 1999, Print.

Shelley, Percy Bysshe. *Shelley's Poetry and Prose: Authoritative Texts, Criticism*, edited by Donald H. Reiman and Sharon B. Powers, W. W. Norton & Company, 1977. Print.

Sindhi, Abdul Majeed, *Mystic Movements in Pakistan*, Sang-e-Meel Publications Lahore, 2000, Print.

Sing, Jagtar. *Bulleh Shah-Jeevan Ate Rachna*. New Delhi: Unister Books.2008.Print.
Srimad Bhagavad Gita. Time Group Books, Coleman and Co. Ltd., 2017, Print.

Sigmund Freud, *Psychoanalysis and Gender: An Introductory Reader*, edited by Rosalind Minsky, Routledge, 1996. Print.

Soroush, Abdul-Karim. *Amorous Gambling: Shams and Mawlana.* Serat Cultural In stitution, 2000. Print.

Stallworthy, John. *Love Poems.* Penguin Book Series. 1981. Print.

Stoddart, William. Sufism: *The Mystical Doctrines and Methods of Islam.* 2nd ed., London: Paragon House of Publishers, 1998, Print.

Strachey, James. *Group Psychology and the Analysis of the Ego.* The Hogarth Press. 1948. Print.

Symons, Arthu. The Symbolist movement in Literature.New York: Heskell house Publishers Ltd., 190, Print.

The Holy Qur'an. Translated by Allahmah Nooruddin. Noor Foundation. 2007. Print.

Tchekhovitch, Tcheslaw. *Gurdjieff: a Master in Life.* Toronto: Dolmen Meadows.2006. Print.

The Bhagavad Gita. Translated by Eknath Easwaran. Jaico Publication House, 2017, Print.

*The Teaching of Guru Nanak.*www.hinduwebsite.com.Accessed 12 Feb. 2018.

Thoreau, David Henry. *Walden; or, Life in the Woods* (1854). Edited by Jeffrey Cramer, New Heaven: Yale University Press, 2004, Print.

Utas, Bo.The Literary Expression of Persian Sufism, in Mysticism*: Based on Papers Read at the Symposium on Mysticism Held at Åbo on the 7th-9th September, 1968*, ed. by Sven S. Hartman and Carl-Martin Edsman, Almqvist & Wiksell, 1970.

Walbridge, John. *The Wisdom of the Mystic East: Suhrawardi and platonic Orientalism,* State University of New York, 2001.

Warren Hastings, *Memoirs of the Life of Warren Hastings.* Edited by G. R. Gleig, vol. 2, Nabu Press. 2011. Print.

Waug, E. Winston. D. *Sufism in Europian and North America.* New York: Rroutledge Chapman & Hall, 2004, Print.

Waugh, Patricia. *An Oxford Guide: Literary Theory and criticism.*Oxford University Press,2016, Print.

Wordsworth, William. *The Major Works: Including the Prelude*, edited by Stephen Gill, Oxford University Press, 2000, Print.

Yusufi, Qolam-Hussein. *The Bright Fountain: A Meeting with Poets.* Elmi Press, 1997. Print.

Journals, Periodicals and Electronic Sources

Azhar, Arieb. *Bulleh Shah: Neither am I Virtuous Nor a Sinner.*

www.dawn.com/new/1040266/. 7 Dec.2014.

Bano, Sara and Mike Unhar. *Reconciliation Religion: Bulleh Shah*, Ralph Waldo Emerson and the American Transcendentalist. Web. 24 Aug. 2014. ir.iwate/u.ac.jp/dspace/bitstream/10140/3564/1/arfe-v69pi-21.pdf.

Barks, Coleman. *Rumi: The Book of Love: Poems of Ecstasy and Longing*. Harper Collins.

E-books.www.venerablilisopus.org/en/books-samael-aun-wear> Accessed 5 Jan.2017.

Basri, Rabia-Al.*In My Soul*.www.Poemhunter.com.Accessed 14 July 2018.

Bashiri, Iraj Hafiz Shirazi Turk‖: AStructuralist Point of View www.angelfire.com/rnb/bashiri/Hafiz/Hafiz.html#72. Accessed 12 August 2017

Ciabattari, Jane. *Why is Rumi the Best-Selling Poet in the US?* www.Kashmirmonitor.in/news-why-is-rumi-the-best-selling-poet-in-us/ Accessed. 3 Nov. 2014.

Curie, P.M., *The Shirine and Cult of Muin al Din Chisti of Ajmer*, Oxford University Press, Delhi, 1992. Print.

Doniger, Wendy. *Merriam-Webster's Encyclopedia of World Religions*. Merriam-Webster, 1999. p. 992.

Emerson, Ralph Waldo. *Nature*.1836.www.emersoncentral.com/nature.htm/.

.... *Self Relience*. First Series.1841.www.emersoncentral.com/selfreliance.htm/. Accessed. 4 Feb.2015.

Hafiz *Essay-E-Notes*. www.eNotes.com. Accessed 8 April 2018.

Introduction: Gneral Characteristics of Punjabi Sufi Poetry. www.wichaar.com. Accessed 9 september 2017.

Lepage, Victorea. *G.I Gurdjieff and the Hidden History of the Sufism*.

www.newdawnmegazine.com. Accessed 15 Jan. 2017.

Lessing, Doris: *The Sufi Connection*.www.opendemocracy.net/mege-galin/doris-lessing-sufi-connection/. Accessed 12 Dec. 2014.

Levis, C.*S.The Four Loves*. ebook.Kindle Version.

Loloi, Parvin Pursglove. *Translations of Hafiz and their Influence on English Poetry since* 1771: A Study and a Critical Bibliography. Doctoral Thesis, University College of Swansea, 1983.Print

Maisam. *Bulleh Shah-A Voice AgainstReligious Bigotry*. lobpak.com. Accessed 16 July 2018.

Marvell, Andrew. *To His Coy Mistress*. www.poetryfoundation.org. Accessed 12 Jan 2017.

Nisarg, Swami Anand. *Gates of Wisdom: The Poems of Hafiz*.mystery-school.net/pdf/hafiz.pdf/. Accesssed 7 Dec. 2014.

Naqvi, Zainab. *Bulleh Shah* (Detailed Analysis) www.wordpress.com accessed n 4th July 2017.

Ode by Hafiz. www.poetryfoundation.org>poems. Accessed 17 June 2018.

Odes From the Divan of Hafiz.www.goodreads.com

Ogden, James. D'Israeli, Isaac (1766-1848), *Oxford Dictionary of National Biography* (Oxford University Press, 2004) www.oxforddnb.com/view/article/7690> Accessed 18 Nov. 2014.

Oueijan, Naji B. *Sufism, Christian Mysticism, and Romanticism*, Presented at the University of Erfort, The German Society for English Romanticism (November 1999).

hojja-nusreddin.livejournal.com/1554161. Accessed 5 Sep. 2014.

Patterson, *William Patrick. Gurdjieff, Sufism, & Muhammad.* Journal The Gurdjieff. Publihed on 17th March 2010.gurdjiefflegacy.wordpress.com. Accessed 26 Jan. 2017.

Persian Literature Influence on English Literature by Javedi.

<Philtar.ucsm.ac.uk/encyclopedia/indon/nahdat.html>.

Perry, Whitall N. *Gurdjieff in the Light of Tradition Part II: The Teaching.* www.Studiesincomparativereligion.com. Accessed on 12 March 2018.

Poem From Hafiz. villanovagtisc.files.wordpress.com. Accessed 12 May 2018.

Power Quotes on Love-80+Christian sayings about Love-cross-walk. www.crosswalk.com.faith>. Accessed 13 Jan 2018.

Puri, T.R., and T.R., *Shangari.* Bulleh Shah: His Life and Poetry.

www.apnaorg.con/poetry/bullahn/. Accessed 4 Nov.2014.

Quote by Rumi. *www.goodreads.com.* Accessed 17 Jan. 2017.

Role-And-Importance-Of-Sufism-In-The-Modern-World. www.ijoart.org/docs/. Accessed 14 Oct. 2014.

*Story of Layla and Majnum: Ecstasy of Love.*www.ecstasyoflove.wordpress.com>. Accssed 8 Jan. 2016.

Tsolak, Nihat. Poem by Rumi-A Buddist Literary.

www.abuddhistlibrary.com>poetry>rumi.Accessed 21 Dec. 2016.

www.biblehub.com. Accessed 17 June 2017.

www.jstor.org/stable/23331264. Accessed 20 June 2017.

Index